GCSE OCR Gateway Additional Science Higher Revision Guide

This book is for anyone doing **GCSE OCR Gateway Additional Science** at higher level.

GCSE Science is all about **understanding how science works**.
And not only that — understanding it well enough to be able to **question** what you hear on TV and read in the papers.

But you can't do that without a fair chunk of **background knowledge**. Hmm, tricky.

Happily this CGP book includes all the **science facts** you need to learn, and shows you how they work in the **real world**. And in true CGP style, we've explained it all as **clearly and concisely** as possible.

It's also got some daft bits in to try and make the whole experience at least vaguely entertaining for you.

What CGP is all about

Our sole aim here at CGP is to produce the highest quality books — carefully written, immaculately presented and dangerously close to being funny.

Then we work our socks off to get them out to you — at the cheapest possible prices.

Contents

Module B3 — Living and Growing

Module C3 — The Periodic Table

Module P3 — Forces for Transport

Module B4 — It's a Green World

Module C4 — Chemical Economics

Module P4 — Radiation for Life

Formulas

Published by Coordination Group Publications Ltd.

From original material by Richard Parsons.

Editors:
Ellen Bowness, Gemma Hallam, Sharon Keeley, Ali Palin, Andy Park, Kate Redmond, Alan Rix, Ami Snelling, Claire Thompson, Julie Wakeling.

Contributors:
Gloria Barnett, Sandy Gardner, Julian Hardwick, Lucy Muncaster, John Myers, Stephen Phillips, Adrian Schmit, Claire Stebbing, Luke Waller

ISBN: 978 1 84146 741 2

With thanks to Vanessa Aris, Barrie Crowther, Ian Francis, John Moseley and Glenn Rogers for the proofreading.
With thanks to Laura Phillips for the copyright research.

Data used to construct stopping distance diagram on page 48 from the Highway Code. Reproduced under the terms of the Click-Use Licence.

Graph on page 50 — based on data from "Road Casualties Great Britain 2004: Annual Report", Department of Transport.

Groovy website: www.cgpbooks.co.uk

Printed by Elanders Ltd, Newcastle upon Tyne.
Jolly bits of clipart from CorelDRAW®

Cells and DNA

Biology's all about living stuff. And all living stuff contains cells. So let's make a start with cells...

Plant and Animal Cells Have Similarities and Differences

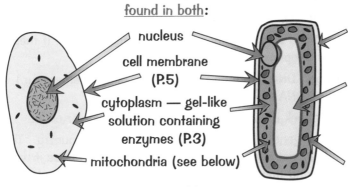

found in both:

nucleus

cell membrane (P.5)

cytoplasm — gel-like solution containing enzymes (P.3)

mitochondria (see below)

just found in plant cells:

rigid cell wall made of cellulose — supports the cell

large vacuole — contains cell sap (a weak solution of sugars and salts) and helps provide support

chloroplasts (see P.57)

Energy for life processes is provided by respiration.

1) Most of the reactions involved in respiration take place in the mitochondria.
2) Respiration turns glucose and oxygen into water and carbon dioxide, and in doing so releases energy.

The Nucleus Contains DNA

1) DNA is found in the nucleus of every cell.
2) It is a double-stranded helix (double spiral). Each of the two strands is made up of lots of small groups called "nucleotides".
3) Each nucleotide contains a small molecule called a "base". DNA has just four different bases.
4) You only need to know the four bases by their first initials — A, C, G and T.
5) Each base forms cross links to a base on the other strand. This keeps the two DNA strands tightly wound together.
6) A always pairs up with T, and C always pairs up with G. This is called complementary base-pairing.

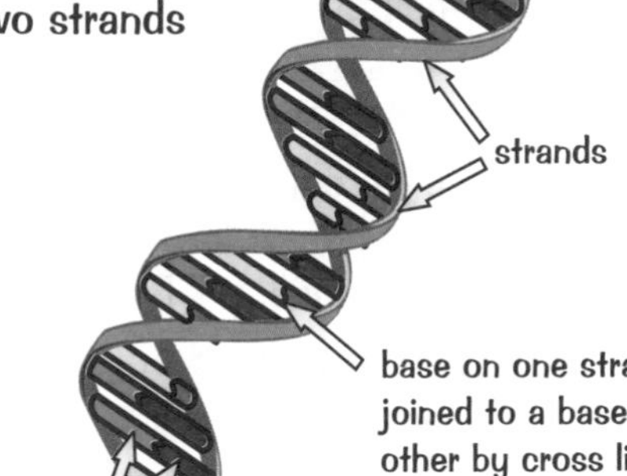
strands
base on one strand is joined to a base on the other by cross links
bases

DNA Can Replicate Itself

1) DNA copies itself every time a cell divides, so that each new cell still has the full amount of DNA.
2) In order to copy itself, the DNA double helix first 'unzips' — to form two single strands.
3) As the DNA unwinds itself, new nucleotides (floating about freely in the nucleus) join on only where the bases fit (A with T and C with G), making an exact copy of the DNA on the other strand.
4) The result is two molecules of DNA identical to the original molecule of DNA.

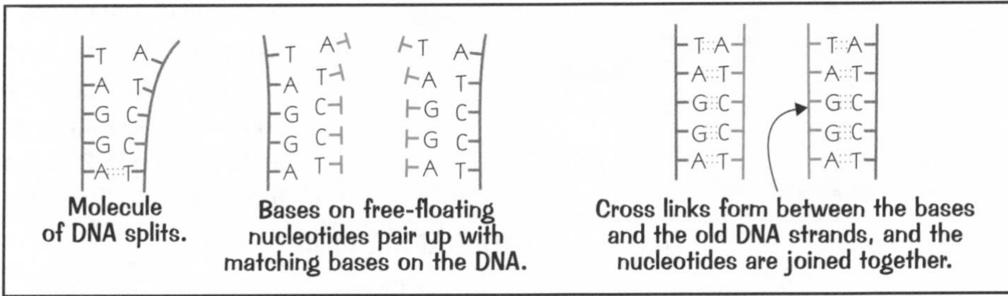
T A
A T
G C
G C
A T
Molecule of DNA splits.
Bases on free-floating nucleotides pair up with matching bases on the DNA.
Cross links form between the bases and the old DNA strands, and the nucleotides are joined together.

Q: What do DNA and a game of rounders have in common...?

Answer: four bases, and don't you forget it. Scientists spent years and years trying to work out the structure of DNA, and in 1953 two of them finally cracked it. They were Francis Crick (British) and James Watson (American) and their discovery of the double helix led to them winning a Nobel Prize in 1962.

DNA Fingerprinting

Now this is more interesting — forensic science being used to catch murderers, just like on the telly.

Genetic Fingerprinting Pinpoints Individuals

1) Your DNA is unique (unless you're an identical twin — then the two of you have identical DNA).
2) DNA fingerprinting (or genetic fingerprinting) is a way of comparing DNA samples to see if they come from the same person or from two different people.
3) DNA fingerprinting is used in forensic science. DNA (from hair, skin flakes, blood, semen etc.) taken from a crime scene is compared with a DNA sample taken from a suspect.
4) It can also be used in paternity tests — to check if a man is the father of a particular child.
5) Some people would like there to be a national genetic database of everyone in the country. That way, DNA from a crime scene could be checked against everyone in the country to see whose it was. But others think this is a big invasion of privacy, and they worry about how safe the data would be and what else it might be used for. There are also scientific problems — false positives can occur if errors are made in the procedure or if the data is misinterpreted.

HOW IT WORKS

1) First you have to isolate the DNA from the cells.
2) Special enzymes are then used to cut the DNA into fragments. They cut it at every place where they recognise a particular order of bases. Where these sections are in the DNA will be different for everyone.
3) If the DNA sample contains that little section of bases lots of times, it'll be cut into lots of little bits. If it only contains it a few times, it'll be left in bigger bits.
4) The DNA bits are separated out using a process a bit like chromatography. They're suspended in a gel, and an electric current is passed through the gel. DNA is negatively charged, so it moves towards the positive anode. Small bits travel faster than big bits, so they get further through the gel.
5) The DNA is "tagged" with a radioactive marker. Then it's placed onto photographic film. The film goes dark where the radioactivity is, revealing the positions of the DNA fragments.

–ve cathode

DNA moves towards the anode, with smallest fragments moving furthest

DNA fragment (invisible)

gel

+ve anode

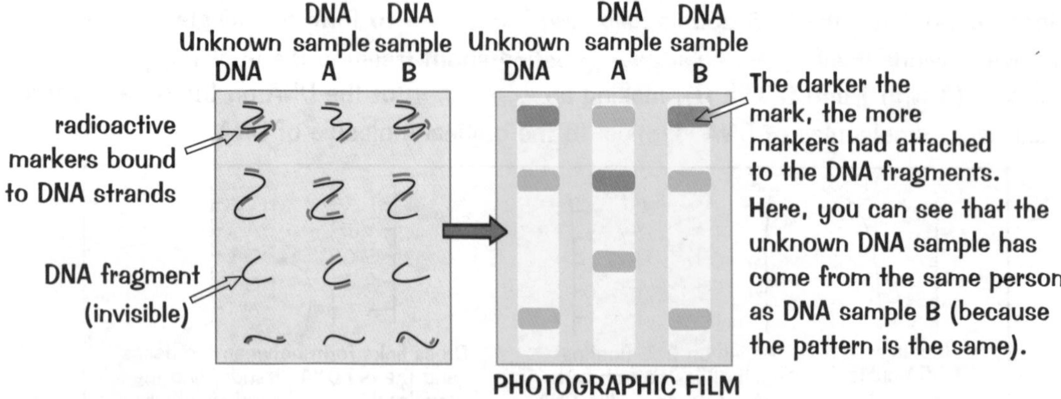

So the trick is — frame your twin and they'll never get you...

In the exam you might have to interpret data on DNA fingerprinting for identification. They'd probably give you a diagram similar to the one at the bottom of this page, and you'd have to say which of the known samples (if any) matched the unknown sample. Pretty easy — it's the two that look the same.

Protein Synthesis and Enzymes

So here's how life works — DNA molecules contain a genetic code which determines which proteins are built. The proteins include enzymes that control all the reactions going on in the body. Simple, eh.

Proteins are Made by Reading the Code in DNA

1) DNA controls the production of proteins (protein synthesis) in a cell.
2) A gene is a section of DNA that 'codes' for a particular protein.
3) Proteins are made up of chains of molecules called amino acids. Each different protein has its own particular number and order of amino acids.
4) This gives each protein a different shape, which means each protein can have a different function.
5) It's the order of the bases in a strand of DNA that decides the order of amino acids in a protein.
6) Each amino acid is coded for by a sequence of three bases in the strand of DNA.
7) Proteins are made from 20 different amino acids, all found in the cytoplasm of cells. They're stuck together to make proteins, following the order of the code on the DNA.

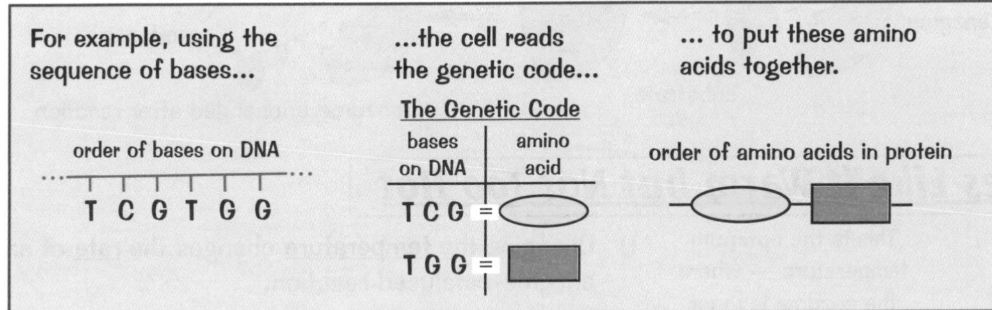

8) We get amino acids from our diet. If we don't take in all the amino acids in the right amounts, our body can change some of them into others. This is called transamination and it happens in the liver.

Enzymes are Catalysts Produced by Living Things

1) Living things have thousands of different chemical reactions going on inside them all the time — like respiration, photosynthesis and protein synthesis.
2) These reactions need to be carefully controlled — to get the right amounts of substances and keep the organism working properly.
3) You can usually make a reaction happen more quickly by raising the temperature. This would speed up the useful reactions but also the unwanted ones too... not good. There's also a limit to how far you can raise the temperature inside a living creature before its cells start getting damaged.
4) So... living things produce enzymes which act as biological catalysts. Enzymes reduce the need for high temperatures and we only have enzymes to speed up the useful chemical reactions in the body.

An ENZYME is a BIOLOGICAL CATALYST which INCREASES the speed of a reaction.

5) Enzymes are all proteins, which is one reason why proteins are so important to living things.
6) Every different biological reaction has its own enzyme designed especially for it.
7) Each enzyme is coded for by a different gene, and has a unique shape which it needs to do its job (see next page).

No horses were harmed in the making of this page...

...it's just our high-tech special effects that give that impression. Enzymes allow us to have a huge amount of control over which chemical reactions go on in our bodies. They're also useful outside the body — where we use them in things like biological washing powders (see page 82).

Enzymes

The enzymes in our body are specific because they have a special shape.

Enzymes are Very Specific

1) Chemical reactions usually involve things either being split apart or joined together.
2) The substrate is the molecule changed in the reaction.
3) Every enzyme has an active site — the part where it joins on to its substrate to catalyse the reaction.
4) Enzymes are really picky — they usually only work with one substrate. The posh way of saying this is that enzymes have a high specificity for their substrate.
5) This is because, for the enzyme to work, the substrate has to fit into the active site. If the substrate's shape doesn't match the active site's shape, then the reaction won't be catalysed. This is called the 'lock and key' mechanism, because the substrate fits into the enzyme just like a key fits into a lock.

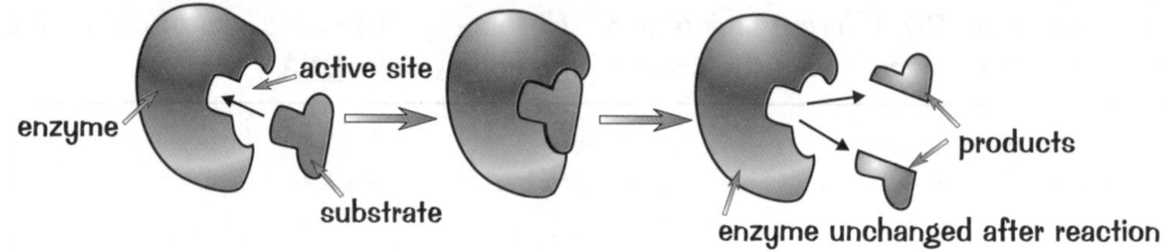

Enzymes Like it Warm but Not Too Hot

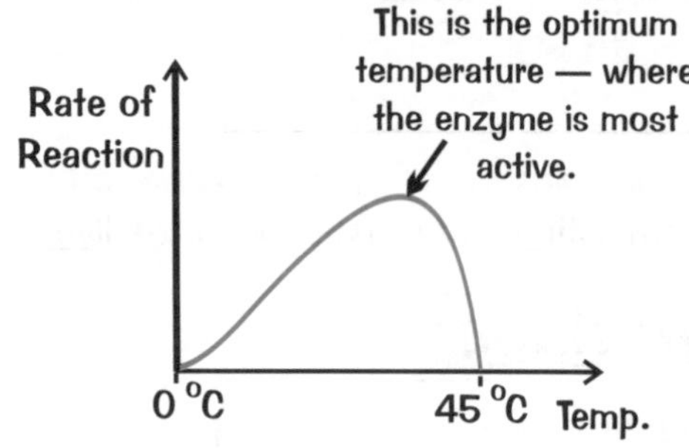

1) Changing the temperature changes the rate of an enzyme-catalysed reaction.
2) Like with any reaction, a higher temperature increases the rate at first. This is because more heat means the enzymes and the substrate particles have more energy. They move about more, so they're more likely to meet up and react.
3) If it gets too hot though, some of the bonds holding the enzyme together break.
4) This makes the enzyme lose its shape. Its active site doesn't fit the shape of the substrate any more, so it can't catalyse the reaction and the reaction stops.
5) The enzyme is now said to be denatured. The shape change is permanent — it won't go back to normal if things cool down again.
6) Each enzyme has its own optimum temperature when the reaction goes fastest. This is the temperature just before it gets too hot and starts to denature. The optimum temperature for the most important human enzymes is about 37 °C — the same temperature as our bodies. Lucky for us.

Enzymes Like it the Right pH Too

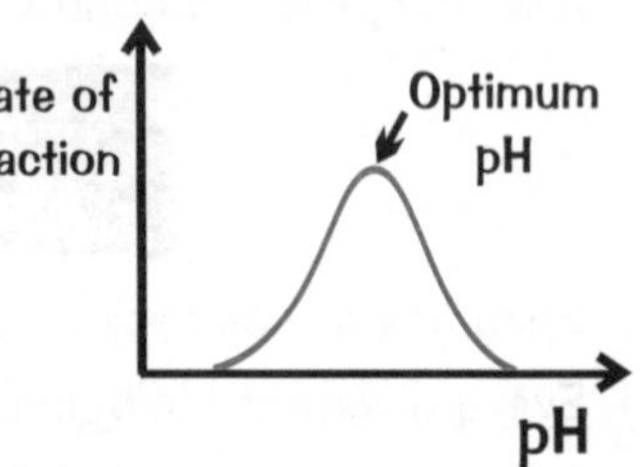

1) The pH also has an effect on enzymes.
2) If the pH is too high or too low, it interferes with the bonds holding the enzyme together. This changes the shape of the active site and denatures the enzyme.
3) All enzymes have an optimum pH that they work best at. It's often neutral pH 7, but not always. For example, pepsin is an enzyme used to break down proteins in the stomach. It works best at pH 2, which means it's well-suited to the acidic conditions in the stomach.

If the lock & key mechanism fails, you get in through a window...

Changing the shape of a protein totally changes it. Egg white contains lots of protein — think what happens when you boil an egg and denature the protein. It goes from clear and runny to white and solid.

Diffusion

Particles move about randomly, and after a bit they end up evenly spaced. And that's how most things move about in our bodies — by "diffusion"...

Don't be Put Off by the Fancy Word

"Diffusion" is simple. It's just the gradual movement of particles from places where there are lots of them to places where there are fewer of them. That's all it is — just the natural tendency for stuff to spread out. Unfortunately you also have to learn the fancy way of saying the same thing, which is this:

DIFFUSION is the PASSIVE MOVEMENT OF PARTICLES from an area of HIGHER CONCENTRATION to an area of LOWER CONCENTRATION

Diffusion happens in both liquids and gases — that's because the particles in these substances are free to move about randomly. The simplest type is when different gases diffuse through each other. This is what's happening when the smell of perfume diffuses through a room:

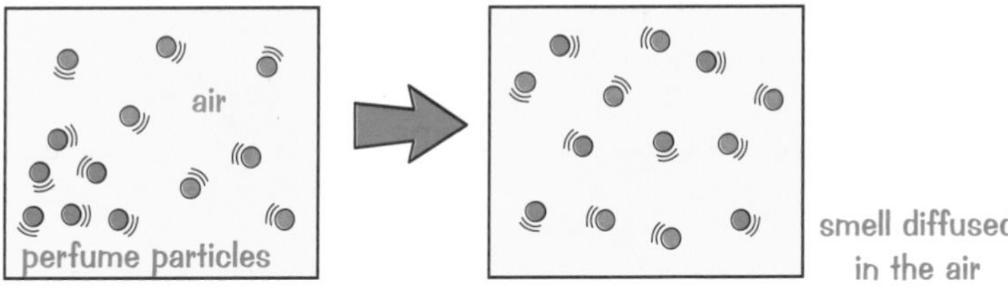

Cell Membranes are Kind of Clever...

They're clever because they hold the cell together BUT they let stuff in and out as well. Only very small molecules can diffuse through cell membranes though — things like simple sugars, water or ions. Big molecules like starch and proteins can't pass through the membrane.

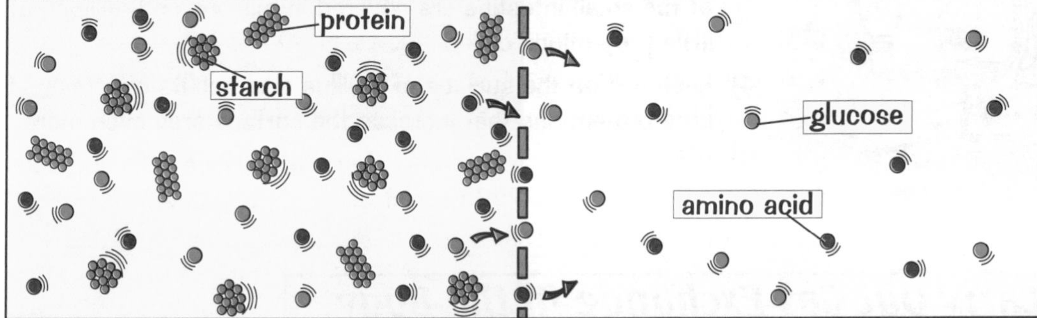

1) Just like with diffusion in air, particles flow through the cell membrane from where there's a higher concentration (a lot of them) to where there's a lower concentration (not such a lot of them).
2) They're only moving about randomly of course, so they go both ways — but if there are a lot more particles on one side of the membrane, there's obviously an overall movement from that side.
3) The rate of diffusion depends on three main things:
   a) Distance — substances diffuse more quickly when they haven't as far to move. Pretty obvious.
   b) Concentration difference (gradient) — substances diffuse faster if there's a big difference in concentration. If there are lots more particles on one side, there are more there to move across.
   c) Surface area — the more surface there is available for molecules to move across, the faster they can get from one side to the other.

Whoever smelt it dealt it... Whoever said the rhyme did the crime...

Because, of course, it's not just perfume that diffuses through a room. Anyway. All living cells have membranes, and their structure allows sugars, water and the rest to drift in and out as needed. Don't forget, the membrane doesn't control diffusion — it happens all by itself.

Diffusion in Cells

You need to know a fair few examples of how diffusion happens in our bodies. There's the small intestine, the lungs, the placenta and synapses. You also need to know how diffusion works in the leaves of plants (covered on page 58).

Small Food Molecules Can Diffuse into the Blood

1) Food is digested in the gut to break it down into pieces small enough to be absorbed into the blood by diffusion.
2) The absorption happens in the small intestine, after big molecules like starch, and proteins have been broken down into small ones like glucose and amino acids.
3) These molecules can diffuse into the blood from the small intestine because their concentration is higher than it is in the blood.
4) When the blood reaches cells that need these substances because their concentration is low, they can diffuse out easily from an area of higher concentration to an area of lower.

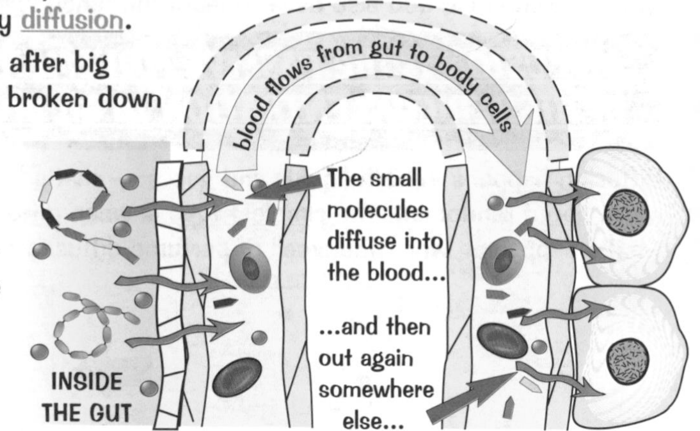

Villi in the Small Intestine Help with Diffusion

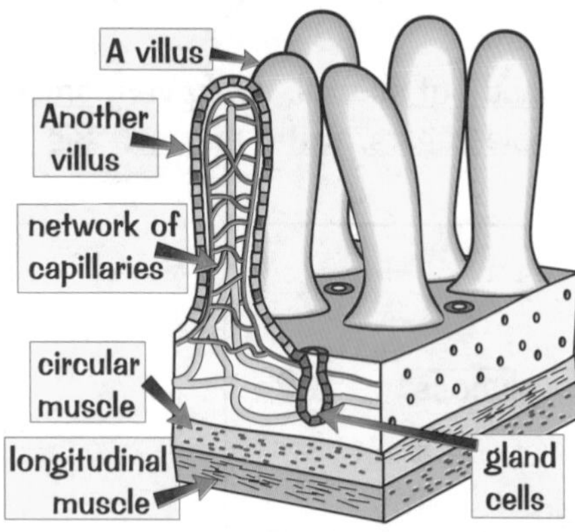

1) The small intestine is adapted for absorption of food.
2) It's very long, so there's time to break down and absorb all the food before it reaches the end.
3) There's a really big surface area for absorption, because the walls of the small intestine are covered in millions and millions of tiny little projections called villi.
4) Each cell on the surface of a villus also has its own microvilli — little projections that increase the surface area even more.
5) Villi have a single permeable layer of surface cells and a very good blood supply to assist quick absorption.

Alveoli Carry Out Gas Exchange in the Body

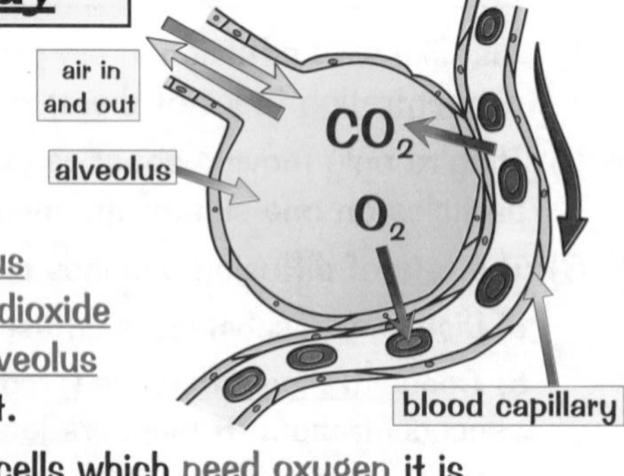

1) The lungs contain millions and millions of little air sacs called alveoli where gas exchange happens.
2) The blood passing next to the alveoli has just returned to the lungs from the rest of the body, so it contains lots of carbon dioxide and very little oxygen. Oxygen diffuses out of the alveolus (high concentration) into the blood (low concentration). Carbon dioxide diffuses out of the blood (high concentration) into the alveolus (low concentration) to be breathed out.

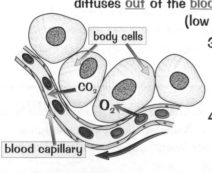

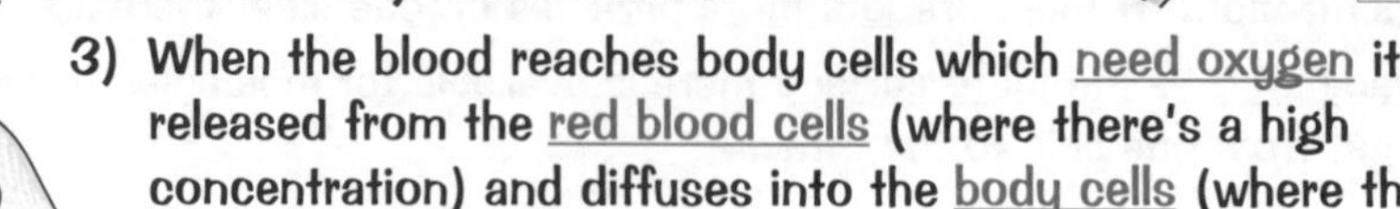

3) When the blood reaches body cells which need oxygen it is released from the red blood cells (where there's a high concentration) and diffuses into the body cells (where the concentration is low).
4) At the same time, carbon dioxide diffuses out of the body cells (where there's a high concentration) into the blood (where there's a low concentration). It's then carried back to the lungs.

Diffusion in Cells

Alveoli are Specialised for Gas Exchange

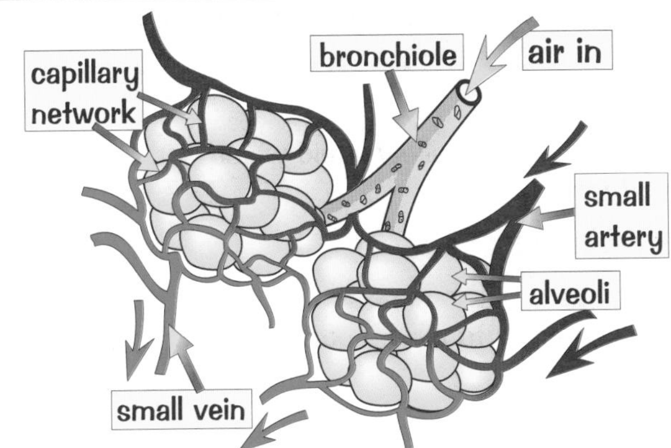

The alveoli are an ideal exchange surface:

1) The huge number of microscopic alveoli gives the lungs an enormous surface area.
2) There's a moist lining for gases to dissolve in.
3) The alveoli have very thin walls — only one cell thick, so the gas doesn't have far to diffuse.
4) They have a great blood supply to maintain a high concentration gradient.
5) The walls are permeable — so gases can diffuse across easily.

Diffusion Also Happens in the Placenta

The placenta is the organ that connects mum and baby when a mammal is pregnant. The placenta is adapted for diffusion:

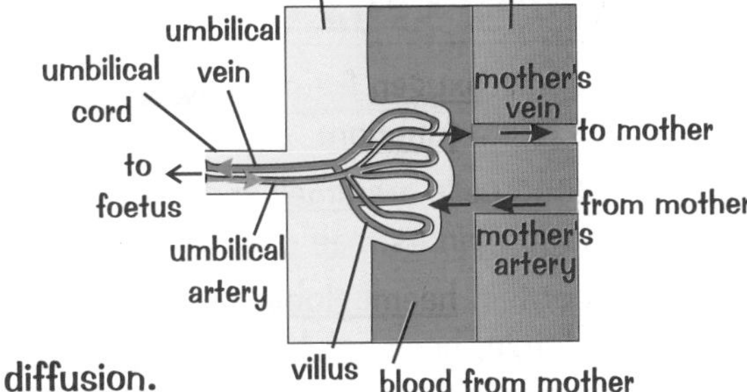

1) There are tiny projections (villi) in the placenta. These give a big surface area. They have capillaries inside containing the foetus's blood.
2) Spaces develop around the villi called sinuses, which become filled with the mother's blood.
3) This lets the mother's blood and the foetus's flow very close to each other so that there's a short distance for diffusion.
4) Food and oxygen diffuse across from the mother's blood to the foetus's when the foetus needs them, from an area of higher concentration to an area of lower concentration.
5) Carbon dioxide and other wastes diffuse across the placenta in the other direction, from foetus to mum. You can probably fill in the high concentration to low concentration bit yourself by now.

And Finally, Diffusion Happens in Synapses

Hopefully you'll remember that neurones (nerves) are connected by synapses. A synapse is just a gap between the end of one neurone and the start of the next. You also need to know:

1) When a nerve impulse arrives at a synapse it triggers the release of a transmitter substance from the end of the neurone into the gap.
2) The transmitter substance diffuses across the gap between the neurones and binds to receptors on the end of the next neurone.
3) This stimulates a new nerve impulse in this neurone. The diffusion of the transmitter substance across the synapse has allowed the nerve impulse to jump the gap and continue on the other side.

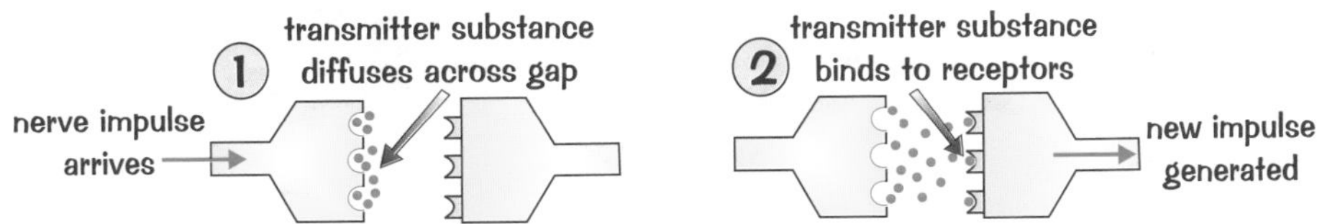

Don't worry — there's still diffusion in a leaf to look forward to...

...just in case you were getting upset at the thought of not hearing any more about it. So that's five examples altogether (including the leaf, see p.58). The process of diffusion is the same in each case.

Functions of the Blood

Blood is very useful stuff. It's a big transport system for moving things around the body. The blood cells do good work too. The red blood cells are responsible for transporting oxygen about, and they carry 100 times more than could be moved just dissolved in the plasma. And as for the white blood cells...

Plasma is the Liquid Bit of Blood

It's basically blood minus the blood cells (see below). Plasma is a pale yellow liquid which carries just about everything that needs transporting around your body:

1) Red and white blood cells (see below) and platelets (used in clotting).
2) Water.
3) Digested food products like glucose and amino acids from the gut to all the body cells.
4) Carbon dioxide from the body cells to the lungs.
5) Urea from the liver to the kidneys (where it's removed in the urine).
6) Hormones — these act like chemical messengers.
7) Antibodies and antitoxins produced by the white blood cells (see below).

Red Blood Cells Have the Job of Carrying Oxygen

They transport oxygen from the lungs to all the cells in the body. The structure of a red blood cell is adapted to its function:

1) Red blood cells are small and have a biconcave shape (which is a posh way of saying they look a little bit like doughnuts, see diagram below) to give a large surface area for absorbing and releasing oxygen.
2) They contain haemoglobin, which is what gives blood its colour — it contains a lot of iron. In the lungs, haemoglobin reacts with oxygen to become oxyhaemoglobin. In body tissues the reverse reaction happens to release oxygen to the cells.
3) Red blood cells don't have a nucleus — this frees up space for more haemoglobin, so they can carry more oxygen.
4) Red blood cells are very flexible. This means they can easily pass through the tiny capillaries (see next page).

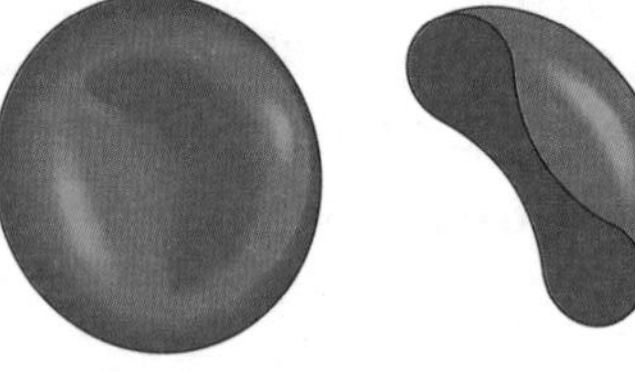

White Blood Cells are Used to Fight Disease

1) Their main role is defence against disease.
2) They produce antibodies to fight microbes.
3) They produce antitoxins to neutralise the toxins produced by microbes.
4) They have a flexible shape, which helps them to engulf any micro-organisms they come across inside the body. Basically the white blood cell wraps around the micro-organism until it's totally surrounded, and then it digests it using enzymes.

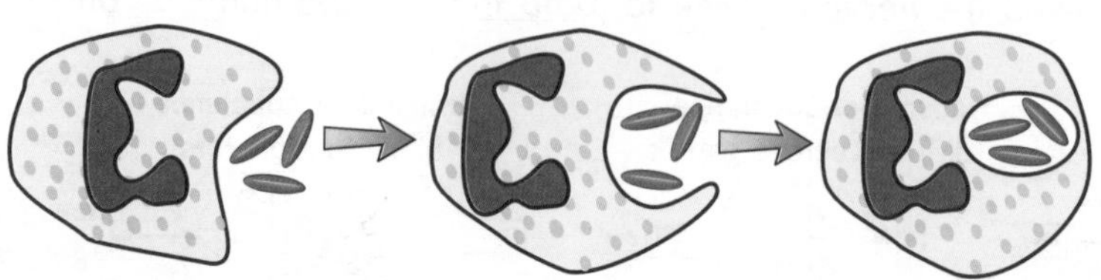

It's all blood, sweat and tears — kind of...

...without the sweat... or the tears... just the blood then... yep... anyway...

The average human body contains about six and a half pints of blood altogether, and every single drop contains millions of cells. There are usually about 500 times more red blood cells than white.

Circulatory System: Blood Vessels

Blood needs a good system to move it around the body — called the circulatory system.

Blood Vessels are Designed for Their Function

There are three different types of blood vessel:

1) ARTERIES — these carry the blood away from the heart.
2) CAPILLARIES — these are involved in the exchange of materials at the tissues.
3) VEINS — these carry the blood to the heart.

Arteries Carry Blood Under Pressure

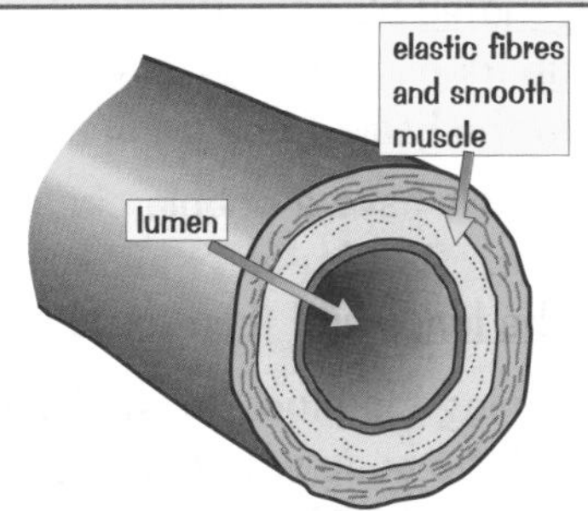

1) The heart pumps the blood out at high pressure so the artery walls are strong and elastic.
2) The walls are thick compared to the size of the hole down the middle (the "lumen" — silly name!). They contain thick layers of muscle to make them strong.

Cholesterol is a fatty substance. Eating a diet high in saturated fat has been linked to high levels of cholesterol in the blood. You need some cholesterol for things like making cell membranes. But if you get too much cholesterol it starts to build up in your arteries. These form plaques in the wall of the lumen, which narrows the artery. This restricts the flow of blood — bad news for the part of the body the artery is supplying with food and oxygen. If an artery supplying the heart or brain is affected, it can cause a heart attack or stroke.

Capillaries are Really Small

thin wall — only one cell thick
very small lumen
nucleus of cell

1) Arteries branch into capillaries.
2) Capillaries are really tiny — too small to see.
3) They carry the blood really close to every cell in the body to exchange substances with them.
4) They have permeable walls, so substances can diffuse in and out.
5) They supply food and oxygen, and take away wastes like CO_2.
6) Their walls are usually only one cell thick. This increases the rate of diffusion by decreasing the distance over which it occurs.

Veins Take Blood Back to the Heart

1) Capillaries eventually join up to form veins.
2) The blood is at lower pressure in the veins so the walls don't need to be as thick as artery walls.
3) They have a bigger lumen than arteries to help the blood flow despite the lower pressure.
4) They also have valves to help keep the blood flowing in the right direction.

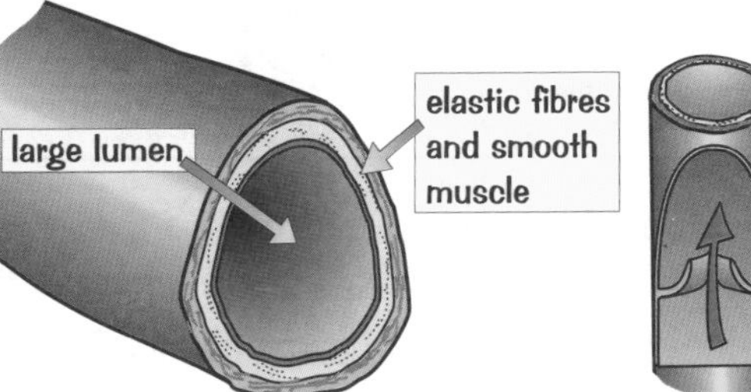

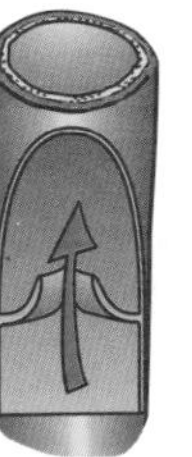

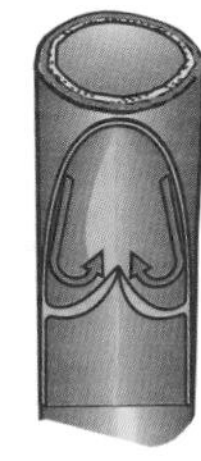

Learn this page — don't struggle in vein...

Here's an interesting fact for you — your body contains about 60 000 miles of blood vessels. That's about six times the distance from London to Sydney in Australia. Of course, capillaries are really tiny, which is how there can be such a big length — they can only be seen with a microscope.

Circulatory System: The Heart

Blood doesn't just move around the body on its own, of course. It needs a pump.

Mammals Have a Double Circulatory System

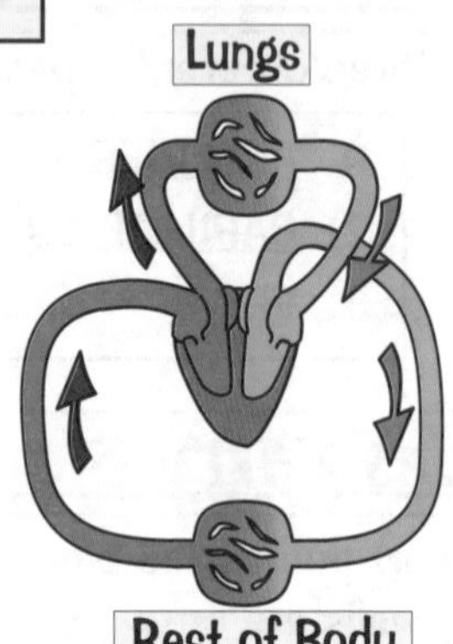

1) The first one connects the heart to the lungs. Deoxygenated blood is pumped to the lungs to take in oxygen. The blood then returns to the heart.
2) The second one connects the heart to the rest of the body. The oxygenated blood in the heart is pumped out to the body. It gives up its oxygen, and then the deoxygenated blood returns to the heart to be pumped out to the lungs again.
3) Not all animals have a double circulatory system — fish don't, for example. So why can't mammals just pump the blood out through the lungs and then on to the rest of the body?
4) Well, returning the blood to the heart after it's picked up oxygen at the lungs means it can be pumped out around the body with much greater force. This is needed so the blood can get to every last tissue in the body and still have enough push left to flow back to the heart through the veins.

Learn This Diagram of the Heart with All Its Labels

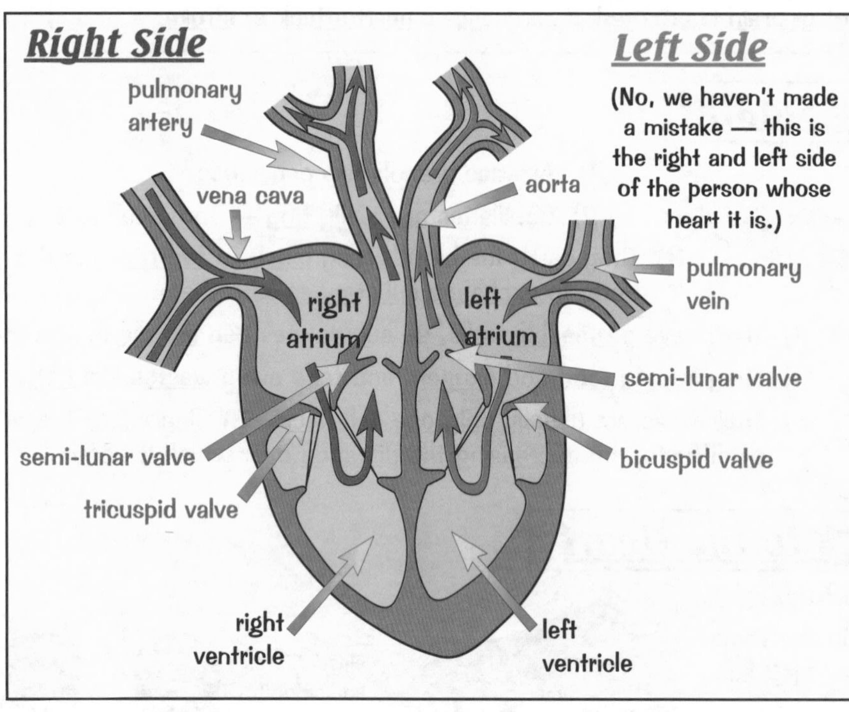

1) The right atrium of the heart receives deoxygenated blood from the body (through the vena cava).
   (The plural of atrium is atria.)
2) The deoxygenated blood moves through to the right ventricle, which pumps it to the lungs (via the pulmonary artery).
3) The left atrium receives oxygenated blood from the lungs (through the pulmonary vein).
4) The oxygenated blood then moves through to the left ventricle, which pumps it out round the whole body (via the aorta).
5) The left ventricle has a much thicker wall than the right ventricle. It needs more muscle because it has to pump blood around the whole body, whereas the right ventricle only has to pump it to the lungs.
6) The semi-lunar, tricuspid and bicuspid valves prevent the backflow of blood.

Okay — let's get to the heart of the matter...

The human heart beats 100 000 times a day on average. You can feel a pulse in your wrist or neck (where the vessels are close to the surface). This is the blood being pushed along by another beat. Doctors use a stethoscope to listen to your heart — it's actually the valves closing that they hear.

Replacement Hearts

Heart disease is one of the main killer diseases of the Western world, but nowadays many people with defective hearts can have surgery to put the problems right.

You Can Just Replace Parts of the Heart

The heart has a pacemaker — a group of cells which determines how fast it beats. If this stops working properly the heartbeat becomes irregular, which can be dangerous. The pacemaker then needs to be replaced with an artificial one. Defective heart valves can also be replaced — either with valves from animals, or with artificial, mechanical valves.

Or You Can Get a Heart Transplant...

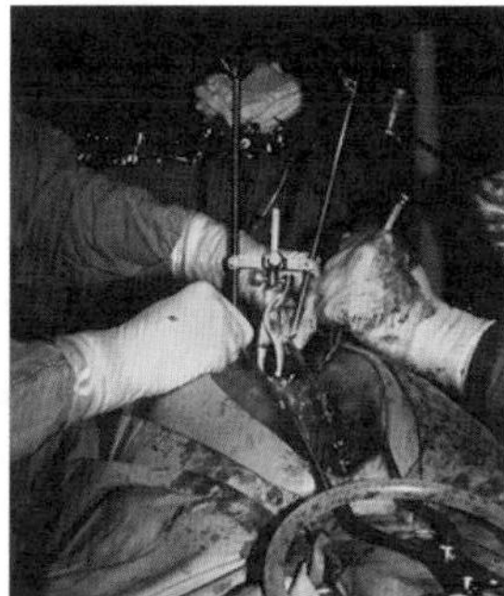

In extreme cases, the whole heart can be removed and replaced by another one from a human donor — this is called a transplant. It involves major surgery and a lifetime course of drugs and medical care. They're only done on patients whose hearts are so damaged that the problems can't be solved in any other way.

...But You Need a Donor

One of the major problems in getting a heart transplant is a shortage of donors.
To be a heart donor, the person must meet these criteria:

1) Relatively young (under 45), so that the heart is as fit and healthy as possible.
2) Tissues must be a close match to those of the patient, or the heart's likely to be rejected (see below).
3) Body weight must be similar to the patient needing the transplant, so the heart is a good 'fit'.
4) Hearts stay usable for no more than 6 hours outside the body — so the donor must have only very recently died or their heart must still be working (i.e. the patient is 'brain dead', but they've been kept 'alive' artificially so their heart hasn't actually stopped yet).
5) Close relatives must give permission.

TRANSPLANTS CAN BE REJECTED One of the main problems with heart transplants is that the patient's immune system often recognises the new heart as 'foreign' and attacks it — this is called rejection. Doctors use drugs that suppress the patient's immune system to help stop the donor heart being rejected, but that leaves the patient more vulnerable to infections. Rejection can also occur with replacement heart valves from animals.

Mechanical Parts aren't Usually Rejected by the Body

1) The main advantage of using artificial parts (valves and pacemakers) is that rejection isn't normally a problem. They're usually made from metals or plastics, which the body can't recognise as foreign in the same way as it does with living tissue.
2) Pacemakers do need a battery, but this is very small and is inserted under the skin. It lasts for about ten years and is easily replaced.
3) Artificial valves need more major surgery and don't work quite as well as healthy natural ones — the blood doesn't flow through them as smoothly, which can cause blood clots and lead to strokes. The patient has to take drugs to thin their blood and make sure this doesn't happen, which can cause problems if they're hurt in an accident.
4) Replacing a valve is a much less drastic procedure than a transplant, and inserting a pacemaker only involves an overnight stay in hospital.

Pity they can't fit me in for a brain transplant before the exam...

The first successful heart transplant took place in South Africa in 1967. They can transplant loads of stuff nowadays — kidneys, lungs, liver, pancreas, corneas, small intestine... but they all need donors.

Multiplying Cells

Cell division — pretty important if you're planning on being bigger than an amoeba. Which I am, one day.

Being Multi-cellular Has Some Important Advantages

There's nothing wrong with single-celled organisms — they're pretty successful. Bacteria, for example, aren't in danger of extinction any time soon. But there are some big advantages in being multi-cellular, and so some organisms have cleverly evolved that way. Here are some advantages you should know:

1) A single large cell has a smaller surface area to volume ratio than lots of small cells do. This reduces the organism's ability to move substances in and out of the cell.
2) Being multi-cellular means you can be bigger. This is great because it means you can travel further, get your nutrients in a variety of different ways, fewer things can eat or squash you, etc.
3) Being multi-cellular allows for cell differentiation. Instead of being just one cell that has to do everything, you can have different types of cells that do different jobs. Your cells can be specially adapted for their particular jobs, e.g. taking in oxygen in the blood, reacting to light in the eyes.
4) This means multi-cellular organisms can be more complex — they can have specialised organs, different shapes and behaviour — and so can be adapted specifically to their particular environment.

Mitosis Makes New Cells for Growth and Repair

"Mitosis is when a cell reproduces itself by splitting to form two identical offspring."

This happens in the body when you want identical cells — e.g. when you want to grow and you need lots of the same type of cell, when you need to repair cells that have been damaged or when you need to replace worn-out cells. The important thing to understand in mitosis is what happens to the DNA.

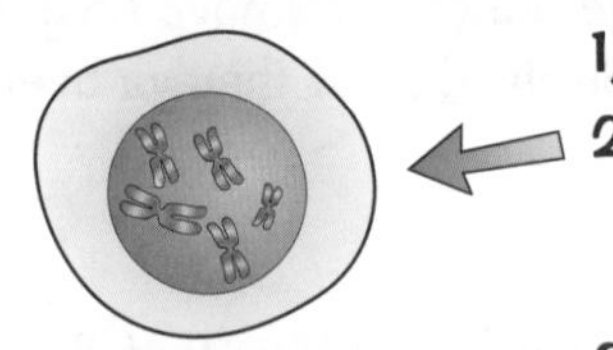

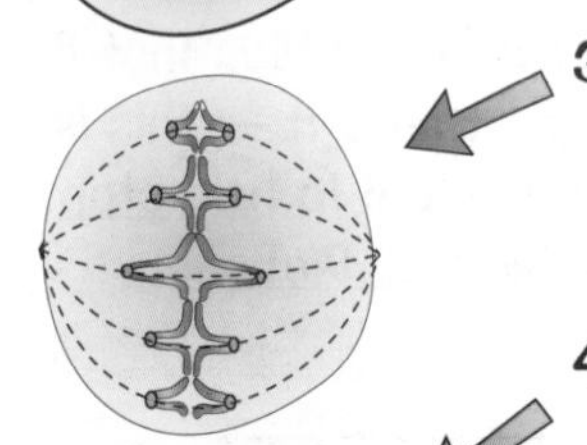

1) Before mitosis starts, the DNA in the cell is replicated (see p.1).
2) Then at the beginning of mitosis, the DNA coils into double-armed chromosomes. These arms are exact duplicates of each other — they contain exactly the same DNA.
3) The chromosomes line up at the centre of the cell, and then cell fibres pull them apart. One arm of each chromosome goes to one end of the cell, and the other goes to the opposite end. Membranes form around each of these two different sets of chromosomes.
4) The cytoplasm divides, and you get two new cells containing exactly the same genetic material.
5) And that's mitosis. You've ended up with two new cells with exactly the same genetic information as each other. Before these can divide again, the DNA has to replicate itself to give each chromosome two arms again.

The Other Type of Cell Division is Meiosis

1) Reproductive cells undergo meiosis to make gametes. These are the sex cells — eggs and sperm.
2) The body cells of mammals are diploid. This means that each of the organism's body cells has two copies of each chromosome in its nucleus — one from the organism's mum, and one from its dad.
3) But sex cells are haploid. They only have one copy of each chromosome (due to the way they divided — see next page). This is so that you can supply one sex cell from the mum (the egg) and one sex cell from the dad (the sperm) and still end up with the usual number of chromosomes in body cells.

Right — now that I have your undivided attention...

There's no denying mitosis and meiosis can seem tricky at first. But don't worry — just go through it slowly, one step at a time. Even if the exam's tomorrow. Panicking and rushing don't help at all.

Sexual Reproduction

People can look very similar to their mum and dad, often a good mix of the two. Here's why.

Meiosis Involves Two Divisions

1) Meiosis starts in exactly the same way as mitosis — the DNA replicates and curls up to form double-armed chromosomes (see previous page).

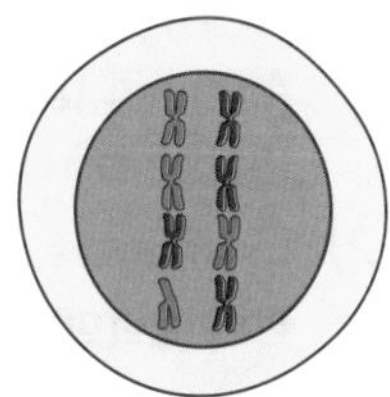

2) After replication the chromosomes arrange themselves into pairs. Humans have 23 pairs of chromosomes, that's 46 altogether. Both chromosomes in a pair contain information about the same features. One chromosome comes from your mum and one from your dad.

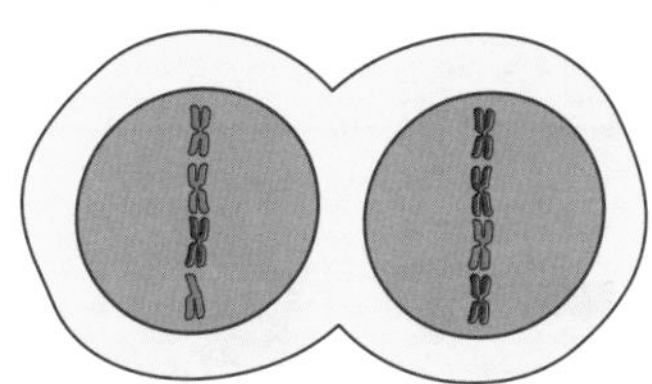

3) In the first division, these pairs split up — some of your dad's chromosomes go with some of your mum's chromosomes. In each of the two new cells, there are no pairs at all — just one of each of the 23 different types. So each new cell has a mixture of your mum's and your dad's genes, but only half the usual number of chromosomes.

4) The second division of meiosis is like mitosis on the last page — each chromosome splits in half and one arm ends up in each new cell.

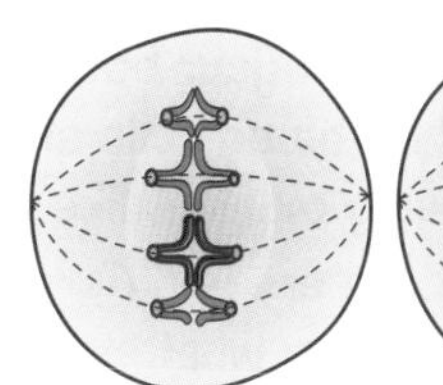

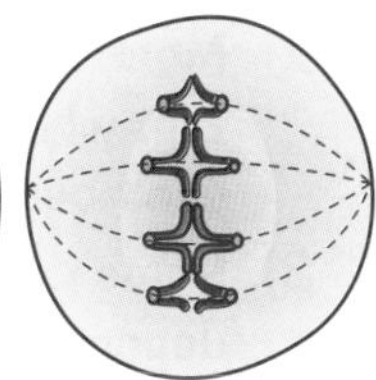

5) And that's meiosis. You've ended up with four new cells — two after the first division, and then each of those splits again. The cells are genetically different from each other because the genes all get shuffled up during meiosis and each gamete only gets half of them, at random.

Sexual Reproduction Creates Variation

SEXUAL REPRODUCTION involves the fusion of male and female gametes (sex cells). Because there are TWO parents, the offspring contains a mixture of their parents' genes.

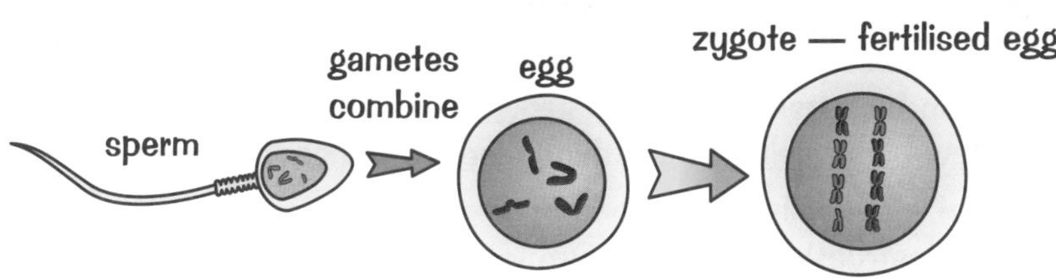

The offspring will have a mixture of the two sets of chromosomes, so it will inherit features from both parents. This is why sexual reproduction produces more variation than asexual reproduction.

Sperm Cells are Adapted for Their Function

The function of a sperm is to transport the male's DNA to the female's egg so that their DNA can combine.

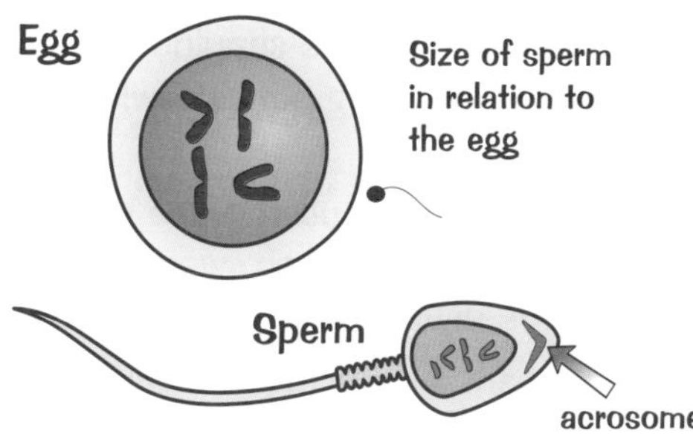

1) Sperm are small and have long tails so they can swim to the egg.
2) Sperm have lots of mitochondria (see page 1) to provide the energy needed to swim this distance.
3) Sperm also have an acrosome at the front of the 'head', where they store the enzymes they need to digest their way through the membrane of the egg cell.
4) They're produced in large numbers to increase the chance of fertilisation.

No sniggering in the back, please...

For many kids in year seven, the mere sight of a sperm is enough to convulse them in giggles. Those of them that don't think it's an innocent tadpole, anyway. But that's not the case for you lot. We hope.

Stem Cells and Differentiation

Plants and animals have different tactics for growth, but they both have stem cells.

Animals Stop Growing, Plants Can Grow Continuously

Plants and animals grow differently:

1) Animals tend to grow while they're young, and then they reach full growth and stop growing. Plants often grow continuously — even really old trees will keep putting out new branches.
2) In animals, growth happens by cell division, but in plants, growth in height is mainly due to cell enlargement (elongation) — cell division usually just happens in the tips of the roots and shoots.

Stem Cells Can Turn into Different Types of Cells

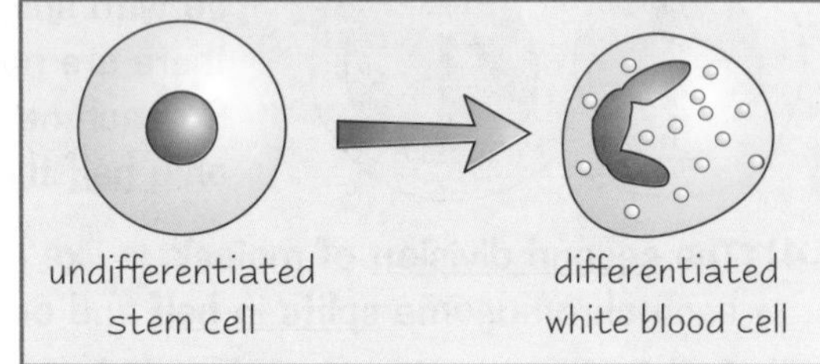

1) Differentiation is the process by which a cell changes to become specialised for its job. In most animal cells, the ability to differentiate is lost at an early stage, but lots of plant cells don't ever lose this ability.
2) Most cells in your body are specialised for a particular job. E.g. white blood cells are brilliant at fighting invaders but can't carry oxygen, like red blood cells.
3) Some cells are undifferentiated. They can develop into different types of cell, tissues and organs depending on what instructions they're given. These cells are called STEM CELLS.
4) Stem cells are found in early human embryos. They're exciting to doctors and medical researchers because they have the potential to turn into any kind of cell at all. This makes sense if you think about it — all the different types of cell found in a human being have to come from those few cells in the early embryo.
5) Adults also have stem cells, but they're only found in certain places, like bone marrow. These aren't as versatile as embryonic stem cells — they can't turn into any cell type at all, only certain ones.

Stem Cells May be Able to Cure Many Disorders

1) Medicine already uses stem cells to cure disease. For example, people with blood disorders (e.g. leukaemia and sickle cell anaemia) can be cured by bone marrow transplants. Bone marrow contains adult stem cells that turn into new blood cells (but nothing else) to replace faulty old ones.
2) Very early human embryos contain a lot of stem cells. Scientists can extract these and grow them. Researchers are trying to find out how to 'instruct' the cells to turn into useful cells, e.g. nerve cells to cure brain damage and spinal injuries, skin cells for skin grafts, etc.
3) Tissues derived from stem cells could be used for drug testing and development, reducing the need for animal testing.

Some People Are Against Stem Cell Research

1) Some people are against stem cell research because they feel that human embryos shouldn't be used for experiments since each one is a potential human life. Others think that curing patients who already exist and who are suffering is more important than the rights of embryos.
2) One fairly convincing argument in favour of this point of view is that the embryos used in the research are usually unwanted ones from fertility clinics which, if they weren't used for research, would probably just be destroyed. But of course, campaigners for the rights of embryos usually want this banned too.
3) Around the world, there are now 'stocks' of stem cells that scientists can use for their research. Some countries (e.g. the USA) won't fund research to make new stem cell stocks, but in the UK it's allowed as long as it follows strict guidelines.

But florists cell stems — and nobody complains about that...

Research has recently been done into getting stem cells from alternative sources. E.g. some researchers think it might be possible to get cells from umbilical cords to behave like embryonic stem cells.

Growth in Humans

Growth in humans is more complicated than just getting born and then getting bigger.

Growth Starts Well Before Birth

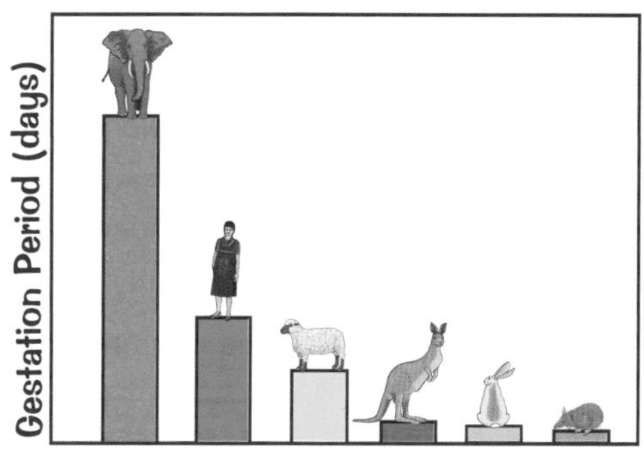

Mammals give birth to live young. So, the baby grows inside it's mothers womb until it reaches a stage where it can survive outside. This period is called gestation and its length varies in different mammals:

Gestation length is usually related to the size of the animal, but also to how developed it is at birth (e.g. kangaroo babies are born relatively undeveloped and so the gestation period is quite short).

The human body doesn't grow evenly in the mother's womb or in early life. Certain organs grow faster than others, and the fastest-growing of all is the brain. This is because a large and well-developed brain gives humans a big survival advantage — it's our best tool for finding food, avoiding predators, etc.

The graphs show that, during the first year of life, a baby's head size increases in proportion with its body weight (the slope of both graphs is about the same). Head growth is actually responsible for much of the weight increase in the baby. Doctors monitor the baby's weight and head circumference. The actual values are not as important as the rate of growth. If the baby is growing too slowly, or if the head is relatively too large or small, it can alert the doctor to possible development problems.

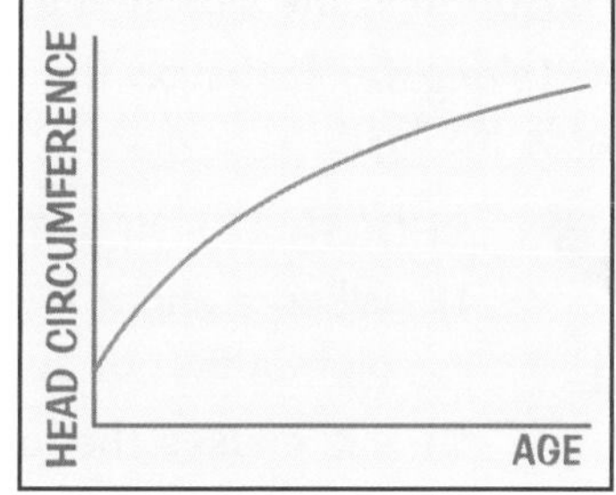

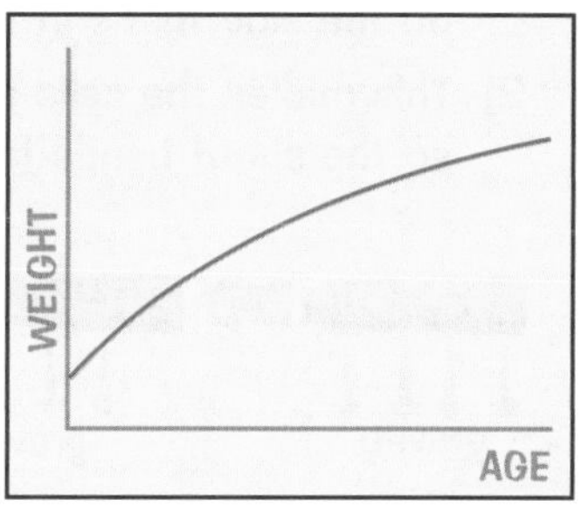

The Human Life Span Has Five Stages

During a normal life span, everyone passes through these five stages. Some of the stages have a clearly defined beginning and end, while others are a bit more vague.

STAGE	DESCRIPTION
Infancy	Roughly the first year of life. Time of rapid growth, child begins to walk.
Childhood	Period between infancy and puberty. Development of the brain.
Adolescence	Begins with puberty and continues until body development and growth are complete.
Maturity/adulthood	Period between adolescence and old age. Cell division for growth stops.
Old age	Usually considered to be between age 65 and death.

You Need to be Able to Interpret Data on Human Growth

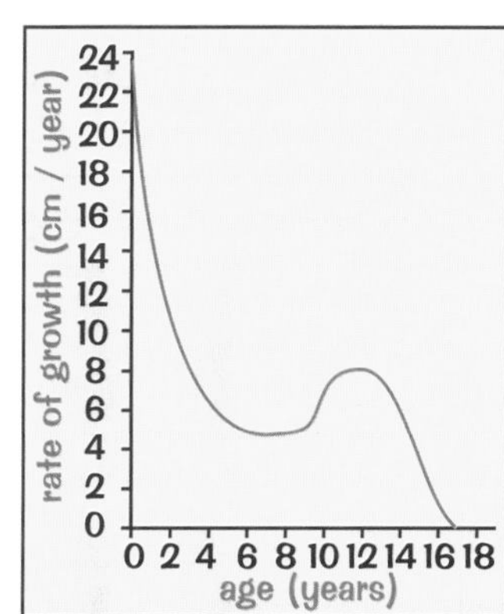

In exams, you may be asked to interpret human growth data. This will usually show growth over a period of time. Be really careful to note whether the data shows actual growth or growth rate (speed of growth).

If it shows actual growth, you can judge the rate of growth by looking at the slope of the graph. In this growth rate example graph, you might be asked to describe changes in the rate of growth, or note key points (e.g. there's a sudden growth spurt at the beginning of puberty).

I'm growing rather sick of this topic...

Listen, you think you're sick of reading these lame jokes? Just think how I feel, having to make them up.

Growth in Plants

Plants don't just grow randomly. Plant hormones make sure they grow in the right direction.

Auxins are Plant Growth Hormones

1) Auxins are plant hormones which control growth at the tips of shoots and roots.
2) Auxin is produced in the tips and diffuses backwards to stimulate the cell elongation process which occurs in the cells just behind the tips.
3) If the tip of a shoot is removed, no auxin will be available and the shoot stops growing.
4) Auxins are involved in the responses of plants to light and gravity.

Auxins Change the Direction of Root and Shoot Growth

You'll see below that extra auxin promotes growth in the shoot but actually inhibits growth in the root — but also note that this produces the desired result in both cases.

SHOOTS ARE POSITIVELY PHOTOTROPIC (grow towards light)

1) When a shoot tip is exposed to light, it accumulates more auxin on the side that's in the shade than the side that's in the light.
2) This makes the cells grow (elongate) faster on the shaded side, so the shoot bends towards the light.

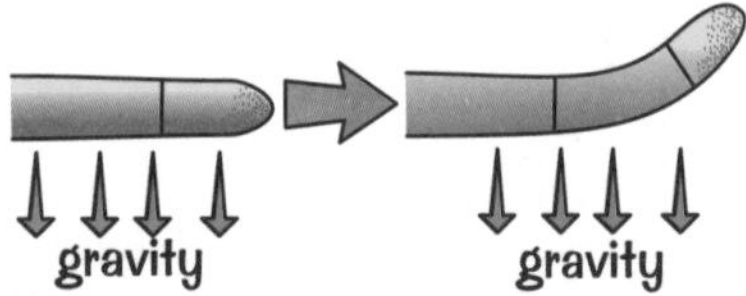

SHOOTS ARE NEGATIVELY GEOTROPIC (grow away from gravity)

1) When a shoot is growing sideways, gravity produces an unequal distribution of auxin in the tip, with more auxin on the lower side.
2) This causes the lower side to grow faster, bending the shoot upwards.

ROOTS ARE POSITIVELY GEOTROPIC (grow towards gravity)

1) A root growing sideways will also have more auxin on its lower side.
2) But in a root the extra auxin inhibits growth. This means the cells on top elongate faster, and the root bends downwards.

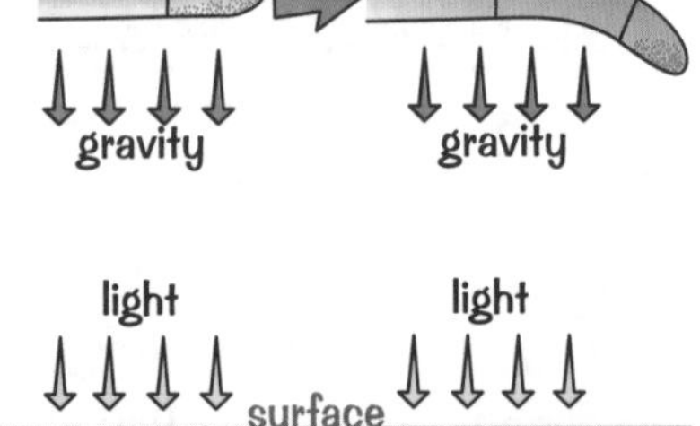

ROOTS ARE NEGATIVELY PHOTOTROPIC (grow away from light)

1) If a root starts being exposed to some light, it's probably getting near the surface — the wrong direction for a root to be going.
2) As in the shoot, more auxin accumulates on the more shaded side. The auxin inhibits cell elongation on the shaded side, so the root bends downwards, back into the ground.

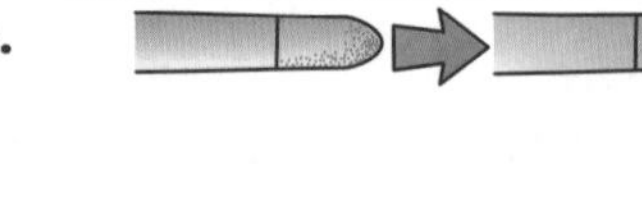

Experiments Have Shown How Auxins Work

The two experiments illustrated show that auxins are produced in the tip of the plant (experiment 1) and cause bending by building up on the shaded side of the shoot (experiment 2).

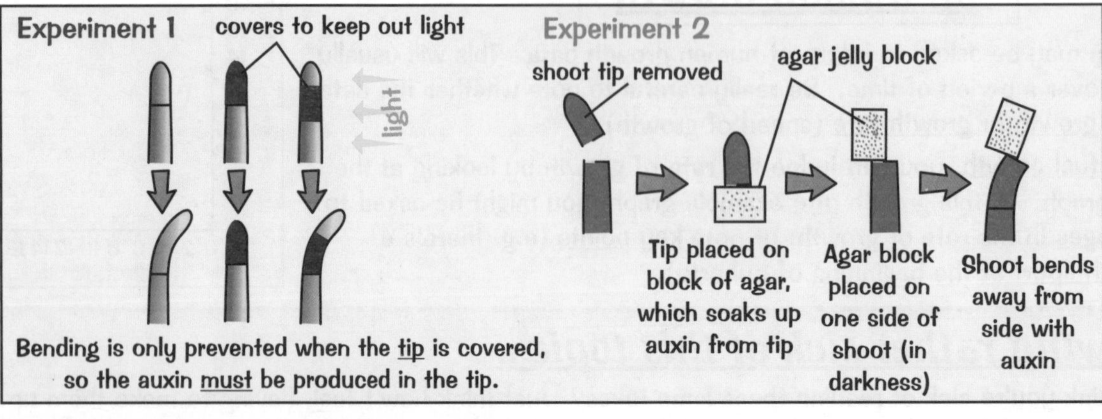

Commercial Use of Plant Hormones

Plant hormones can be extracted and used by people, or artificial copies can be made. They can then be used to do all kinds of useful things, including killing weeds, growing cuttings and ripening fruit.

1) As Selective Weedkillers

1) Most weeds growing in fields of crops or in a lawn are broad-leaved, in contrast to grasses and cereals which have very narrow leaves.
2) Selective weedkillers have been developed from plant growth hormones which only affect the broad-leaved plants.
3) They totally disrupt their normal growth patterns, which soon kills them, whilst leaving the grass and crops untouched.

2) Growing from Cuttings with Rooting Powder

1) A cutting is part of a plant that has been cut off it, like the end of a branch with a few leaves on it.
2) Normally, if you stick cuttings in the soil they won't grow, but if you add rooting powder, which contains a plant growth hormone, they will produce roots rapidly and start growing as new plants.
3) This enables growers to produce lots of clones (exact copies, see page 23) of a really good plant very quickly.

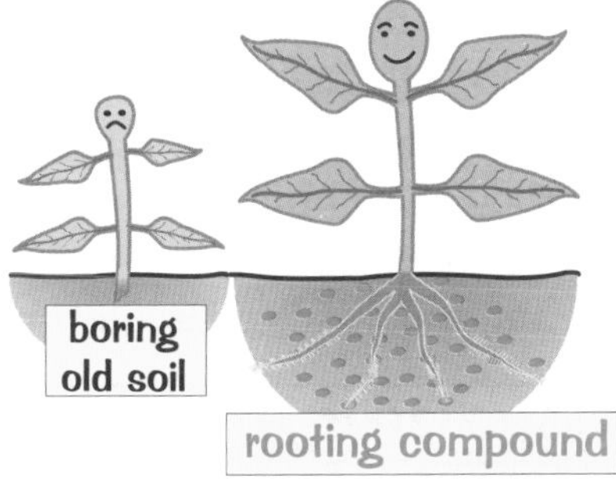

3) Controlling the Ripening of Fruit

1) The ripening of fruits can be controlled either while they are still on the plant, or during transport to the shops.
2) This allows the fruit to be picked while it's still unripe (and therefore firmer and less easily damaged).
3) Ripening hormone is then added and the fruit will ripen on the way to the supermarket and be perfect just as it reaches the shelves.

4) Controlling Dormancy

1) Lots of seeds won't germinate (start growing) until they've been through certain conditions (e.g. a period of cold or of dryness). This is called dormancy.
2) Another hormone called gibberellin is what breaks this dormancy and allows the seeds to germinate.
3) Commercial growers can treat seeds with gibberellin to make them germinate at times of year when they wouldn't normally. It also helps to make sure all the seeds in a batch germinate at the same time.

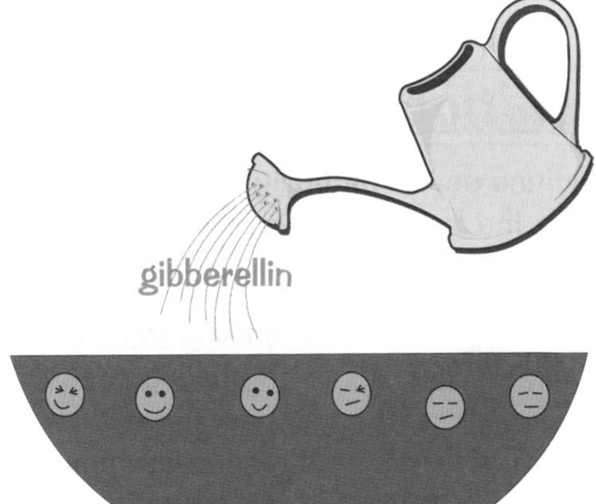

You will ripen when I SAY you can ripen — and NOT BEFORE...

If you want some fruit to ripen, put them into a paper bag with a banana. The banana releases a ripening hormone called ethene which causes the fruit to ripen. Bad apples also release lots of ethene. Unfortunately this means if you've got one bad apple in a barrel, you'll soon have lots of bad apples.

Mutation

Mutations are really common — but sadly, they hardly ever give any of us superpowers.

Gene Mutations are Changes to Genes

A MUTATION is a change in the DNA base sequence.

1) There are several things that cause mutations — they even occur spontaneously.
2) These things change the base sequence of the DNA (see P.1). If this change becomes permanent (the DNA replicates before it's fixed) it becomes a mutation.
3) If the mutation occurs within a gene, it means that when the code is read in order to make proteins, you end up with either a different protein or no protein at all.

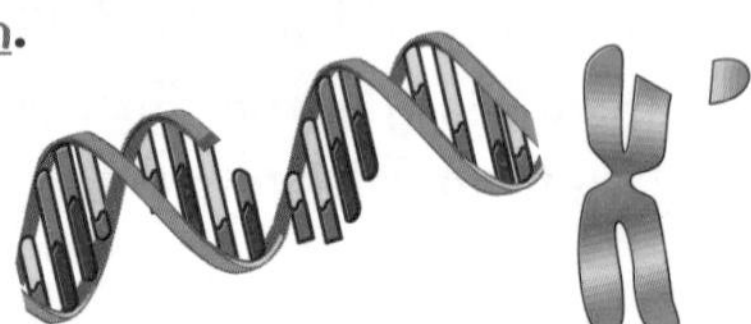

Most Mutations are Harmful

1) Making the wrong protein or no protein at all can be a bit of a disaster — especially if the protein is an important enzyme or something.
2) If a mutation occurs in reproductive cells, then the offspring might develop abnormally or die at an early stage of their development.
3) If a mutation occurs in body cells, the mutant cells can sometimes start to multiply in an uncontrolled way and invade other parts of the body. This is what we know as cancer.

Some Mutations are Beneficial, Giving Us Evolution

1) Occasionally, a different protein might be produced after a mutation that actually benefits the organism — the new protein is an improvement on the one it was supposed to be.
2) This gives the organism a survival advantage over the rest of the population. It passes on the mutated DNA to its offspring, and they survive better too, so soon the mutation becomes common in the population. This is natural selection and evolution at work. A good example is a mutation in a bacterium that makes it resistant to antibiotics, so the mutant gene lives on, creating a resistant "strain" of bacteria.
3) Blue budgies appeared suddenly as a mutation amongst yellow budgies. This is a good example of a neutral effect. It didn't harm its chances of survival and so it remained in the population (and at one stage, every grandma in Britain had one).

Radiation and Certain Chemicals Cause Mutations

Mutations occur 'naturally', caused by 'natural' background radiation (from the Sun, and rocks etc.) or just by the laws of chance that every now and then the DNA doesn't quite copy itself properly. However the chance of mutation is increased if you're exposed to:

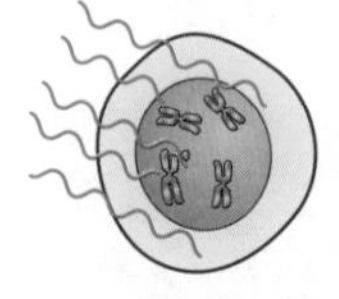

1) ionising radiation, including X-rays and ultraviolet light (which are the highest-frequency parts of the EM spectrum), together with radiation from radioactive substances. For each of these examples, the greater the dose of radiation, the greater the chance of mutation.

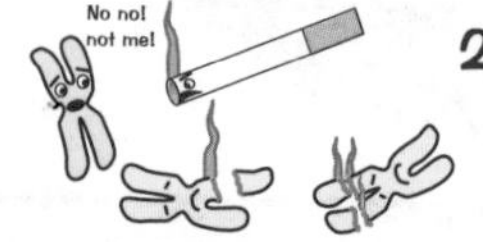

2) certain chemicals which are known to cause mutations. Such chemicals are called mutagens. If the mutations produce cancer then the chemicals are often called carcinogens. Cigarette smoke contains chemical mutagens (or carcinogens).

Run, run, it's a mutant! Run from the terrible blue budgie...

All living organisms have experienced mutation at some point in their evolutionary history. That's why we don't all look the same. They're not usually as dramatic as turning you into a human torch either.

Selective Breeding

'Selective breeding' sounds like it has the potential to be a tricky topic, but it's actually dead simple. You take the best plants or animals and breed them together to get the best possible offspring. That's it.

Selective Breeding is Very Simple

Organisms are selectively bred to develop the best features, which are things like:

A) Maximum yield of meat, milk, grain etc.

B) Good health and disease resistance.

C) In animals, other qualities like temperament, speed, fertility, good mothering skills, etc.

D) In plants, other qualities like attractive flowers, nice smell, etc.

Selective breeding is also called artificial selection, because humans artificially select the plants or animals that are going to breed and have their genes remain in the population, according to what we want from them. This is the basic process involved in selective breeding:

1) From your existing stock select the ones which have the best characteristics.
2) Breed them with each other.
3) Select the best of the offspring, and breed them together.
4) Continue this process over several generations, and the desirable trait gets stronger and stronger. In farming, this will give the farmer gradually better and better yields.

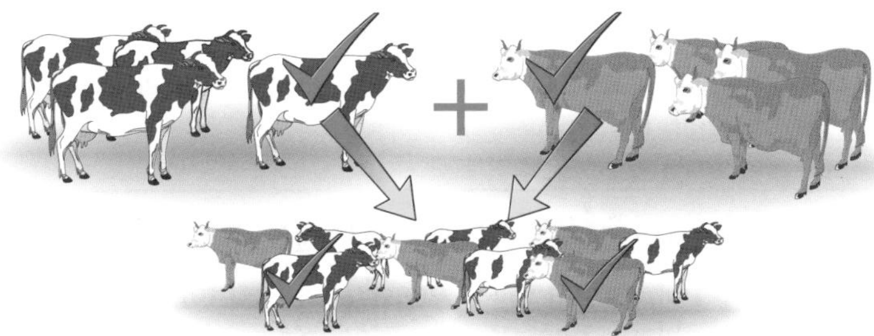

The Main Drawback is a Reduction in the Gene Pool

1) The main problem with selective breeding is that it reduces the number of different alleles (forms of a gene) in a population because the farmer keeps breeding from the "best" animals or plants — the same ones all the time.
2) There's more chance of the organisms developing genetic disorders when the gene pool is limited like this. This is because lots of these conditions are recessive — you need two alleles to be the same for it to have an effect. Related individuals are more likely to share the same alleles.
3) There can also be serious problems if a new disease appears, because there's little variety in the population. All the stock are closely related to each other, so if one of them is going to be killed by a new disease, the others are also likely to succumb to it.

Selective Breeding  Reduction in the number of different alleles (genes)  Less chance of any resistant alleles being present in the population  Nothing to selectively breed a new strain from

I use the same genes all the time too — they flatter my hips...

Selective breeding's not a new thing. People have been doing it for yonks. That's how we ended up with something like a poodle from a wolf. Somebody thought 'I really like this small, woolly, yappy wolf — I'll breed it with this other one'. And after thousands of generations, we got poodles. Hurrah.

Genetic Engineering

Genetic engineering — playing around with genes. Cool.

Genetic Engineering is Great — Hopefully

This is a young science with exciting possibilities (but potential dangers too). The basic idea is to move sections of DNA (genes) from one organism to another so that it produces useful biological products.

You need to be able to explain some of the advantages and risks involved in genetic engineering.

1) The main advantage is that you can produce organisms with new and very useful features. There are some examples of this below — make sure you learn them.
2) The main risk is that the inserted gene might have unexpected harmful effects. For example, genes are often inserted into bacteria so they produce useful products. If these bacteria mutated and became pathogenic (disease-causing), the foreign genes might make them more harmful and unpredictable. People also worry about the engineered DNA 'escaping' — e.g. weeds could gain rogue genes from a crop that's had genes for herbicide resistance inserted into it. Then they'd be unstoppable. Eeek.

Genetic Engineering Involves These Important Stages:

1) First the gene that's responsible for producing the desirable characteristic is selected (say the gene for human insulin).
2) It's then 'cut' from the DNA using enzymes, and isolated.
3) The useful gene is inserted into the host DNA of a bacterium.
4) The host bacterium is now cultivated and soon there are millions of similar bacteria all producing, say, human insulin.

Learn These Three Examples of Genetic Engineering:

1) In some parts of the world, the population relies heavily on rice for food. In these areas, vitamin A deficiency can be a problem, because rice doesn't contain much of this vitamin, and other sources are scarce. Genetic engineering has allowed scientists to take a gene that controls beta-carotene production from carrot plants, and put it into rice plants. Humans can then change the beta-carotene into Vitamin A. Problem solved.
2) The gene for human insulin production has been put into bacteria. These are cultured in a fermenter, and the human insulin is simply extracted from the medium as they produce it. Great.
3) Some plants have resistance to things like herbicides, frost damage and disease. Unfortunately, it's not always the plants we want to grow that have these features. But now, thanks to genetic engineering, we can cut out the gene responsible and stick it into any useful plant we like. Splendid.

There's Moral and Ethical Issues Involved

All this is nice, but you need to be able to weigh up these benefits against the moral and ethical issues:

1) Some people think it's wrong to genetically engineer other organisms purely for human benefit. This is a particular problem in the genetic engineering of animals, especially if the animal suffers as a result.
2) People worry that we won't stop at engineering plants and animals. Those who can afford it might decide which characteristics they want their children to have, creating a 'genetic underclass'.
3) The evolutionary consequences of genetic engineering are unknown, so some people think it's irresponsible to carry on when we're not sure what the impact on future generations might be.
4) There are concerns about 'playing God', and meddling with things that should be left well alone.

Barry played God in the school nativity — I was a sheep...

You can do great things with genetic engineering. But some people worry that we don't know enough about it, or that some maniac is going to come along and combine Cherie Blair with a grapefruit. Possibly.

Cloning: Embryo Transplants

Eeek, cloning. People get even more worked up about this than they do about genetic engineering. But embryo transplants are pretty widely used now — people don't get as upset when it's just farm animals.

Cloning is Making an Exact Copy of Another Organism

Learn this definition of clones:

Clones are genetically identical organisms.

Clones occur naturally in both plants and animals. Identical twins are clones of each other. These days clones are very much a part of the high-tech farming industry.

You Need to Know About Embryo Transplants in Cows

Normally, farmers only breed from their best cows and bulls. However, such traditional methods would only allow the prize cow to produce one new offspring each year. These days the whole process has been transformed using embryo transplants:

1) Sperm are taken from the prize bull. They can also be frozen and used at a later date.
2) Selected prize cows are given hormones to make them produce lots of eggs.
3) The cows are then artificially inseminated.
4) The fertilised eggs divide to give a ball of genetically identical cells which develops into an embryo.
5) The embryos are taken from the prize cows. Their sex is checked and they're screened for genetic defects.
6) The embryos are then split into separate cells before any cells become specialised. Each cell grows into a new embryo which is a clone of the original one.
7) The offspring are clones of each other, NOT clones of their parents.
8) These embryos are implanted into other cows, called 'surrogate mothers', where they grow. They can also be frozen and used at a later date.

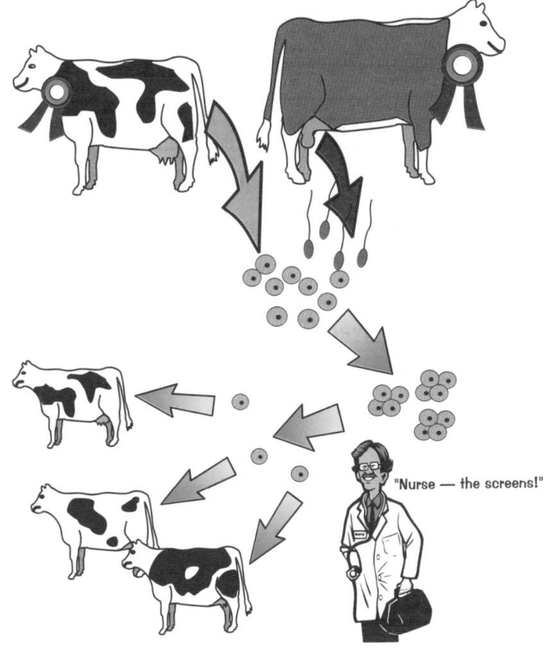

Advantages of Embryo Transplants — Hundreds of Ideal Offspring

a) Hundreds of "ideal" offspring can be produced every year from the best bull and cow.
b) The original prize cow can keep producing prize eggs all year round.

Disadvantages — Reduced Gene Pool

The main problem is that the same alleles keep appearing (and many others are lost). So there's a greater risk of genetic disorders, and a disease could wipe out an entire population if there are no resistant alleles (see page 19).

Thank goodness they didn't do that with my little brother...

It seems strange that you can pull apart a growing embryo and not harm it. But at that stage, the cells are all the same — they haven't started to differentiate into different cells with different jobs to do yet. So if you can separate them gently enough that the cells aren't damaged, they keep dividing quite happily.

Adult Cloning

Ah, Dolly the sheep. It seems a long time ago now, but she was the first mammal cloned from an adult cell. She was born in 1996, the only success of 277 attempts by the team who created her.

Cloning an Adult is Done by Transplanting a Cell Nucleus

The first mammal to be successfully cloned from an adult cell was a sheep called "Dolly".
This is the method that was used to produce Dolly:

1) The nucleus of a sheep's egg cell was removed — this left the egg cell without any genetic information.
2) Another nucleus was inserted in its place. This was a diploid nucleus from an udder cell of a different sheep (the one being cloned) and had all its genetic information.
3) The cell was stimulated so that it started dividing by mitosis, as if it was a normal fertilised egg.
4) The dividing cell was implanted into the uterus of another sheep to develop until it was ready to be born.
5) The result was Dolly, a clone of the sheep from which the udder cell came.

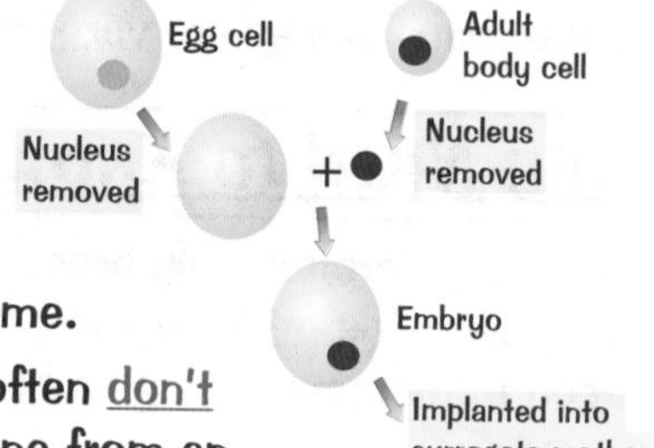

There are risks with cloning. Embryos formed by cloning from adult cells often don't develop normally. There had been many failed attempts at producing a clone from an adult before the success with Dolly.

There are Both Benefits and Risks Involved in Cloning

There are many possible benefits of cloning:

1) Animals that can produce medicines in their milk could be cloned. Researchers have managed to transfer human genes that produce useful proteins into sheep and cows, so that they can produce, for example, the blood clotting agent factor VIII used for treating haemophilia. With cloning, you only need to transfer the genes once, and then you could clone the animal as many times as you liked.
2) Animals (probably pigs) that have organs suitable for organ transplantation into humans (xenotransplantation) could be developed by genetic engineering and then cloned in the same way.
3) The study of animal clones and cloned cells could lead to greater understanding of the development of the embryo and of ageing and age-related disorders.
4) Cloning could be used to help preserve endangered species.

But there are risks too:

1) There is some evidence that cloned animals might not be as healthy as normal ones.
2) Cloning is a new science and it might have consequences that we're not yet aware of.
3) People are worried that humans might be produced by cloning if research continues.

Cloning Humans is a Possibility — with a Lot of Ethical Issues

As the technology used to clone mammals improves, it becomes more and more likely that humans could one day be cloned as well. However, there are still enormous difficulties to be overcome, and it might well involve women willing to donate hundreds of eggs. There would have to be lots of surrogate pregnancies, probably with high rates of miscarriage and stillbirth. The problems scientists have had with other mammals (see below) have shown that the human clones produced could well be unhealthy and die prematurely. There are also worries that if we clone humans we will be 'playing God', and meddling with things we don't fully understand. Even if a healthy clone were produced, it might be psychologically damaged by the knowledge that it's just a clone of another human being.

A whole lamb from a single cell? Pull the udder one...

Since Dolly, scientists have successfully cloned all kinds of mammals including goats, cows, mice, pigs, cats, rabbits, horses and dogs. Many of these clones suffered health problems and died young — Dolly seemed normal, but died aged just six (when the breed has a life expectancy of 11-12).

Cloning Plants: Asexual Reproduction

Many Plants Produce Clones — All by Themselves

This means they produce exact genetic copies of themselves without involving another plant.

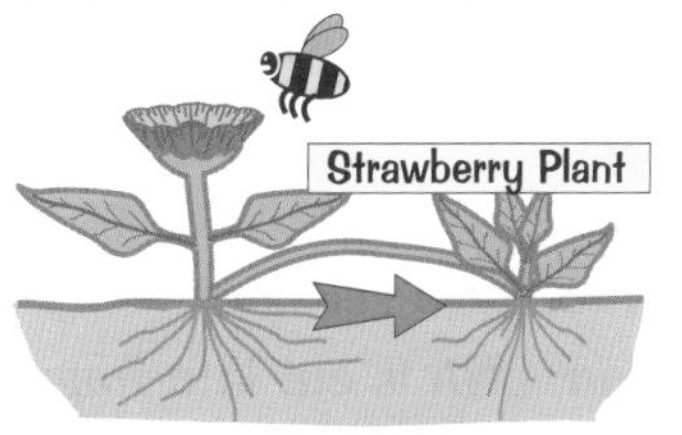

1) Strawberry plants produce runners.

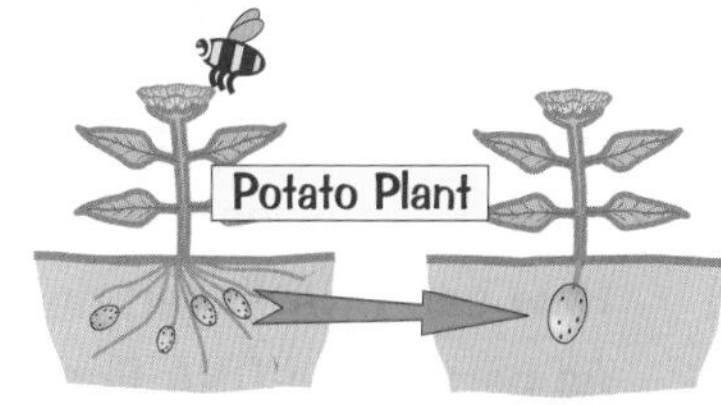

2) Tubers grow on plants like potatoes and give clones of the parent plant.

Gardeners are familiar with taking cuttings from good parent plants, and then planting them to produce identical copies (clones) of the parent plant. Cloning plants is easier than cloning animals because many plant cells keep their ability to differentiate (see page 14) — animal cells lose this at an early stage.

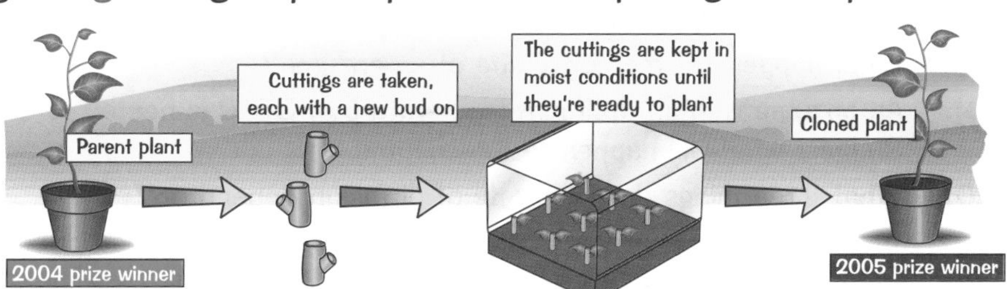

Commercial Cloning Often Involves Tissue Culture

1) First you choose the plant you want to clone based on its characteristics — e.g. a beautiful flower, a good fruit crop.
2) You remove a small amount of tissue from the parent plant. Because you only need a tiny amount, you can remove tissue from several points to give several clones. You get the best results if you take tissue from fast-growing root and shoot tips.
3) You grow the tissue in a medium containing nutrients and growth hormones. This is done under aseptic (sterile) conditions to prevent growth of microbes that could harm the plants.
4) As the tissues produce shoots and roots they can be moved to potting compost to carry on growing.

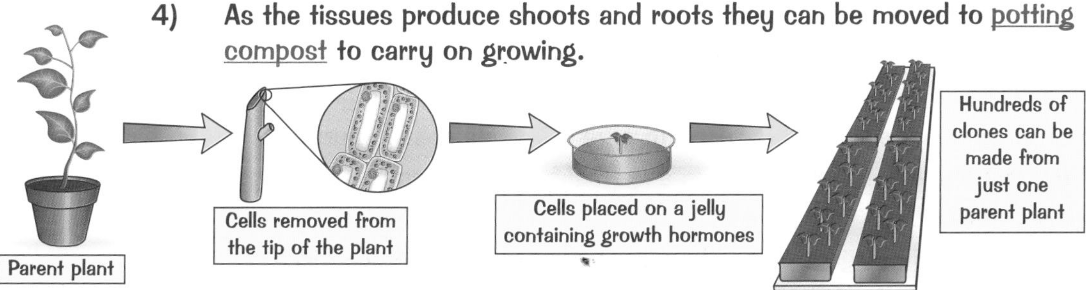

Commercial Use of Cloned Plants Has Pros and Cons

1) You can be fairly sure of the characteristics of the plant because it'll be genetically identical to the parent — so you'll only get good ones, and won't waste time and money growing duds.
2) It's possible to mass-produce plants that are hard to grow from scratch.
3) But, if the plants suffer from a disease or start doing badly because of a change in environment, they'll all have the same problems because they all have the same genes.
4) And there are the usual problems with lack of genetic variation (see page 19).

Stop cloning around — just learn it...

Plants are much better at being cloned than mammals are. They don't start dropping dead or having health problems, they just get on with it. And nobody seems that bothered about ethics when it's a tulip.

Revision Summary for Module B3

Well, just look at this — it's your first Revision Summary page. There's one of these little fellas at the end of every section, and my, they're a right bundle of laughs. No really, they're hilarious. Just look at question one there — "Where in a cell does respiration happen?" HAAAAH HAR HAR HAR. Good one.

1) Where in a cell does respiration happen?
2) What is a nucleotide?
3) How can DNA fingerprinting be used in forensic science?
4) As part of the DNA fingerprinting method, DNA is cut into fragments. How is this done?
5) The DNA is then suspended in a gel and an electric current is passed through it. How does this separate out the DNA fragments?
6) What is transamination?
7) What name is given to biological catalysts?
8) What happens at the active site of an enzyme?
9) An enzyme with an optimum temperature of 37 °C is heated to 60 °C. Suggest what will happen to the enzyme.
10) What three things does the rate of diffusion depend on?
11) Give three ways that the small intestine is adapted for absorption.
12) Why does oxygen enter the blood in the alveoli, and leave it when it reaches a respiring tissue?
13) Name two substances that diffuse through the placenta from the foetus to the mother.
14) Name six things that blood plasma transports around the body.
15) Name the substance formed in red blood cells when haemoglobin reacts with oxygen.
16) Why do arteries need very muscular, elastic walls?
17) Explain how capillaries are adapted to their function.
18) Name the blood vessel that joins to the right ventricle of the heart. Where does it take the blood?
19) Why does the left ventricle have a thicker wall than the right ventricle?
20) What must doctors consider when deciding if someone is a suitable donor for a heart transplant?
21) How many cells are produced after a mitotic division? Are they genetically identical?
22) How many cells are produced after a meiotic division? Are they genetically identical?
23) Give three ways that sperm cells are adapted for their function.
24) Describe two differences in the way plant cells and animal cells grow and develop.
25) Explain how stem cells could be used to cure a serious spinal injury.
26) List the five stages of growth seen in a normal human life span.
27) What are auxins?
28) Shoots are negatively geotropic. How are auxins responsible for this?
29) Give three ways that plant growth hormones are used commercially.
30) Why are mutations in an organism's DNA often harmful to that organism?
31) Give two things that increase the rate of mutation if you are exposed to them.
32) Suggest three features that you might selectively breed for in a dairy cow.
33) Give two disadvantages of selective breeding.
34) Give three ways that genetic engineering has been used successfully in crop plants.
35) What are the advantages and disadvantages of the cloning technique used in embryo transplants?
36) Three sheep were used to produce Dolly. One provided the egg cell she grew from, another provided the nucleus for this cell, and the last gave birth to her. Which sheep was Dolly a clone of?
37) Give three potential benefits and three potential risks of continuing to clone mammals.
38) In plants, where should you take the tissue from to get the best results from a tissue culture?

Chemical Equations

These can get real tricky, real fast, so practise them now until they're perfect...

A chemical reaction can be described by the process reactants → products.

e.g. magnesium + oxygen → magnesium oxide

which means magnesium reacts with oxygen to produce magnesium oxide.

You have to know how to write these reactions in both words and symbols, as shown below:

The Symbol Equation Shows the Atoms on Both Sides:

Magnesium + Oxygen → Magnesium oxide

$2Mg + O_2 \rightarrow 2MgO$

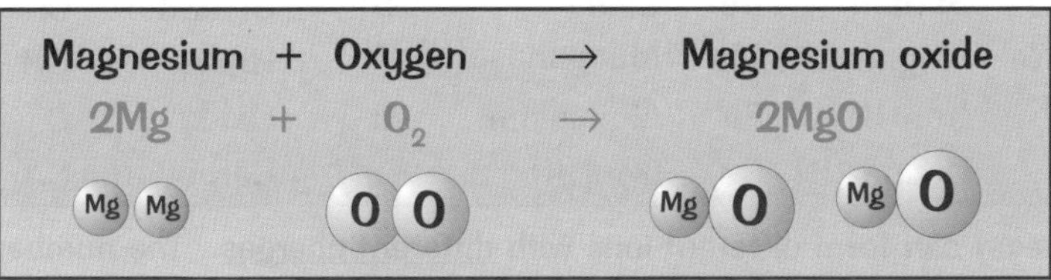

Methane + Oxygen → Water + Carbon Dioxide

$CH_4 + 2O_2 \rightarrow 2H_2O + CO_2$

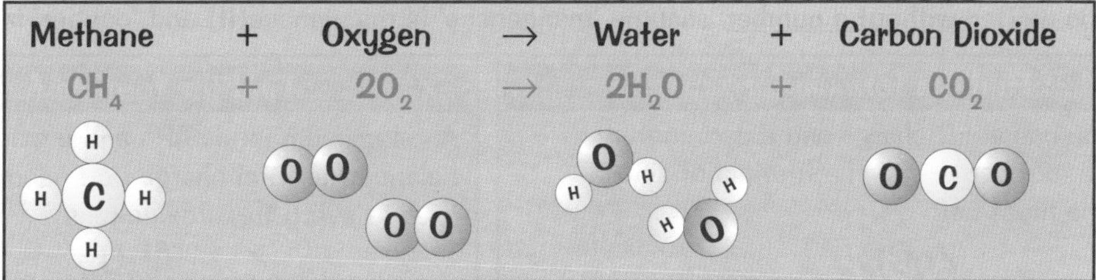

You Need to Know How to Write Out Any Equation

You really do need to know how to write out chemical equations. In fact, you need to know how to write out equations for pretty much all the reactions in this book.

That might sound like an awful lot, but there aren't nearly as many as you think. Have a look.

You also need to know the formula for all the ionic and covalent compounds in here too. Lovely.

Displayed Formulas Show the Bonds in a Molecule

A molecule's displayed formula's really useful because it shows all the atoms and all the covalent bonds (see p.36).

Finding the molecular formula from it is really easy — all you have to do is add up the number of each different type of atom.

The molecule on the right has a single carbon and four hydrogen atoms, so the molecular formula is CH_4.

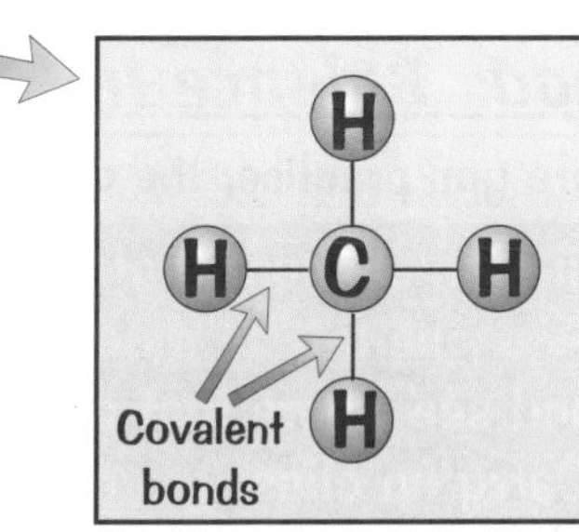

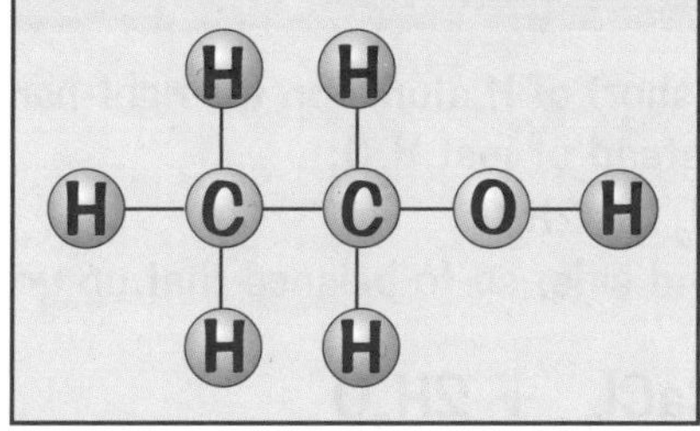

Here is the displayed formula for ethanol. Its molecular formula is C_2H_6O.

Chemistry's just full of formulas...

Keep practising chemical equations throughout this section. After all, practice makes perfect. It's tricky imagining all those little molecules zooming about in the air we breathe or seeing water as an oxygen with two hydrogens. But you will — just give it time...

Balancing Equations

For full marks you're going to need to know how to balance chemical equations...

You Need to Know These Chemical Formulas

Before you can balance anything, you need to be able to write down the right chemical formulas.
That means you have to learn the stuff in this table and how to use it.
The main thing to remember is that in compounds the total charge must always add up to zero.

Common Substances		Positive Ions						Negative Ions	
Water	H_2O	Lithium	Li^+	Barium	Ba^{2+}	Zinc	Zn^{2+}	Chloride	Cl^-
Carbon dioxide	CO_2	Sodium	Na^+	Magnesium	Mg^{2+}	Manganese(II)	Mn^{2+}	Hydroxide	OH^-
Methane	CH_4	Potassium	K^+	Iron(II)	Fe^{2+}	Aluminium	Al^{3+}	Oxide	O^{2-}
Silver nitrate	$AgNO_3$			Copper(II)	Cu^{2+}	Iron(III)	Fe^{3+}	Carbonate	CO_3^{2-}

Some metals (e.g. copper, iron and manganese) can form different ions with different charges. The number in brackets after the name tells you the size of the positive charge on the ion. If you ever see them in compounds written without a number, assume 'manganese' is manganese(II) and 'copper' is copper(II).

EXAMPLE: Find the formula for zinc carbonate.

A zinc ion has a +2 charge and a carbonate ion has a –2 charge. So the formula of zinc carbonate must be:

$$ZnCO_3$$

EXAMPLE: Find the formula for aluminium oxide.

An aluminium ion is Al^{3+} and a oxide ion is O^{2-}. To balance the total charge you need two aluminium ions to every three oxide ions.

$$Al_2O_3$$

Balancing the Equation — Match Them Up One by One

1) There must always be the same number of atoms on both sides — they can't just disappear.
2) You balance the equation by putting numbers in front of the formulas where needed.
   Take this equation for reacting calcium hydroxide with hydrochloric acid:

$$Ca(OH)_2 + HCl \rightarrow CaCl_2 + H_2O$$

The formulas are all correct but the numbers of some atoms don't match up on both sides.
You can't change a formula like $Ca(OH)_2$ to $Ca(OH)_3$. You can only put numbers in front of them:

Method: Balance Just ONE Type of Atom at a Time

The more you practise, the quicker you get, but all you do is this:

1) Find an element that doesn't balance and pencil in a number to try and sort it out.
2) See where it gets you. It may create another imbalance, but pencil in another number and see where that gets you.
3) Carry on chasing unbalanced elements and it'll sort itself out pretty quickly.

I'll show you. In the equation above you soon notice we're short of H atoms on the right-hand side.

1) The only thing you can do about that is make it $2H_2O$ instead of just H_2O:

$$Ca(OH)_2 + HCl \rightarrow CaCl_2 + 2H_2O$$

2) But that now causes too many H atoms on the right-hand side, so to balance that up you could try putting 2HCl on the left-hand side:

$$Ca(OH)_2 + 2HCl \rightarrow CaCl_2 + 2H_2O$$

3) And suddenly there it is. Everything balances. And you'll notice the Cl just sorted itself out.

A balanced diet — a biscuit in one hand, an apple in the other...

It's all maths, this page. What's the charge on the positive ion... what's the charge on the negative ion... how many atoms on the left... how many on the right... just make sure they're equal and you'll fly by.

Atoms

There are quite a few different (and equally useful) models of the atom — but chemists tend to like this model best. You can use it to explain pretty much the whole of chemistry... which is nice.

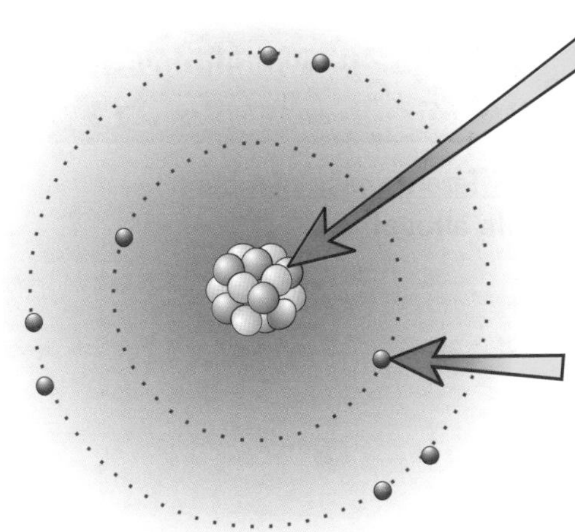

The Nucleus

1) It's in the middle of the atom.
2) It contains protons and neutrons.
3) It has a positive charge because of the protons.
4) Almost the whole mass of the atom is concentrated in the nucleus.
5) But size-wise it's tiny compared to the rest of the atom.

The Electrons

1) Move around the nucleus.
2) They're negatively charged.
3) They're tiny, but they cover a lot of space.
4) The volume of their orbits determines how big the atom is.
5) They have virtually no mass.
6) They occupy shells around the nucleus.
7) These shells explain the whole of chemistry.

Atoms are really tiny, don't forget. They're too small to see, even with a very high power microscope.

PARTICLE	MASS	CHARGE
Proton	1	+1
Neutron	1	0
Electron	0.0005	–1

Protons are heavy and positively charged
Neutrons are heavy and neutral
Electrons are tiny and negatively charged (Electron mass is often taken as zero.)

Number of Protons Equals Number of Electrons

1) Neutral atoms have no charge overall.
2) The charge on the electrons is the same size as the charge on the protons — but opposite.
3) This means the number of protons always equals the number of electrons in a neutral atom.
4) If some electrons are added or removed, the atom becomes charged and is then an ion.

Atomic Number and Mass Number Describe an Atom

These two numbers tell you how many of each kind of particle an atom has.

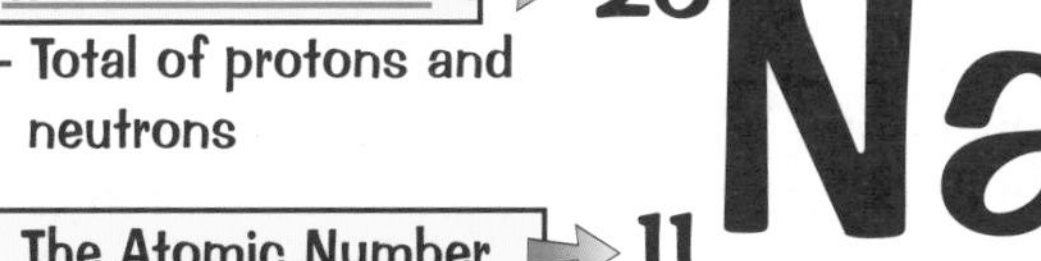

1) The atomic (proton) number tells you how many protons there are.
2) Atoms of the same element all have the same number of protons — so atoms of different elements will have different numbers of protons.
3) To get the number of neutrons, just subtract the atomic number from the mass number.
4) The mass (nucleon) number is always the biggest number. On a periodic table the mass number is actually the relative atomic mass.
5) The mass number tends to be roughly double the proton number.
6) Which means there's about the same number of protons as neutrons in most nuclei.

Number of protons = number of electrons...

This stuff might seem a bit useless at first, but it should be permanently engraved into your mind. If you don't know these basic facts, you've got no chance of understanding the rest of chemistry. So learn it now, and watch as the Universe unfolds and reveals its timeless mysteries to you...

Isotopes, Elements and Compounds

And the question on everybody's lips is — what are isotopes...

Isotopes are the Same Except for an Extra Neutron or Two

Isotopes are: different atomic forms of the same element, which have the SAME number of PROTONS but a DIFFERENT number of NEUTRONS.

1) The upshot is: isotopes must have the same atomic number but different mass numbers.
2) If they had different atomic numbers, they'd be different elements altogether.
3) A very popular pair of isotopes are carbon-12 and carbon-14.

Carbon-12

$^{12}_{6}C$

6 PROTONS
6 ELECTRONS
6 NEUTRONS

Carbon-14

$^{14}_{6}C$

6 PROTONS
6 ELECTRONS
8 NEUTRONS

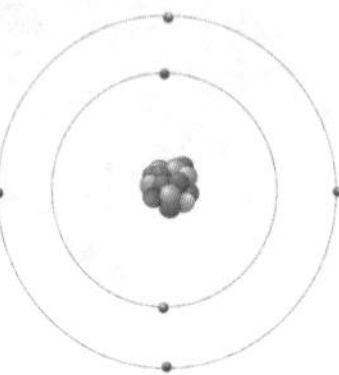

The number of electrons decides the chemistry of the element. If the atomic number is the same, then the number of protons is the same, so the number of electrons is the same, so the chemistry is the same. The different number of neutrons in the nucleus doesn't affect the chemical behaviour at all.

Elements Consist of One Type of Atom Only

Elements cannot be broken down chemically. Quite a lot of everyday substances are elements:

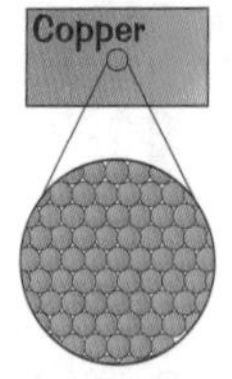

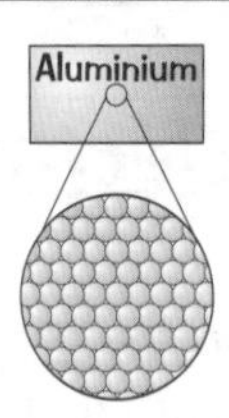

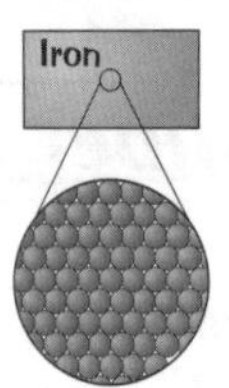

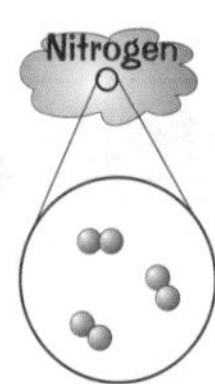

Compounds are Chemically Bonded

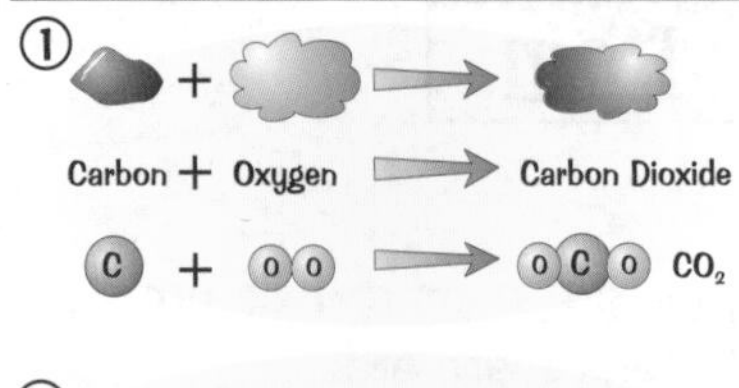

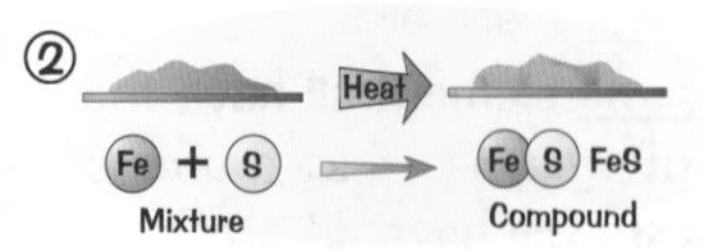

1) Carbon dioxide is a compound formed from a chemical reaction between carbon and oxygen.
2) It's very difficult to separate the two original elements again.
3) The properties of a compound are totally different from the properties of the original elements.
4) If iron and sulfur react to form iron sulfide, the compound formed is a grey solid lump, and doesn't behave anything like either iron or sulfur.

There are two types of chemical bonding:

1) Ionic Bonding — the attraction between positive and negative particles called ions.
2) Covalent Bonding — sharing a pair of electrons.

   You'll find out more about these types of bond later in this section.
   Until then, you'll just have to hold your breath...

Don't mix these up — it'll only compound your problems...

There are loads of natural isotopes out there. Radioactive ones, non-radioactive ones... they have their uses as well. Carbon's in every living organism, carbon-13 and carbon-14 are both radioactive (great stuff), and what's more, carbon-14's used to date old materials... wonder if it'd work on my Dad...

The Periodic Table

The periodic table is a chemist's bestest friend — start getting to know it now... seriously...

The Periodic Table is a Table of All Known Elements

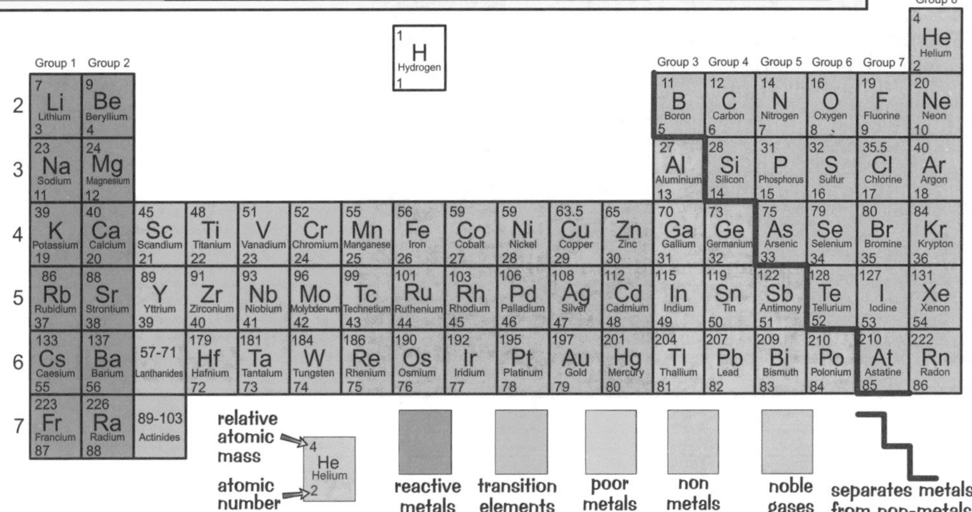

1) There are 100ish elements, which all materials are made of. More are still being 'discovered'.
2) The modern periodic table shows the elements in order of ascending atomic number.
3) The periodic table is laid out so that elements with similar properties form columns.
4) These vertical columns are called groups and roman numerals are often (but not always) used for them.
5) The group to which the element belongs corresponds to the number of electrons it has in its outer shell. E.g. Group 1 elements have 1 outer shell electron, Group 7 elements have 7 outer shell electrons, and so on.
6) Some of the groups have special names. Group 1 elements are called alkali metals. Group 7 elements are called halogens, and Group 8 elements are called the noble gases.
7) The rows are called periods. Each new period represents another full shell of electrons (see page 30).
8) The period to which the element belongs corresponds to the number of shells of electrons it has.

Elements in a Group Have the Same Number of Outer Electrons

1) The elements in each group all have the same number of electrons in their outer shell.
2) That's why they have similar properties. And that's why we arrange them in this way.
3) When only a small number of elements were known, the periodic table was made by looking at the properties of the elements and arranging them in groups — the same groups that they are in today.
4) This idea is extremely important to chemistry — so make sure you understand it.

The properties of the elements are decided entirely by how many electrons they have.
Atomic number is therefore very significant because it is equal to the number of electrons each atom has.
But it's the number of electrons in the outer shell which is the really important thing.

Electron Shells are Just Totally Brill

The fact that electrons form shells around atoms is the basis for the whole of chemistry.
If they just whizzed round the nucleus any old how and didn't care about shells or any of that stuff there'd be no chemical reactions. No nothing in fact — because nothing would happen.
The atoms would just slob about, all day long. Just like teenagers.
But amazingly, they do form shells (if they didn't, we wouldn't even be here to wonder about it), and the electron arrangement of each atom determines the whole of its chemical behaviour.
Phew. I mean electron arrangements explain practically the whole Universe. They're just totally brill.

This table comes up periodically...

Physicists are still producing new elements in particle accelerators, but they're all radioactive.
Most only last a fraction of a second before they decay — they're up to element 118 at the moment.

Electron Shells

Electron shells... orbits electrons zoom about in.

Electron Shell Rules:

1) Electrons always occupy shells (sometimes called energy levels).
2) The lowest energy levels are always filled first.
3) Only a certain number of electrons are allowed in each shell:
   1st shell: 2 2nd Shell: 8 3rd Shell: 8
4) Atoms are much happier when they have full electron shells.
5) In most atoms the outer shell is not full and this makes the atom want to react.

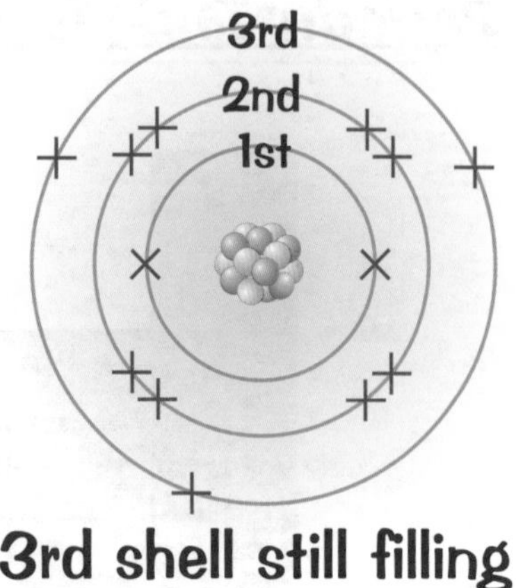

3rd shell still filling

Working Out Electron Configurations

You need to know the electron configurations for the first 20 elements. They're shown in the diagram below — but they're not hard to work out. For a quick example, take nitrogen. Follow the steps...

1) The periodic table tells you that nitrogen has seven protons... so it must have seven electrons.
2) Follow the 'Electron Shell Rules' above. The first shell can only take 2 electrons and the second shell can take a maximum of 8 electrons.
3) So the electron configuration for nitrogen must be 2,5 — easy peasy.
4) Now you try it for argon.

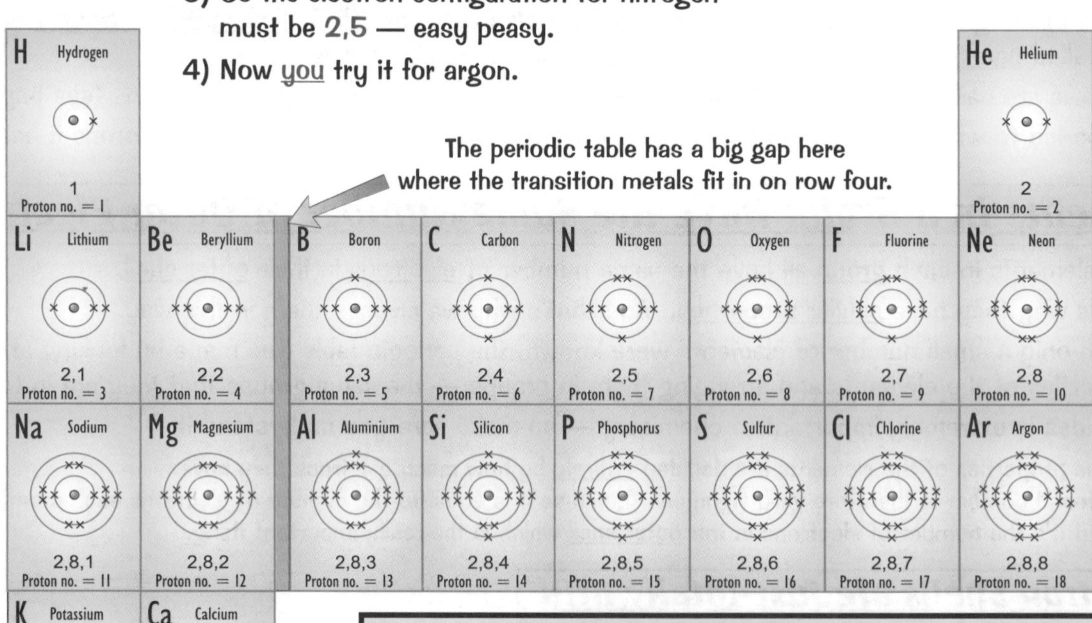

Answer: To calculate the electron configuration of argon, follow the rules. It's got 18 protons, so it must have 18 electrons. The first shell must have 2 electrons, the second shell must have 8, and so the third shell must have 8 as well. It's as easy as 2, 8, 8.

One little duck and two fat ladies — 2, 8, 8...

You need to know enough about electron shells to draw out that whole diagram at the bottom of the page without looking at it. Obviously, you don't have to learn each element separately, just learn the pattern. Cover the page: using a periodic table, find the atom with the electron configuration 2, 8, 6.

Ionic Bonding

Ionic Bonding — Transferring Electrons

In ionic bonding, atoms lose or gain electrons to form charged particles (or ions) which are then strongly attracted to one another (because of the attraction of opposite charges, + and –).

A Shell with Just One Electron is Well Keen to Get Rid...

All the atoms over at the left-hand side of the periodic table, such as sodium, potassium, calcium etc., have just one or two electrons in their outer shell. And basically they're pretty keen to get shot of them, because then they'll only have full shells left, which is how they like it.
So given half a chance they do get rid, and that leaves the atom as an ion instead.
Now ions aren't the kind of things to sit around quietly watching the world go by.
They tend to leap at the first passing ion with an opposite charge and stick to it like glue.

A Nearly Full Shell is Well Keen to Get That Extra Electron...

On the other side of the periodic table the elements in Group 6 and Group 7, such as oxygen and chlorine, have outer shells which are nearly full. They're obviously pretty keen to gain that extra one or two electrons to fill the shell up. When they do of course they become ions — you know, not the kind of things to sit around, and before you know it, pop, they've latched onto the atom (ion) that gave up the electron a moment earlier. The reaction of sodium and chlorine is a classic case:

① The sodium atom gives up its outer electron and becomes an Na^+ ion.

② The chlorine atom picks up the spare electron and becomes a Cl^- ion.

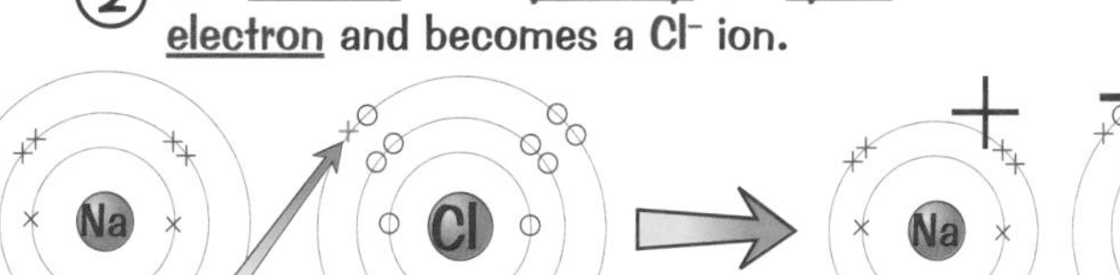

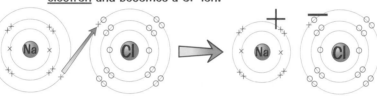

③ **POP!**

An ionic bond is formed.

Simple Ions — Groups 1 & 2 and 6 & 7

1) Ions are charged particles — they can be single atoms (e.g. Cl^-) or groups of atoms (e.g. NO_3^-).
2) When atoms lose or gain electrons to form ions, all they're trying to do is get a full outer shell (a stable octet). Atoms like full outer shells — it's atom heaven.
3) When metals form ions, they lose electrons to form positive ions. Loss of electrons is called oxidation.
4) When non-metals form ions, they gain electrons to form negative ions. Gain of electrons is called reduction.
5) So when a metal and a non-metal combine, they form ionic bonds.
6) You need to know the positive and negative ions in the table on the right.
7) To work out the formula of an ionic compound, you have to balance the +ve and the –ve charges.

Positive (+ve) ions		Negative (–ve) ions	
Group 1	Group 2	Group 6	Group 7
Li^+	Be^{2+}	O^{2-}	F^-
Na^+	Mg^{2+}		Cl^-
K^+	Ca^{2+}		

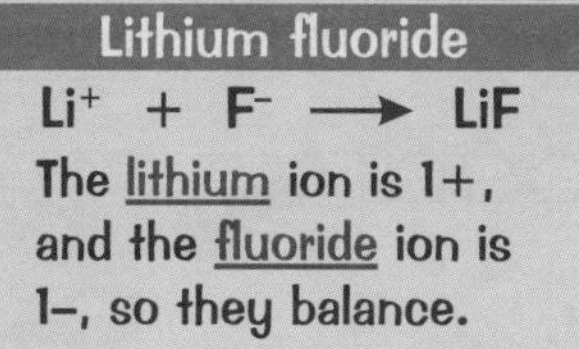
Lithium fluoride

$Li^+ + F^- \longrightarrow LiF$

The lithium ion is 1+, and the fluoride ion is 1–, so they balance.

Potassium oxide

$2\,K^+ + O^{2-} \longrightarrow K_2O$

The potassium ion is 1+, and the oxygen ion is 2–, so you need two K^+ ions to balance the O^{2-} ion.

Magnesium chloride

$Mg^{2+} + 2\,Cl^- \longrightarrow MgCl_2$

The magnesium ion is 2+, and the chloride ion is 1–, so you need two Cl^- ions to balance the Mg^{2+} ion.

Full Shells — it's the name of the game...

Here's where you can get a little practice working out formulas for molecules. Remember to balance them, or you'll lose marks. Some elements like to gain electrons, some like to lose electrons, but they all want to have a full outer shell. Poor little electron shells, all they want in life is to be full...

Ions and Ionic Compounds

Electronic Structure of Some Simple Ions

'Dot and cross' diagrams show what happens to the electrons in ionic bonds:

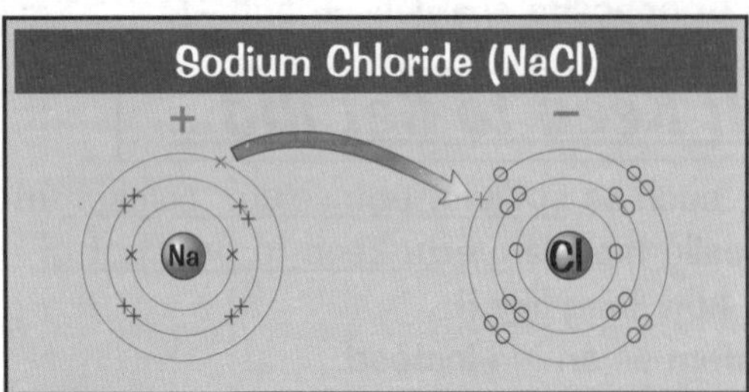

The sodium atom gives up its outer electron, becoming an Na^+ ion. The chlorine atom picks up the electron, becoming a Cl^- (chloride) ion.

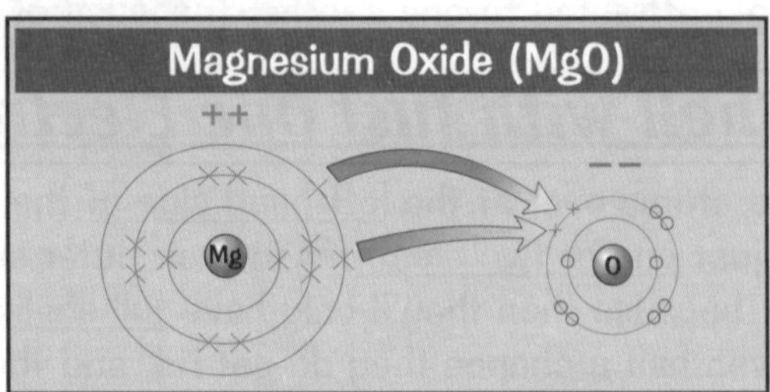

The magnesium atom gives up its two outer electrons, becoming an Mg^{2+} ion. The oxygen atom picks up the electrons, becoming an O^{2-} (oxide) ion.

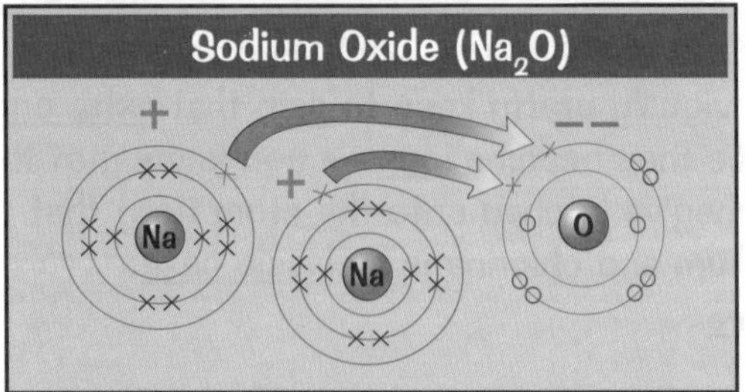

Two sodium atoms give up their outer electrons, becoming two Na^+ ions. The oxygen atom picks up the two electrons, becoming an O^{2-} ion.

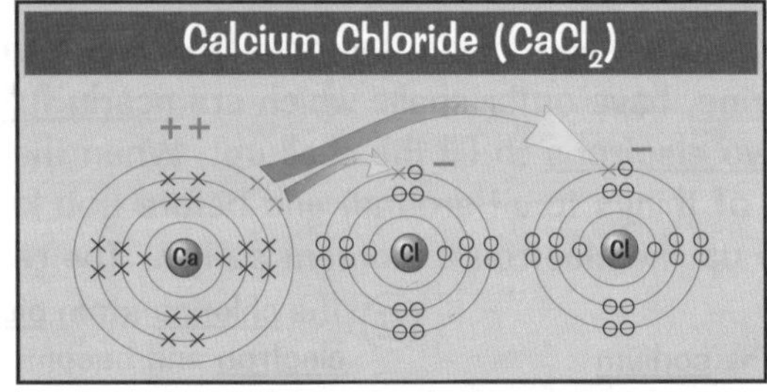

The calcium atom gives up its two outer electrons, becoming a Ca^{2+} ion. The two chlorine atoms pick up one electron each, becoming two Cl^- (chloride) ions.

Notice that all the atoms end up with full outer shells as a result of this giving and taking of electrons.

NaCl and MgO Form Giant Ionic Lattices

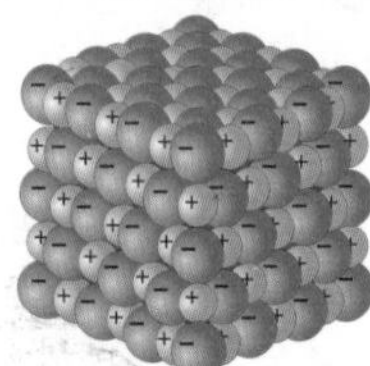

1) Ionic bonds always produce giant ionic structures.
2) The ions form a closely packed regular lattice arrangement. The ions are not free to move though, so these compounds do not conduct electricity when solid.
3) There are very strong chemical bonds between all the ions.
4) A single crystal of sodium chloride (salt) is one giant ionic lattice, which is why salt crystals tend to be cuboid in shape.

1) They Have High Melting Points and Boiling Points...

...due to the very strong chemical bonds between all the ions in the giant structure.

2) NaCl Dissolves to Form a Solution That Conducts Electricity

When dissolved the ions separate and are all free to move in the solution, so obviously they'll carry electric current.
(Not all ionic compounds dissolve in water — MgO is insoluble.)

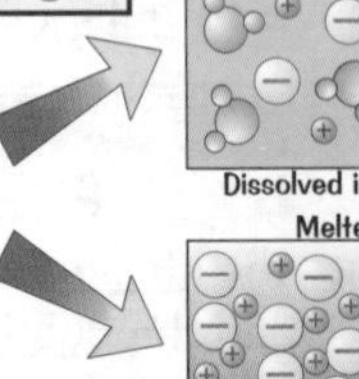

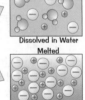

3) They Conduct Electricity When Molten

When it melts, the ions are free to move and they'll carry electric current.

Giant ionic lattices — all over your chips...

Because they conduct electricity when they're dissolved in water, ionic compounds are used to make some types of battery. In the olden days, most batteries had actual liquid in, so they tended to leak all over the place. Now they've come up with a sort of paste that doesn't leak but still conducts. Clever.

Group 1 — Alkali Metals

Group 1 Metals are Known as the 'Alkali Metals'

Group 1 metals include lithium, sodium and potassium... know those three names real well. They could also ask you about rubidium and caesium.

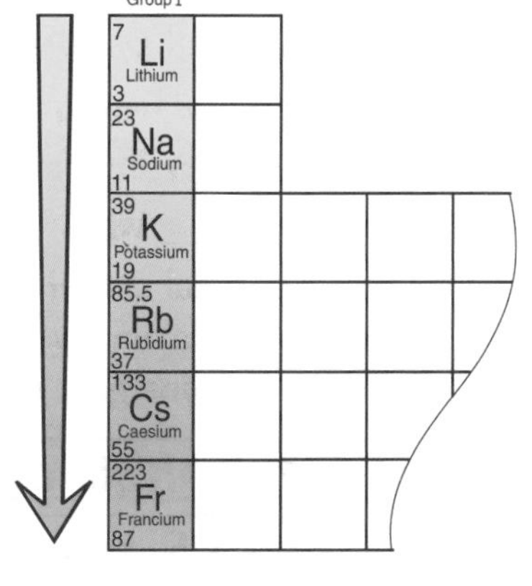

As you go DOWN Group 1, the alkali metals become more reactive — the outer electron is more easily lost, because it's further from the nucleus.

1) The alkali metals all have ONE outer electron. This makes them very reactive and gives them all similar properties.
2) They all have the following physical properties:
   - Low melting point and boiling point (compared with other metals),
   - Low density — lithium, sodium and potassium float on water,
   - Very soft — they can be cut with a knife.
3) The alkali metals always form ionic compounds. They are so keen to lose the outer electron there's no way they'd consider sharing, so covalent bonding is out of the question.

Oxidation is the Loss of Electrons

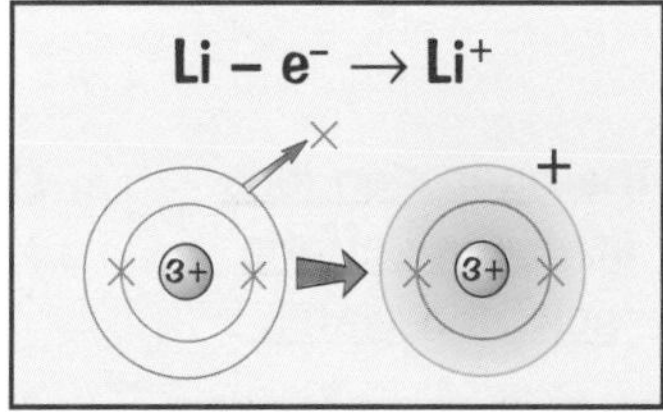

1) Group 1 metals are keen to lose an electron to form a 1^+ ion with a stable electronic structure.
2) The more reactive the metal the happier it is to lose an electron.
3) Loss of electrons is called OXIDATION.

Reaction with Cold Water Produces Hydrogen Gas

1) When lithium, sodium or potassium are put in water, they react very vigorously.
2) They move around the surface, fizzing furiously.
3) They produce hydrogen.
4) The reactivity with water increases down the group — the reaction with potassium gets hot enough to ignite it.
5) Sodium and potassium melt in the heat of the reaction.
6) They form a hydroxide in solution, i.e. aqueous OH^- ions.

A lighted splint will indicate hydrogen by producing the notorious "squeaky pop" as the H_2 ignites.

Squeaky pop!!

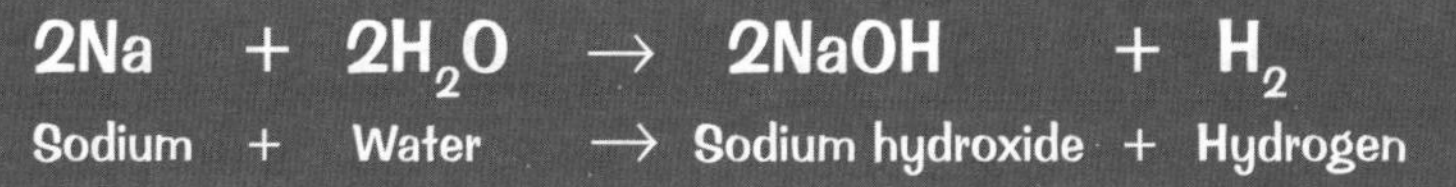

$$2Na + 2H_2O \rightarrow 2NaOH + H_2$$

Sodium + Water → Sodium hydroxide + Hydrogen

The solution becomes alkaline, which changes the colour of the pH indicator (see C4, page 73) to purple.

Alkali Metal Compounds Burn with Characteristic Colours

1) Dip a wire loop into some hydrochloric acid to clean it.
2) Put the loop into a powered sample of the compound to be tested, then place the end in a blue Bunsen flame.
3) Alkali metal ions will give pretty coloured flames — the colour of the flame tells you which alkali metal is present.

Lithium:	Red flame
Sodium:	Yellow/orange flame
Potassium:	Lilac flame

Red and orange and pink and green — or something like that...

Alkali metals are really reactive. They're so reactive in fact they have to be stored in oil — otherwise they just react with the air. Learn the trends and characteristics of alkali metals before turning over.

Electrolysis and the Half-Equations

Electrolysis Means 'Splitting Up with Electricity'

1) Electrolysis is the breaking down of a substance using electricity.
2) It needs a liquid to conduct the electricity, called the electrolyte.
3) Electrolytes are usually free ions dissolved in water, e.g. dilute acids like H_2SO_4, and dissolved salts like NaCl.
4) It's the free ions which conduct the electricity and allow the whole thing to work.
5) For an electrical circuit to be complete, there's got to be a flow of electrons. In electrolysis, electrons are taken away from ions at the positive anode and given to other ions at the negative cathode. As ions gain or lose electrons they become atoms or molecules and are released.

The Electrolysis of Sulfuric Acid Solution

Water contains hydrogen and oxygen — two elements that are very useful gases.
But, pure water doesn't conduct electricity very well, which makes its electrolysis difficult.
If you add a little sulfuric acid it conducts a lot better.

In solution, the molecules will split into their ions:

$$H_2O \rightleftharpoons H^+ + OH^-$$
$$H_2SO_4 \rightleftharpoons 2H^+ + SO_4^{2-}$$

The hydrogen ions are from sulfuric acid and water.

+ve ions are called CATIONS because they're attracted to the –ve cathode.

Hydrogen is produced at the –ve cathode.

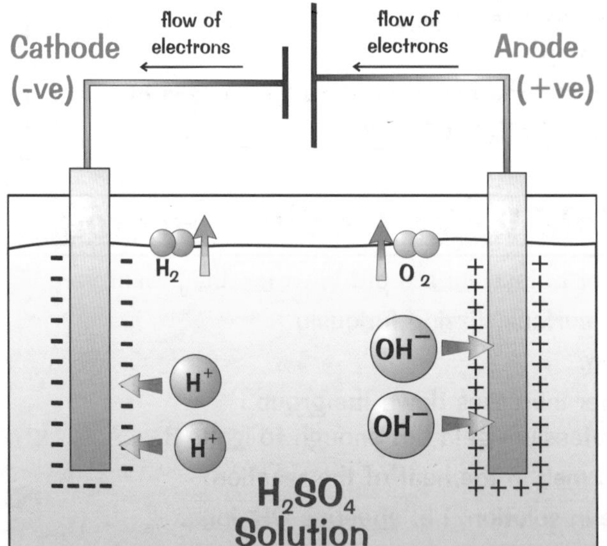

All the hydroxide ions come from water.

–ve ions are called ANIONS because they're attracted to the +ve anode.

Oxygen is produced at the +ve anode.

1) At the cathode, two hydrogen ions accept two electrons to become one hydrogen molecule.
2) At the anode, four hydroxide (OH^-) ions lose their electrons and become one oxygen molecule and two water molecules.

The Half-Equations — Make Sure the Electrons Balance

The main thing is to make sure the charges balance on each side of each half-equation.
For the above cell the half-equations are:

Cathode: $2H^+ + 2e^- \rightarrow H_2$

Anode: $4OH^- \rightarrow 2H_2O + O_2 + 4e^-$

Cations — sounds like a useful form of pet control...

So you need a bit of acid to split water into hydrogen and oxygen. Hydrogen gas is used in the Haber process, which makes ammonia — you'll learn all about this on page 80. Oxygen is just generally great, you know, for breathing and stuff...

Extracting Aluminium

Electrolysis Removes Aluminium from Its Ore

1) Aluminium's a very abundant metal, but it is always found naturally in compounds.
2) The main ore is bauxite, and after mining and purifying, a white powder is left.
3) This is pure aluminium oxide, Al_2O_3.
4) As aluminium's more reactive than carbon, it has to be extracted from its ore using electrolysis.

Cryolite is Used to Lower the Temperature (and Costs)

1) Al_2O_3 has a very high melting point of over 2000 °C — so melting it would be very expensive.
2) Instead the aluminium oxide is dissolved in molten cryolite (a less common ore of aluminium).
3) This brings the temperature down to about 900 °C, which makes it much cheaper and easier.
4) The electrodes are made of graphite, a good conductor of electricity.

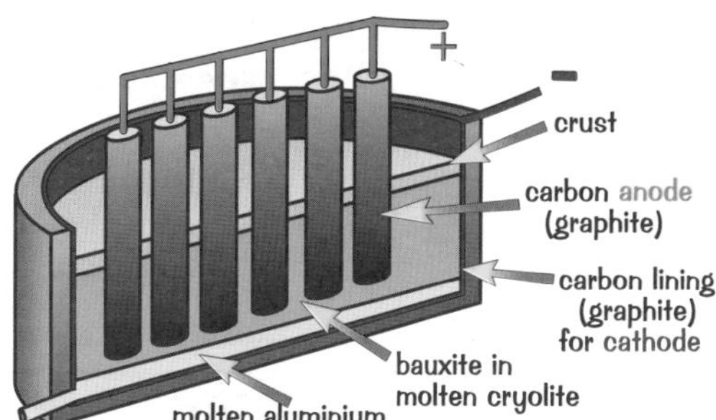

Electrolysis — Turning IONS into the ATOMS You Want

1) Molten aluminium oxide contains free ions — so it'll conduct electricity.
2) The positive Al^{3+} ions are attracted to the cathode where they pick up electrons and "zup", they turn into aluminium atoms. These then sink to the bottom.
3) The negative O^{2-} ions are attracted to the anode where they lose electrons. The oxygen atoms will then react together to form O_2, or with the carbon anode as well to form CO_2.
4) As the carbon anode is constantly getting worn down, it often needs replacing.

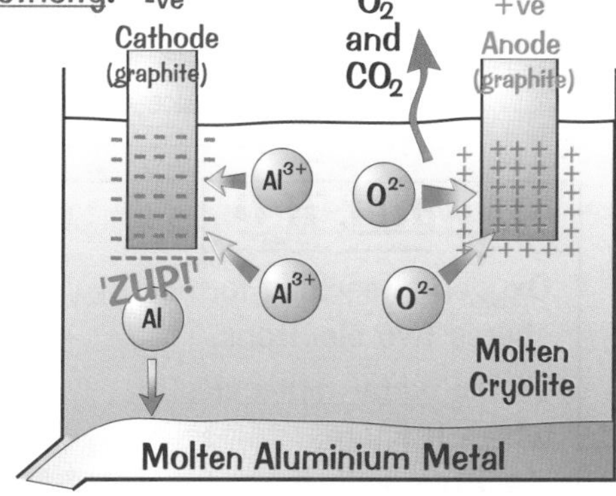

Overall, this is a REDOX reaction and you need to know the reactions at both electrodes:

At the Cathode (–ve):

$$Al^{3+} + 3e^- \rightarrow Al$$

(Reduction — a gain of electrons)

At the Anode (+ve):

$$2O^{2-} \rightarrow O_2 + 4e^-$$

(Oxidation — a loss of electrons)

The complete equation for the decomposition of aluminium oxide is then:

Aluminium oxide → Aluminium + Oxygen

Electrolysis is Expensive — It's All That Electricity...

1) Electrolysis uses a lot of electricity and that can make it pretty expensive.
2) Energy is also needed to heat the electrolyte mixture to 900 °C. This is expensive too.
3) The disappearing anodes need frequent replacement. That costs money as well.
4) But in the end, aluminium now comes out as a reasonably cheap and widely-used metal. A hundred years ago it was a very rare metal, simply because it was so hard to extract.

Faster shopping at Tesco — use Electrolleys...

Electrolysis is fantastic for removing any unwanted hairs from your body. Great for women with moustaches, or men with hairy backs. And even better for the beauty clinic, as they'll get to charge a small fortune for the treatment. After all it's a very expensive process...

Covalent Bonding

Covalent Bonds — Sharing Electrons

1) Sometimes atoms prefer to make covalent bonds by sharing electrons with other atoms.
2) This way both atoms feel that they have a full outer shell, and that makes them happy.
3) Each covalent bond provides one extra shared electron for each atom.
4) Each atom involved has to make enough covalent bonds to fill up its outer shell.
5) Learn these important examples:

1) Hydrogen Gas, H_2

Hydrogen atoms have just one electron. They only need one more to complete the first shell...

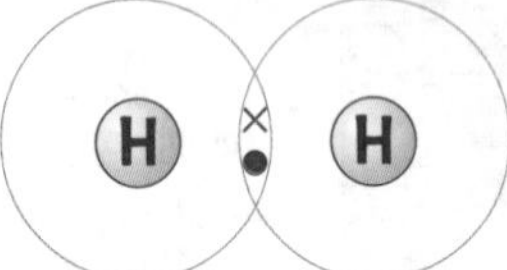

...so they often form single covalent bonds to achieve this.

2) Chlorine Gas, Cl_2

Each chlorine atom needs just one more electron to complete the outer shell...

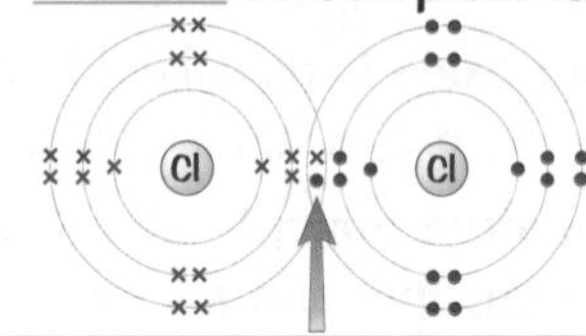

...so they form a single covalent bond and together share one pair of electrons.

3) Methane, CH_4

Carbon has four outer electrons, which is a half full shell.

To become a 4+ or a 4– ion is hard work so it forms four covalent bonds to make up its outer shell.

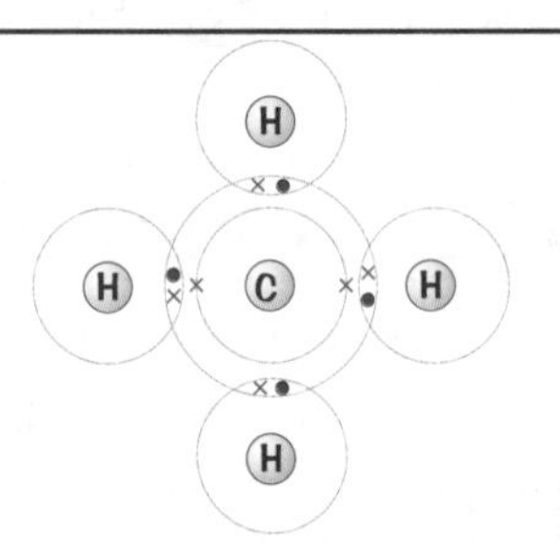

4) Water, H_2O

Oxygen cheerfully forms covalent bonds and shares two electrons.

Like in water molecules, where it shares electrons with the hydrogen atoms.

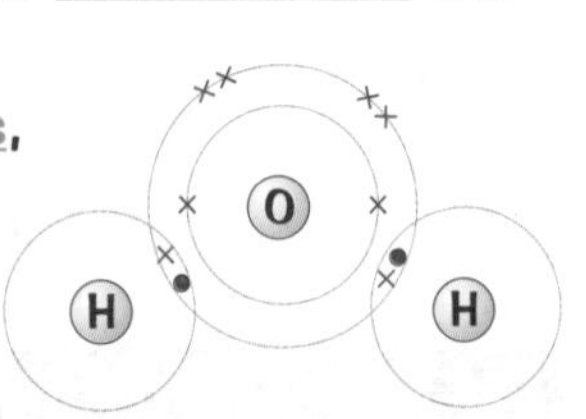

5) Carbon Dioxide, CO_2

Carbon needs four more electrons to fill it up, oxygen needs two. So two double covalent bonds are formed.

A double covalent bond has two shared pairs of electrons.

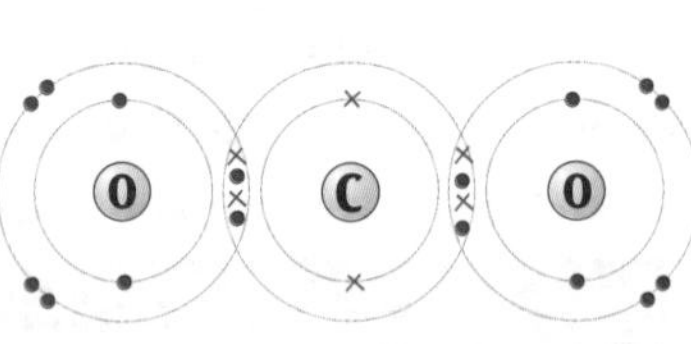

Simple Molecular Substances

1) Substances formed from covalent bonds usually have simple molecular structures, like CO_2 and H_2O.
2) The atoms within the molecules are held together by very strong covalent bonds.
3) By contrast, the forces of attraction between these molecules are very weak.

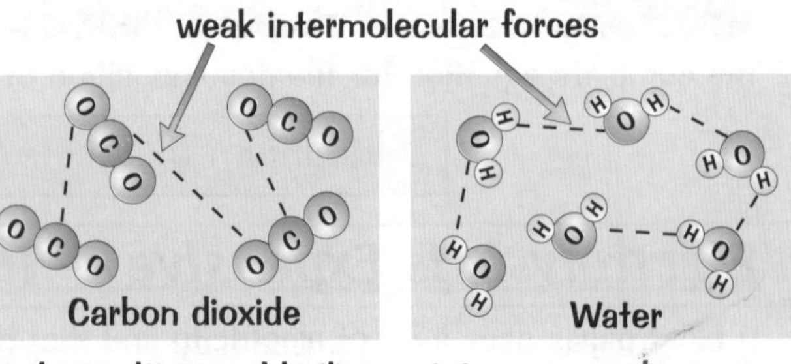

4) The result of these feeble intermolecular forces is that the melting and boiling points are very low, because the molecules are easily parted from each other.
5) Most molecular substances are gases or liquids at room temperature.
6) Molecular substances don't conduct electricity, simply because there are no free electrons or ions.

It's good to share — especially when it's somebody else's...

Make sure you can draw all five of those examples. You never know when they'll come in handy... (hint: in your exam). You also get giant covalent structures (see page 85) — they're totally different from the simple molecular ones. You've got to know the details, and examples. Learn them now.

Group 7 — Halogens

Group 7 Elements are Known as the 'Halogens'

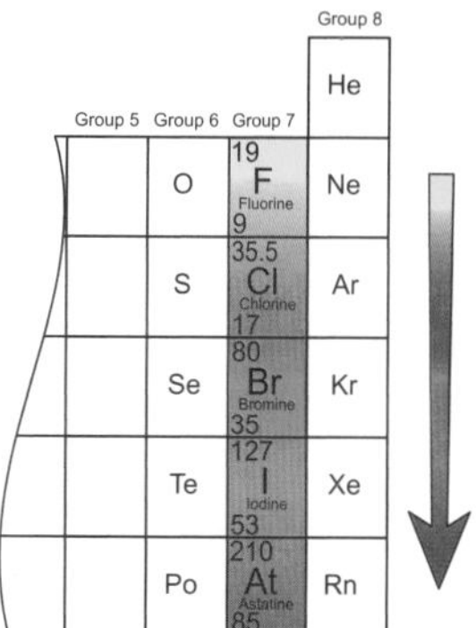

Group 7 is made up of fluorine, chlorine, bromine, iodine and astatine.

All Group 7 elements have 7 electrons in their outer shell — so they've all got similar properties.

As you go DOWN Group 7, the halogens become less reactive — there's less inclination to gain the extra electron to fill the outer shell when it's further out from the nucleus.

Chlorine is a fairly reactive, poisonous, dense green gas.
Bromine is a dense, poisonous, orange liquid.
Iodine is a dark grey crystalline solid.

Iodine

Halogens Do Both Covalent and Ionic Bonding

Halogens form covalent bonds with themselves and in various molecular compounds like this:

Cl_2 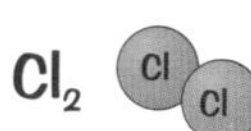 Br_2 Br Br I_2 I I Hydogen chloride 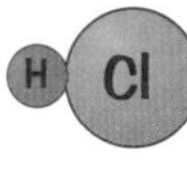

Or, they can form ionic bonds with other elements like the alkali metals to form ions with a 1– charge: Cl^- Br^- I^- as in Na^+Cl^- or $Fe^{3+}Br_3^-$

Reduction is the Gain of Electrons

1) Halogens are keen to gain an electron to form a 1^- ion with a stable electronic structure.
2) The more reactive the halogen the happier it is to gain an electron.
3) Gain of electrons is called REDUCTION.

$$Cl_2 + 2e^- \rightarrow 2Cl^-$$

Halogen molecule → Halide ion

The Halogens React with Alkali Metals to Form Salts

They react vigorously with alkali metals to form salts called 'metal halides'.

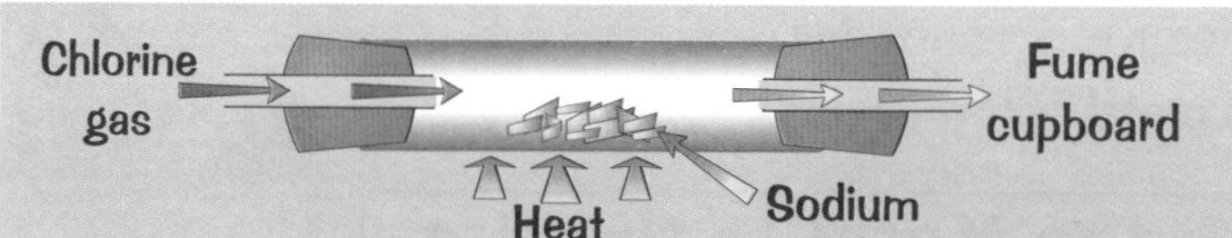

$$2Na + Cl_2 \rightarrow 2NaCl$$

Sodium + Chlorine → Sodium chloride

$$2K + Br_2 \rightarrow 2KBr$$

Potassium + Bromine → Potassium bromide

More Reactive Halogens Will Displace Less Reactive Ones

Chlorine can displace bromine and iodine from a solution of bromide or iodide.
Bromine will also displace iodine because of the trend in reactivity.

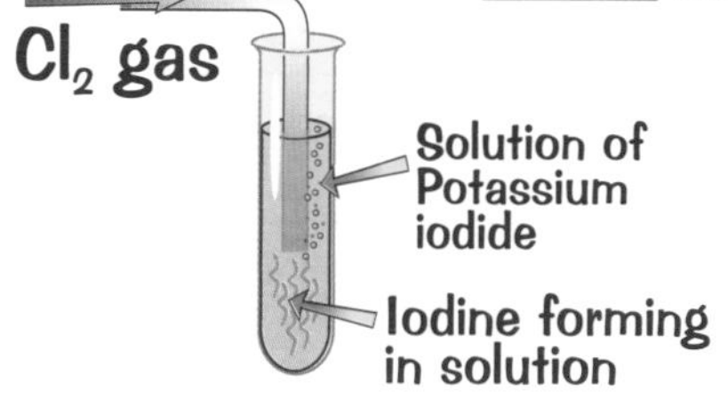

$$Cl_2 + 2KI \rightarrow I_2 + 2KCl$$

Chlorine + Potassium iodide → Iodine + Potassium chloride

$$Cl_2 + 2KBr \rightarrow Br_2 + 2KCl$$

Chlorine + Potassium bromide → Bromine + Potassium chloride

Halogens — one electron short of a full shell...

The halogens are another group from the periodic table, and just like the alkali metals (p.33) you've got to learn their trends and the equations on this page. Learn them, cover up the page, scribble, check.

Metals

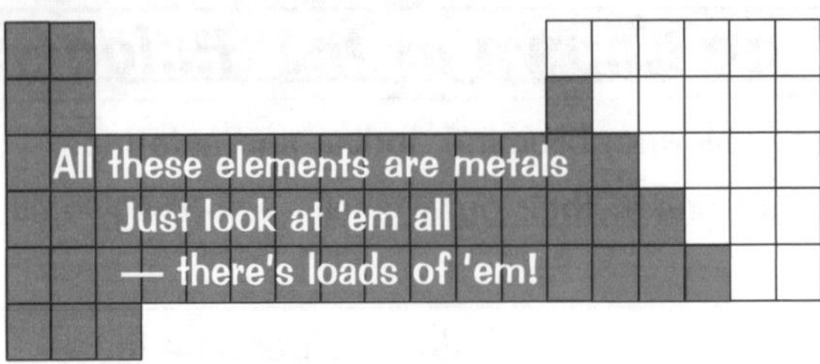

Metals Have a Crystal Structure

1) All metals have the same basic properties.
2) These are due to the special type of bonding that exists in metals.
3) Metals consist of a giant structure of atoms held together with metallic bonds.
4) These special bonds allow the outer electron(s) of each atom to move freely.
5) This creates a 'sea' of free electrons throughout the metal which is what gives rise to many of the properties of metals.

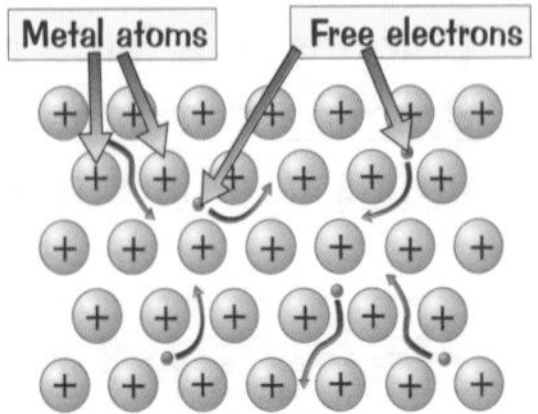

Most Have High Melting and Boiling Points, and High Density

1) Metals are very dense and lustrous (i.e. shiny).
2) There's a strong attraction between the free electrons and the closely packed positive ions — causing very strong metallic bonding.
3) You're going to have to get them pretty hot to melt them, e.g. iron melts at 1538 °C and boils at 2860 °C. (Mercury is an exception — it's liquid at room temp.)

They're Strong, but Also Bendy and Malleable

1) Metals have a high tensile strength — in other words they're strong and hard to break.
2) But they can also be hammered into a different shape (they're malleable).

They're Good Conductors of Heat and Electricity

This is entirely due to the sea of free electrons.

1) They carry the current — so conduct electricity.
2) They also carry the heat energy through the metal.

Don't try this at home. You'll die.

You've Got to be Able to Match the Metal to the Use

Use	Properties	Metal
Saucepans	Good conductor of heat, doesn't rust easily	Stainless Steel — and it's cheap too.
Electrical Wiring	Good conductor of electricity, easily bent	Copper. One of the best conductors around.
Aeroplanes	Low density (light), strong, doesn't corrode	Aluminium. Titanium's sometimes used, but it's a lot more expensive.
Bridges	Strong	Steel — this is mostly iron, but it's got a little bit of carbon in it, which makes it a lot less brittle.

Metal Fatigue? — yeah, we've all had enough of this page now...

It's not just the main structure of an aeroplane that's made of aluminium — parts of the engines, the seat supports and even the cabin crew's trolleys are all made of aluminium. And because aluminium doesn't corrode, planes don't have to be painted, saving hundreds of kilograms on a big commercial jet.

Superconductors and Transition Metals

Oooooo, some interesting stuff...

At Very Low Temperatures, Some Metals are Superconductors

1) Normally, all metals have some electrical resistance — even really good conductors like copper.
2) That resistance means that whenever electricity flows through them, they heat up, and some of the electrical energy is wasted as heat.
3) If you make some metals cold enough, though, their resistance disappears completely. The metal becomes a superconductor.
4) Without any resistance, none of the electrical energy is turned into heat, so none of it's wasted.
5) That means you could start a current flowing through a superconducting circuit, take out the battery, and the current would carry on flowing forever.

So What's the Catch...

1) Using superconducting wires you can make:
   a) Power cables that transmit electricity without any loss of power.
   b) Really strong electromagnets that don't need a constant power source.
   c) Electronic circuits that work really fast, because there's no resistance to slow them down.
2) But here's the catch — when I said cold, I meant REALLY COLD. Metals only start superconducting at less than –265 °C! Getting things that cold is very hard, and very expensive.
3) Scientists are trying to develop room temperature superconductors now. So far, they've managed to get some weird metal oxide things to superconduct at about –135 °C, which is a much cheaper temperature to get down to. They've still got a long way to go, though.

Metals in the Middle of the Periodic Table are Transition Metals

A lot of everyday metals are transition metals (e.g. copper, iron, zinc, gold, silver, platinum) — but there are loads of others as well. Transition metals have typical 'metallic' properties.

If you get asked about a transition metal you've never heard of — don't panic. These 'new' transition metals follow all the properties you've already learnt for the others. It's just that some folk get worried by the unfamiliar names.

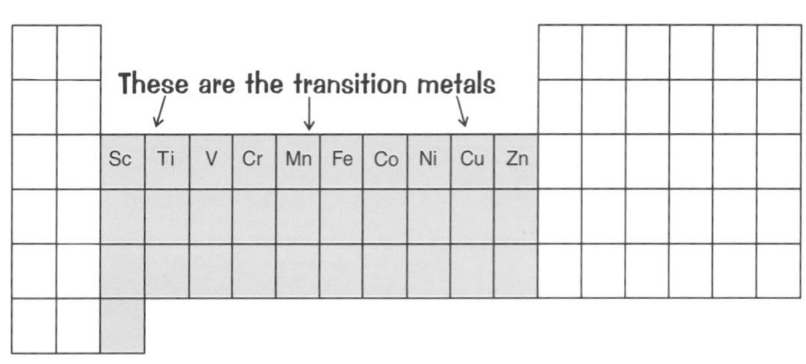

Transition Metals and Their Compounds Make Good Catalysts

1) Iron is the catalyst used in the Haber process for making ammonia.
2) Nickel is useful for the hydrogenation of alkenes (e.g. to make margarine).

The Compounds are Very Colourful

The compounds are colourful due to the transition metal ion they contain.

e.g. Iron(II) compounds are usually light green.
Iron(III) compounds are usually orange/brown (e.g. rust).
Copper compounds are often blue.

Mendeleev and his amazing technicoloured periodic table...

Superconducting magnets are used in magnetic resonance image (MRI) scanners in hospitals. That way, the huge magnetic fields they need can be generated without using up a load of electricity. Great stuff...

Thermal Decomposition and Precipitation

1) Thermal Decomposition — Breaking Down with Heat

1) Thermal decomposition is when a substance breaks down into simpler substances when heated.
2) Transition metal carbonates break down on heating. Transition metal carbonates are things like copper carbonate ($CuCO_3$), iron(II) carbonate ($FeCO_3$), zinc carbonate ($ZnCO_3$) and manganese carbonate ($MnCO_3$), i.e. they've all got a CO_3 bit in them.
3) They break down into a metal oxide (e.g. copper oxide, CuO) and carbon dioxide. This usually results in a colour change.

EXAMPLE: The thermal decomposition of copper carbonate.

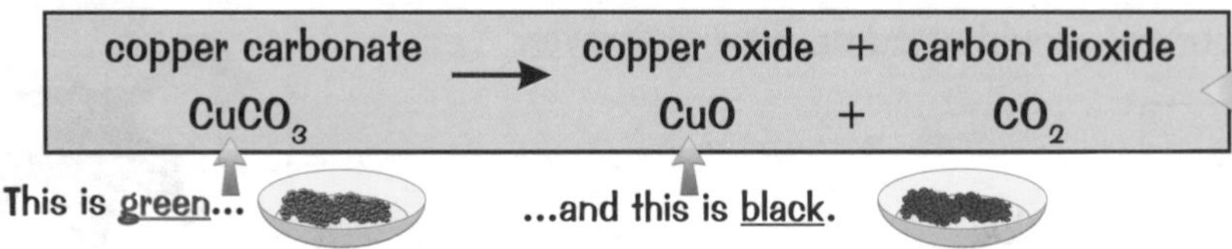

The reactions for the thermal decomposition of:
(i) iron(II) carbonate,
(ii) manganese carbonate,
(iii) zinc carbonate,
are the same — although the colours are different.

Use Limewater to Test for Carbon Dioxide

1) You can easily check that the gas given off is carbon dioxide.
2) Bubble the gas through limewater — if it is carbon dioxide, the limewater turns milky.

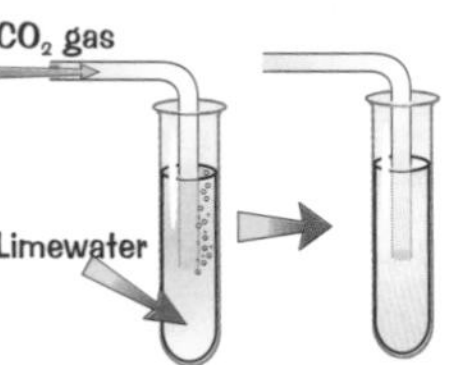

2) Precipitation — A Solid Forms in Solution

1) A precipitation reaction is where two solutions react and an insoluble solid forms in the solution.
2) The solid is said to 'precipitate out' and, confusingly, the solid is also called 'a precipitate'.
3) Some soluble transition metal compounds react with sodium hydroxide to form an insoluble hydroxide, which then precipitates out.

EXAMPLE: Soluble copper sulfate reacts with sodium hydroxide to form insoluble copper hydroxide.

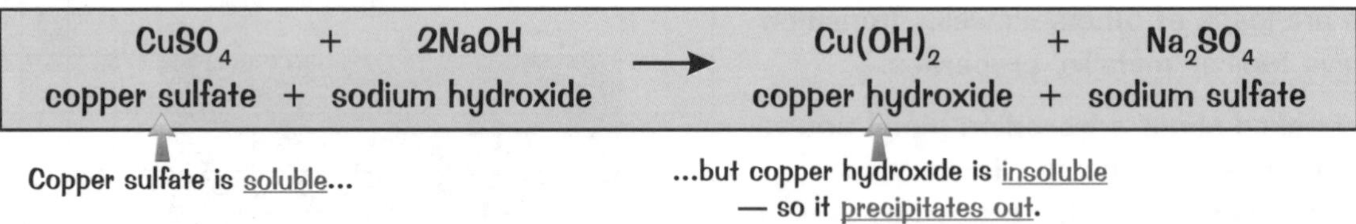

4) Since copper hydroxide is blue, you get a distinctive blue precipitate forming in the test tube.
5) You can also write the above equation in terms of ions:

$$Cu^{2+} + 2OH^- \longrightarrow Cu(OH)_2$$

The Cu^{2+} ions and the hydroxide ions combine to give you the insoluble copper hydroxide.

Use Precipitation to Test for Transition Metal Ions

1) Some insoluble transition metal hydroxides have distinctive colours.
2) You can use this fact to test which transition metal ions a solution contains.

Copper hydroxide is a blue solid.
Iron(II) hydroxide is a dark grey/green solid.
Iron(III) hydroxide is an orange solid.

3) For example, if you add sodium hydroxide to an unknown soluble salt, and an orange precipitate forms, you know you had iron(III) ions in the solution.

My duffel coat's worn out — thermal decomposition...

Limewater isn't actually water with limes dissolved in it. Disappointing isn't it. It's named because it's made from treating quicklime with water, which is named from... umm... well definitely not the fruit. Impress the examiner by learning these equations and the colours of the precipitates.

Revision Summary for Module C3

These certainly aren't the easiest questions you're going to come across. That's because they test what you know without giving you any clues. At first you might think they're impossibly difficult. Eventually you'll realise that they simply test whether you've learnt the stuff or not.
If you're struggling to answer these then you need to do some serious learning.

1)* Give three rules for balancing equations, then try balancing these equations:
a) $CaCO_3 + HCl \rightarrow CaCl_2 + H_2O + CO_2$ b) $Ca + H_2O \rightarrow Ca(OH)_2 + H_2$
c) $H_2SO_4 + KOH \rightarrow K_2SO_4 + H_2O$ d) $Fe_2O_3 + H_2 \rightarrow Fe + H_2O$
2) What are the three particles found in an atom? What are their relative masses and charges?
3) What do the mass number and atomic number represent?
4) Explain what an isotope is. Give a well-known example.
5) What's the difference between elements and compounds?
6) What feature of atoms determines the order of the modern periodic table?
7) What are the periods and groups? Explain their significance in terms of electrons.
8) List five facts (or 'rules') about electron shells.
9) Calculate the electron configuration for each of the following elements: ${}^{4}_{2}He$, ${}^{12}_{6}C$, ${}^{31}_{15}P$, ${}^{39}_{19}K$.
10) Draw diagrams to show the electron arrangements for the first 20 elements.
11) What is ionic bonding? Which kind of atoms like to do ionic bonding? Why is this?
12) The atoms of which groups form 1+, 1–, 2+ and 2– ions?
13) Sketch dot and cross diagrams for:
a) sodium chloride
b) magnesium oxide
c) sodium oxide
d) magnesium chloride
14) Draw a diagram of a giant ionic lattice and give three features of giant ionic structures.
15) Which group are the alkali metals? What is their outer shell like?
16) Give details of the reactions of the alkali metals with water.
17) List four physical properties and two chemical properties of the alkali metals.
18) How is aluminium extracted from its ore?
Give four operational details, draw a diagram and give the two equations.
19) Explain three reasons why this process is so expensive.
20) Describe the trends in appearance and reactivity of the halogens as you go down the group.
21)* Write word equations and balanced symbol equations for the reactions between:
a) bromine and lithium,   b) chlorine and potassium,   c) iodine and sodium.
22) Give details, with an equation, of a displacement reaction involving the halogens.
23) What is oxidation? What is reduction?
24) What is a superconductor? Describe some useful applications of superconductors.
25) List two properties of transition metal compounds.
26) Name six transition metals, and give uses for two of them.
27) What are thermal decomposition reactions?
28) What type of reaction between two liquids results in the formation of a solid?
What are these solid products called?
29) Describe a way to test solutions for transition metal ions.

* Answers on page 108

Speed and Acceleration

Speed is Just the Distance Travelled in a Certain Time

1) To find the speed of an object, you need to measure the distance it travels (in metres) and the time it takes (in seconds). Then the speed is calculated in metres per second (m/s).
2) You really ought to get pretty slick with this very easy formula:

If the speed isn't constant, this equation gives the average speed.

$$\text{Speed} = \frac{\text{Distance}}{\text{Time}}$$

d / s × t

As usual the formula triangle version makes it all a bit of a breeze.
You just need to try and think up some interesting word for remembering the order of the letters in the triangle, s^{d}t. Errm... sedit, perhaps... well, I'm sure you can think up something better...

EXAMPLE: A cat skulks 20 metres in 35 seconds.
Find: a) its speed, b) how long it will take to skulk 75 m.

ANSWER: Using the formula triangle: a) s = d/t = 20/35 = 0.5714 = 0.57 m/s
b) t = d/s = 75/0.5714 = 131 s = 2 min 11 s

Speed Cameras Measure the Speed of Cars

1) Speed cameras can be used to catch speeding motorists at dangerous accident spots.
2) Lines are painted on the road at a certain distance apart to measure the distance travelled by the car.
3) A photo of the car is taken as it passes the first line and a second photo is taken a certain time later.
4) These photos can then be used to measure the distance travelled by the car in this time.

Example: a speed camera takes two photos of a car. The photos are taken 0.5 s apart and from the marked lines on the road the distance it travels is measured as 5 m. What is the speed of the car?

Answer: $\text{Speed} = \frac{\text{distance}}{\text{time}} = \frac{5\text{ m}}{0.5\text{ s}} = 10\text{ m/s}$

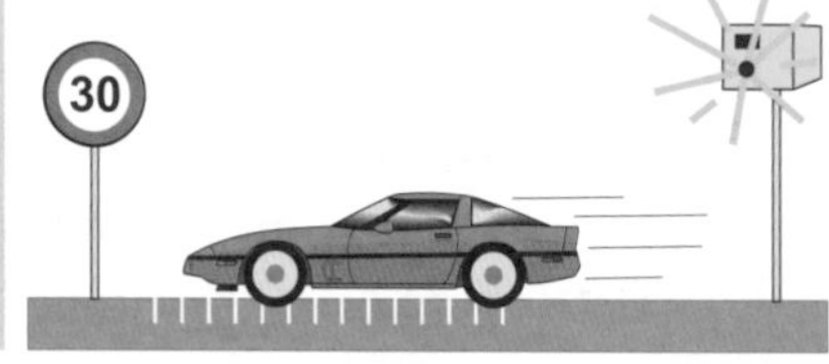

Distance-Time Graphs

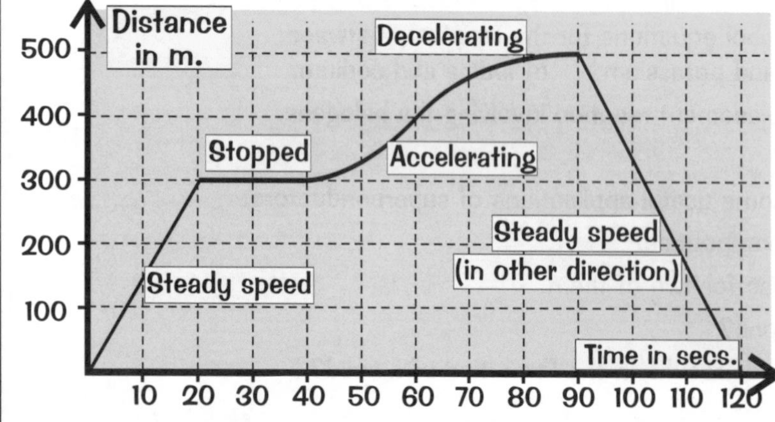

Very Important Notes:

1) GRADIENT = SPEED.
2) Flat sections are where it's stopped.
3) The steeper the graph, the faster it's going.
4) 'Downhill' sections mean it's coming back toward its starting point.
5) Curves represent acceleration or deceleration.
6) A steepening curve means it's speeding up (increasing gradient).
7) A levelling off curve means it's slowing down (decreasing gradient).

Calculating Speed from a Distance-Time Graph — It's Just the Gradient

For example the speed of the return section of the graph is:

$$\text{Speed} = \text{gradient} = \frac{\text{vertical}}{\text{horizontal}} = \frac{500}{30} = 16.7\text{ m/s}$$

Don't forget that you have to use the scales of the axes to work out the gradient. Don't measure in cm.

Speed and Acceleration

Acceleration is How Quickly You're Speeding Up

Acceleration is definitely not the same as speed.

1) Acceleration is how quickly the speed is changing.
2) You also accelerate when you CHANGE DIRECTION without changing speed. (You just need to remember this bit of the definition — you won't have to use it to do any calculations.)

Speed is a simple idea. Acceleration is altogether more subtle, which is why it's confusing.

Acceleration — The Formula:

$$\text{Acceleration} = \frac{\text{Change in Speed}}{\text{Time Taken}}$$

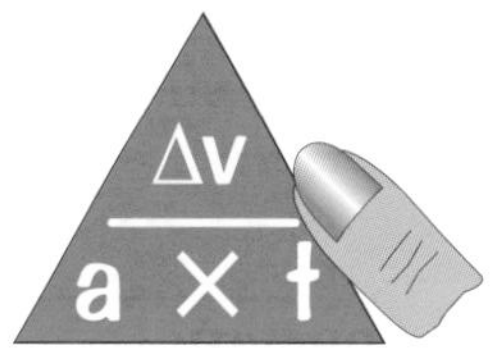

Well, it's just another formula. Just like all the others. Three things in a formula triangle.
Mind you, there are two tricky things with this one. First there's the 'Δv', which means working out the 'change in speed', as shown in the example below, rather than just putting a simple value for speed in.
Secondly there's the units of acceleration, which are m/s^2.
Not m/s, which is speed, but m/s^2. Got it? No? Let's try once more: Not m/s, but m/s^2.

EXAMPLE: A skulking cat accelerates from 2 m/s to 6 m/s in 5.6 s. Find its acceleration.
ANSWER: Using the formula triangle: $a = \Delta v/t = (6 - 2) / 5.6 = 4 \div 5.6 = 0.71\ m/s^2$

Speed-Time Graphs

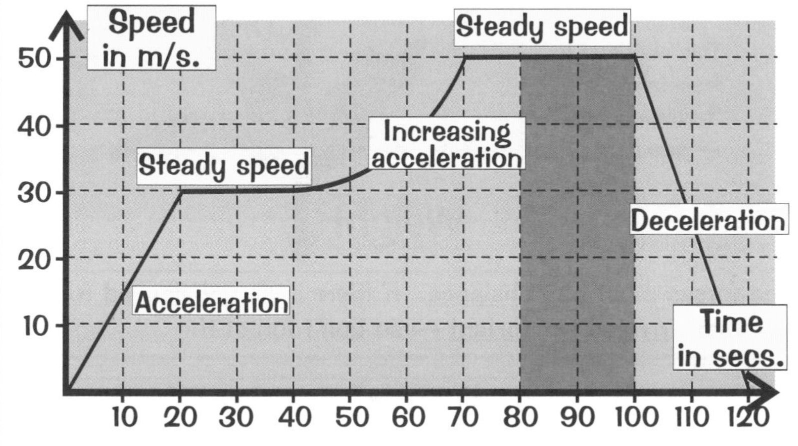

Very Important Notes:

1) GRADIENT = ACCELERATION.
2) Flat sections represent steady speed.
3) The steeper the graph, the greater the acceleration or deceleration.
4) Uphill sections (/) are acceleration.
5) Downhill sections (\) — deceleration.
6) The area under any section of the graph (or all of it) is equal to the distance travelled in that time interval.
7) A curve means changing acceleration.

Calculating Acceleration, Speed and Distance from a Speed-Time Graph

1) The acceleration represented by the first section of the graph is:

$$\text{Acceleration} = \text{gradient} = \frac{\text{vertical}}{\text{horizontal}} = \frac{30}{20} = 1.5\ m/s^2$$

2) The speed at any point is simply found by reading the value off the speed axis.
3) The distance travelled in any time interval is equal to the area. For example, the distance travelled between t = 80 and t = 100 is equal to the shaded area which is equal to 1000 m.

Speed-time graphs — more fun than gravel (just)...

The tricky thing about these two types of graph is that they can look pretty much the same but represent totally different kinds of motion. Make sure you learn the difference between speed and acceleration and know how to calculate both of them. They're easy marks in the exam.

Forces

A force is simply a push or a pull. There are only six different forces for you to know about:

1) GRAVITY or WEIGHT always acting straight downwards.
   (On Earth, gravity makes all things accelerate towards the ground at about $10\ m/s^2$.)
2) REACTION FORCE from a surface, usually acting straight upwards.
3) THRUST or PUSH or PULL due to an engine or rocket speeding something up.
4) DRAG or AIR RESISTANCE or FRICTION which is slowing the thing down.
5) LIFT due to an aeroplane wing.
6) TENSION in a rope or cable.

And there are basically only five different force diagrams:

1) Stationary Object — All Forces in Balance

1) The force of GRAVITY (or weight) is acting downwards.
2) This causes a REACTION FORCE from the surface pushing up on the object.
3) This is the only way it can be in BALANCE.
4) Without a reaction force, it would accelerate downwards due to the pull of gravity.
5) The two HORIZONTAL forces must be equal and opposite otherwise the object will accelerate sideways.

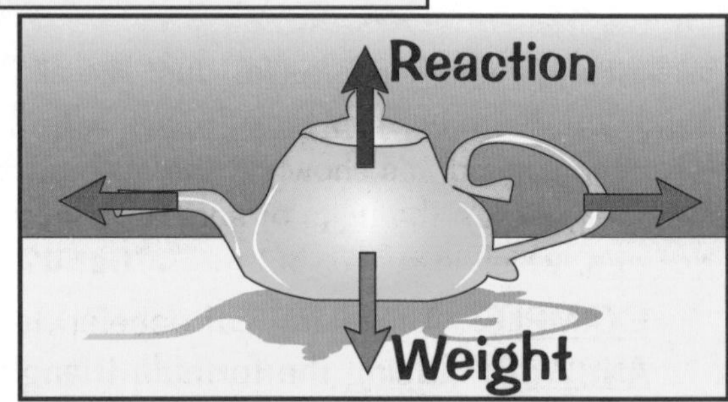

2) Steady Horizontal Speed — All Forces in Balance!

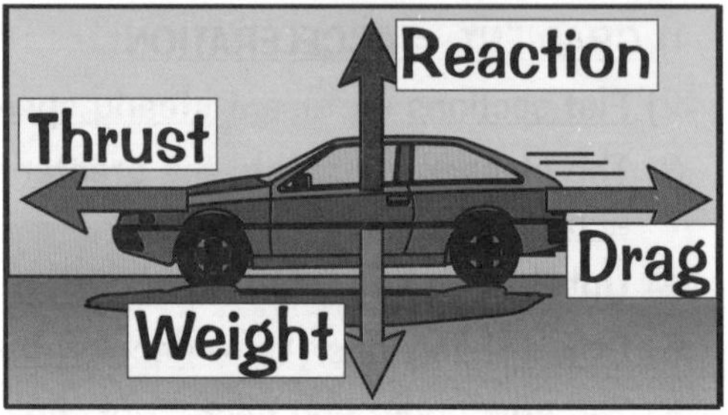

3) Steady Vertical Speed — All Forces in Balance!

This skydiver is free-falling at 'terminal speed' — see next page.

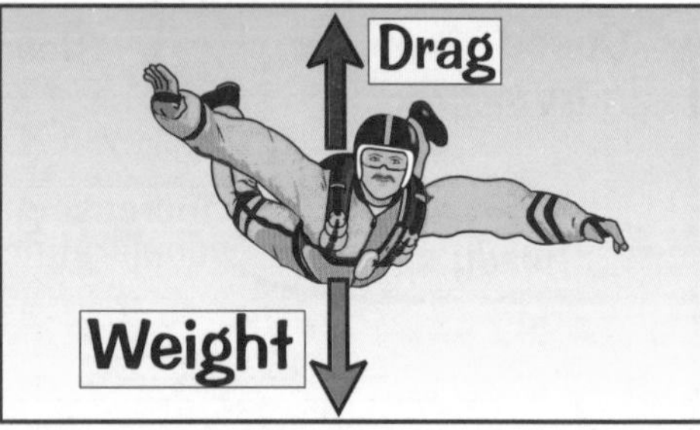

Take note — to move with a steady speed the forces must be in balance. If there is an unbalanced force then you get acceleration, not steady speed. That's rrrreally important — so don't forget it.

4) Horizontal Acceleration — Unbalanced Forces

5) Vertical Acceleration — Unbalanced Forces

1) You only get acceleration with an overall resultant (unbalanced) force.
2) The bigger this unbalanced force, the greater the acceleration.

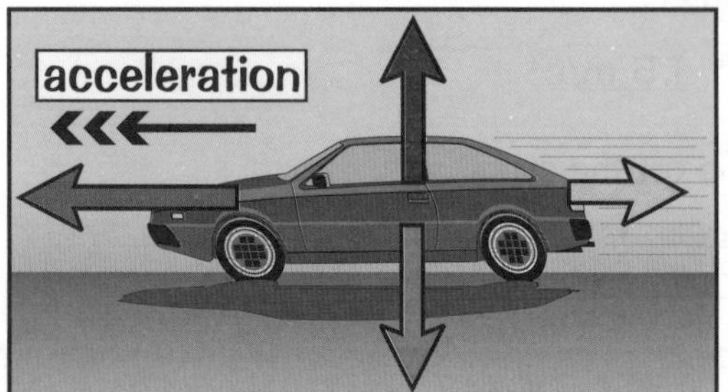

Note that the forces in the other direction (up and down) are still balanced.

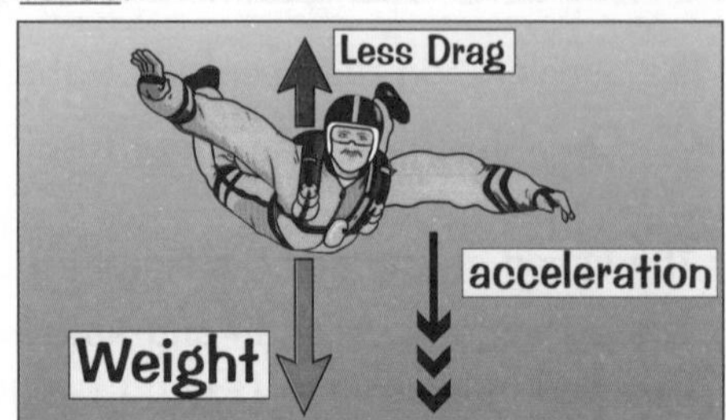

Just after dropping out of the plane, the skydiver accelerates — see next page.

Accelerate your learning — force yourself to revise...

So, things only accelerate in a particular direction if there's an overall force in that direction. Simple.

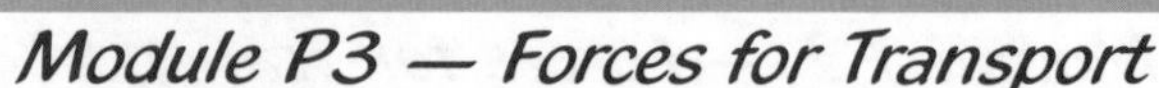

Friction Forces and Terminal Speed

Friction is Always There to Slow things Down

1) If an object has no force propelling it along, it will always slow down and stop because of friction (unless you're out in space where there's no friction).
2) To travel at a steady speed, things always need a driving force to counteract the friction.
3) Friction occurs in three main ways:

a) FRICTION BETWEEN SOLID SURFACES WHICH ARE GRIPPING (static friction)

static friction

b) FRICTION BETWEEN SOLID SURFACES WHICH ARE SLIDING PAST EACH OTHER

You can reduce both these types of friction by putting a lubricant like oil or grease between the surfaces.

sliding friction

c) RESISTANCE OR "DRAG" FROM FLUIDS (LIQUIDS OR GASES, e.g. AIR)

The most important factor by far in reducing drag in fluids is keeping the shape of the object streamlined, like sports cars or boat hulls. Lorries and caravans have "deflectors" on them to make them more streamlined and reduce drag.
Roof boxes on cars spoil this shape and so slow them down.
For a given thrust, the higher the drag the lower the top speed of the car.

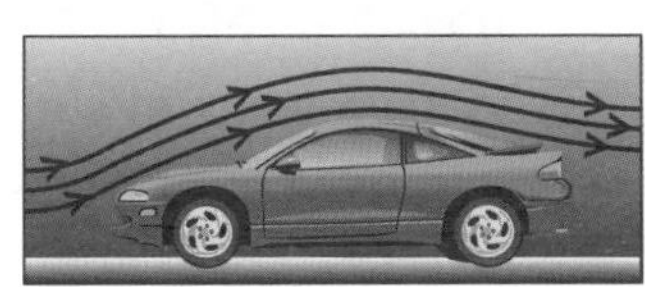

The opposite extreme to a sports car is a parachute which is about as high drag as you can get — which is, of course, the whole idea.

In a fluid: FRICTION ALWAYS INCREASES AS THE SPEED INCREASES — and don't you forget it.

Free-Fallers Reach a Terminal Speed

When free-falling objects first set off they have much more force accelerating them than resistance slowing them down.
As the speed increases the resistance builds up.
This gradually reduces the acceleration until eventually the resistance force is equal to the accelerating force and then it won't be able to accelerate any more.
It will have reached its maximum speed or terminal speed.

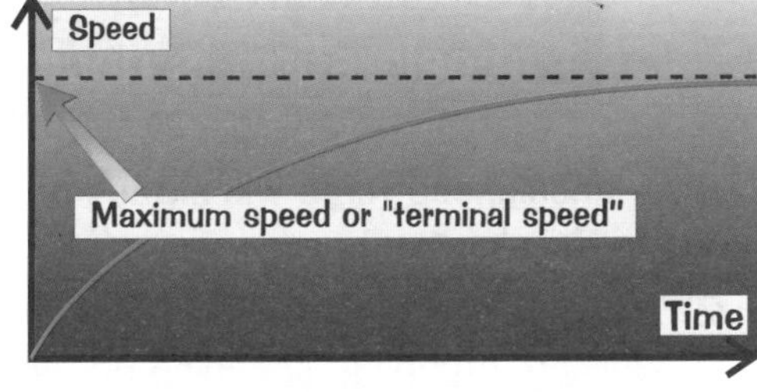

The Terminal Speed of Falling Objects Depends on Their Shape and Area

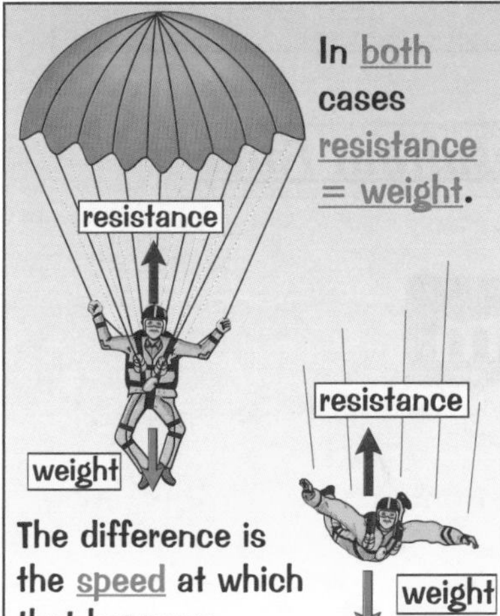

The accelerating force acting on all falling objects is gravity and it would make them all accelerate at the same rate, if it wasn't for air resistance.

To prove this, on the Moon, where there's no air, hamsters and feathers dropped simultaneously will hit the ground together. However, on Earth, air resistance causes things to fall at different speeds, and the terminal speed of any object is determined by its drag compared to its weight. The drag depends on its shape and area.

The most important example is the human skydiver. Without his parachute open he has quite a small area and a force equal to his weight pulling him down. He reaches a terminal speed of about 120 mph.
But with the parachute open, there's much more air resistance (at any given speed) and still only the same force pulling him down.
This means his terminal speed comes right down to about 15 mph, which is a safe speed to hit the ground at.

Air resistance — it can be a real drag...

As well as stopping parachutists ending up as nasty messes on the floor, friction's good for other stuff too. Without friction, you wouldn't be able to walk or run or skip or write... hmm, not all bad then.

Forces and Acceleration

Things only accelerate or change direction if you give them a push. Makes sense.

A Balanced Force Means Steady Speed and Direction

If the forces on an object are all BALANCED, then it'll keep moving at the SAME SPEED in the SAME DIRECTION (so if it starts off still, it'll stay still).

1) When a train or car or bus or anything else is moving at a constant speed, without changing direction, then the forces on it must all be balanced.
2) Never let yourself entertain the ridiculous idea that things need a constant overall force to keep them moving — NO NO NO NO NO NO!
3) To keep going at a steady speed, there must be zero resultant (overall) force — and don't you forget it.

A Resultant Force Means Acceleration

If there is an UNBALANCED FORCE, then the object will ACCELERATE in the direction of the force. The size of the acceleration is decided by the formula: F = ma (see below).

1) An unbalanced force will always produce acceleration (or deceleration).
2) This 'acceleration' can take five different forms: starting, stopping, speeding up, slowing down and changing direction.
3) On a force diagram, the arrows will be unequal:

The Overall Unbalanced Force is Often Called the Resultant Force

Any resultant force will produce acceleration and this is the formula for it:

$$F = ma \quad \text{or} \quad a = F/m$$

m = mass, a = acceleration, F is always the resultant force

Three Points Which Should be Obvious:

1) The bigger the force, the greater the acceleration or deceleration.
2) The bigger the mass, the smaller the acceleration.
3) To get a big mass to accelerate as fast as a small mass, it needs a bigger force. Just think about pushing heavy trolleys and it should all seem fairly obvious, I would hope.

Forces and Acceleration

Resultant Force is Real Important — Especially for "F = ma"

The notion of resultant force is a really important one for you to get your head round. It's not especially tricky, it's just that it seems to get kind of ignored. In most real situations there are at least two forces acting on an object along any direction. The overall effect of these forces will decide the motion of the object — whether it will accelerate, decelerate or stay at a steady speed. If the forces all point along the same direction, the "overall effect" is found by just adding or subtracting them. The overall force you get is called the resultant force. And when you use the formula "F = ma", F must always be the resultant force.

Example: A car of mass of 1750 kg has an engine which provides a driving force of 5200 N.
At 70 mph the drag force acting on the car is 5150 N.
Find its acceleration a) when first setting off from rest b) at 70 mph.

ANSWER: 1) First draw a force diagram for both cases (no need to show the vertical forces):

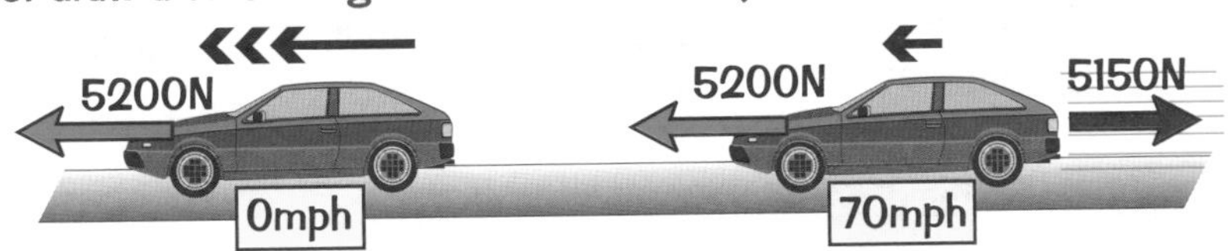

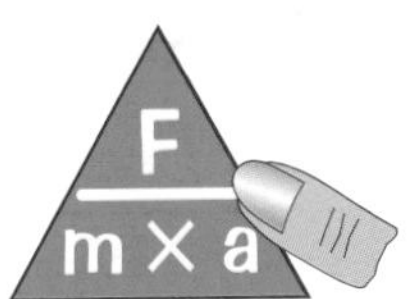

2) Work out the resultant force in each case, and apply "F = ma" using the formula triangle:

Resultant force = 5200 N
$a = F/m = 5200 \div 1750 = \underline{3.0 \text{ m/s}^2}$

Resultant force = 5200 – 5150 = 50 N
$a = F/m = 50 \div 1750 = \underline{0.03 \text{ m/s}^2}$

The Third Law — Reaction Forces

If object A exerts a force on object B then object B exerts the exact opposite force on object A.

1) That means if you push something, say a shopping trolley, the trolley will push back against you, just as hard.
2) And as soon as you stop pushing, so does the trolley. Kinda clever really.
3) So far so good. The slightly tricky thing to get your head round is this — if the forces are always equal, how does anything ever go anywhere? The important thing to remember is that the two forces are acting on different objects. Think about a pair of ice skaters:

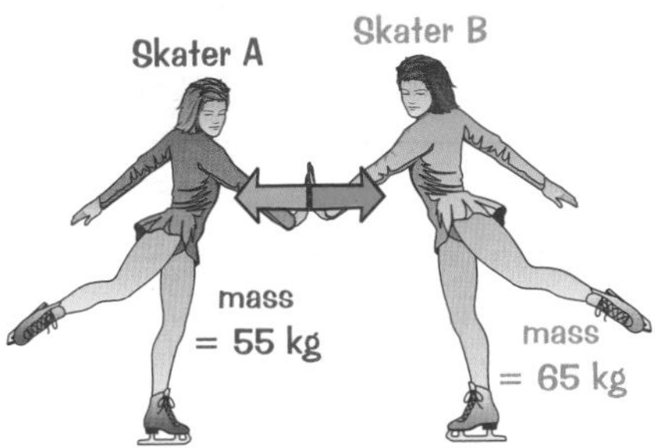

When skater A pushes on skater B (the 'action' force), she feels an equal and opposite force from skater B's hand (the 'reaction' force). Both skaters feel the same sized force, in opposite directions, and so accelerate away from each other.

Skater A will be accelerated more than skater B, though, because she has a smaller mass — remember F = ma.

4) It's the same sort of thing when you go swimming. You push back against the water with your arms and legs, and the water pushes you forwards with an equal-sized force in the opposite direction.

I have a reaction to forces — they bring me out in a rash...

This is the real deal. Like... proper Physics. It was pretty fantastic at the time — suddenly people understood how forces and motion worked, they could work out the orbits of planets and everything. Inspired? No? Shame. Learn them anyway — you're really going to struggle in the exam if you don't.

Stopping Distances

The stopping distance of a car is the distance covered in the time between the driver first spotting a hazard and the car coming to a complete stop. They're pretty keen on this for exam questions, so make sure you learn it properly.

Many Factors Affect Your Total Stopping Distance

The distance it takes to stop a car is divided into the THINKING DISTANCE and the BRAKING DISTANCE.

1) Thinking Distance

"The distance the car travels in the time between the driver noticing the hazard and applying the brakes."

It's affected by TWO MAIN FACTORS:

a) How FAST you're going — obviously. Whatever your reaction time, the faster you're going, the further you'll go.

b) How DOPEY you are — This is affected by tiredness, drugs, alcohol, old age, and a careless blasé attitude.

The figures below for typical stopping distances are from the Highway Code. It's frightening to see just how far it takes to stop when you're going at 70 mph.

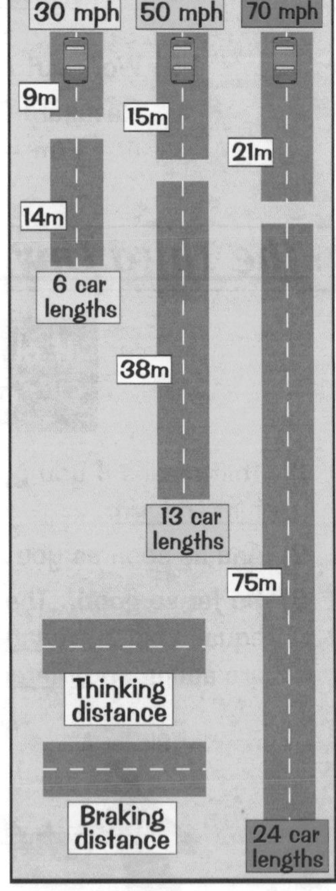

2) Braking Distance

"The distance the car travels during its deceleration whilst the brakes are being applied."

It's affected by FOUR MAIN FACTORS:

a) How FAST you're going — The faster you're going the further it takes to stop. More details on page 52.

b) How HEAVILY LOADED the vehicle is — With the same brakes, a heavily laden vehicle takes longer to stop. A car won't stop as quickly when it's full of people and luggage and towing a caravan.

c) How good your BRAKES are — All brakes must be checked and maintained regularly. Worn or faulty brakes will let you down catastrophically just when you need them the most, i.e. in an emergency.

d) How good the GRIP is — This depends on THREE THINGS:

1) road surface, 2) weather conditions, 3) tyres.

So even at 30 mph, you should drive no closer than 6 or 7 car lengths away from the car in front — just in case. This is why speed limits are so important, and some residential areas are now 20 mph zones.

Leaves and diesel spills and muck on t'road are serious hazards because they're unexpected. Wet or icy roads are always much more slippy than dry roads, but often you only discover this when you try to brake hard! Tyres should have a minimum tread depth of 1.6 mm. This is essential for getting rid of the water in wet conditions. Without tread, a tyre will simply ride on a layer of water and skid very easily. This is called 'aquaplaning' and isn't nearly as cool as it sounds.

Bad visibility can also be a major factor in accidents — lashing rain, thick fog, bright oncoming lights, etc. might mean that a driver doesn't notice a hazard until they're quite close to it — so they have a much shorter distance available to stop in.

Stop right there — and learn this page...

Scary stuff. Makes you think, doesn't it. Learn all the details and write yourself a mini-essay to see how much you really know. You might have to interpret charts of stopping distances in your exam.

Car Safety

When a Car is Moving It Has Kinetic Energy

1) A moving car can have a lot of kinetic energy. To slow a car down this kinetic energy needs to be converted into other types of energy (using the law of conservation of energy).
2) Car brakes slow a car down by turning its kinetic energy into heat energy. This means that when a driver uses the brakes to slow down, the brake pads can become extremely hot.

Cars are Designed to Convert Kinetic Energy Safely in a Crash

1) If a car crashes it will slow down very quickly — this means that a lot of kinetic energy is converted into other forms of energy in a short amount of time, which can be dangerous for the people inside.
2) Cars are designed to convert the kinetic energy of the car and its passengers in a way that is safest for the car's occupants.
3) Crumple zones are parts of the car at the front and back that crumple up in a collision. Some of the car's kinetic energy is converted into other forms of energy by the car body as it changes shape.
4) Seat belts and air bags slow the passengers down safely by converting their kinetic energy into other forms of energy over a longer period of time (see below). These safety features also prevent the passengers from hitting hard surfaces inside the car.

Seat belts absorb energy by stretching the material of the belt. The seat belt won't be as strong after a crash so it has to be replaced.

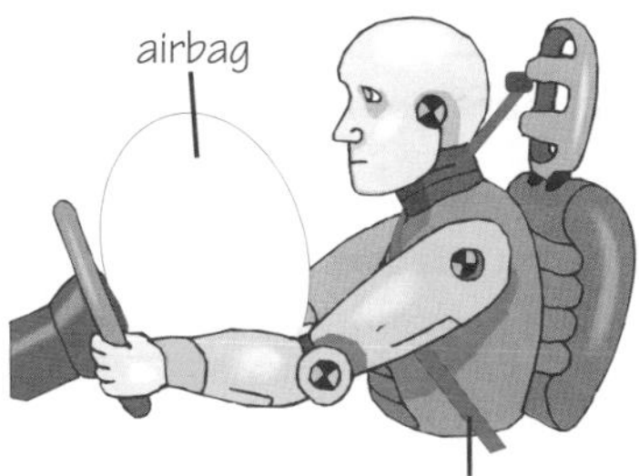

Safety Features Reduce the Forces Acting in Accidents

Cars have many safety features that are designed to reduce the forces acting on people involved in an accident. Smaller forces mean less severe injuries.

1) In a collision the force on the object can be lowered by slowing the object down over a longer time (you can see this by using the formula $F = ma$ — for the same mass, reducing the deceleration, a, reduces the size of the force, F).

2) Safety features in a car increase the collision time to reduce the forces on the passengers — e.g. crumple zones allow the car to slow down more gradually as parts of it change shape.
3) Roads can also be made safer by placing structures like crash barriers and escape lanes in dangerous locations (like on sharp bends or steep hills). These structures increase the time of any collision — which means the collision force is reduced.

Active Safety Features Take Control in an Emergency

1) Many cars have active safety features — these are features that interact with the way the car drives to help to avoid a crash, e.g. power assisted steering, traction control etc.
2) ABS brakes are an active safety feature that prevent skidding. They help the driver to stay in control of the car when braking sharply. They can also give the car a shorter stopping distance.

Actively learn this — it's the safest way to pass the exam...

The most important thing to learn here is that the forces acting on someone in a crash can be reduced by increasing the collision time — and there are loads of different safety features designed to do this...

Car Safety

Not all safety features help avoid accidents — there are many different ways to make driving safer...

Passive Safety Features Protect People from Injury

1) A passive safety feature is any non-interactive feature of a car that helps to keep the occupants of the car safe — e.g. seat belts, air bags, headrests etc.
2) A safety cage is a passive safety feature that surrounds the people in a car. This rigid cage protects the passengers because it doesn't easily change shape, even in a severe collision.
3) It's important that the driver of a car is not distracted when driving — and there are many features in a car that have been designed to keep the driver's attention firmly focused on the road.
4) Many cars now have more of their controls either placed on the steering wheel or on control paddles located near the steering wheel. These features allow drivers to stay safely in control of the vehicle while operating the stereo, electric windows, cruise control etc.
5) Cars are also designed to keep drivers comfortable and in the correct driving position with features like adjustable seats, ventilation etc.

Here are some examples of passive safety features in cars...

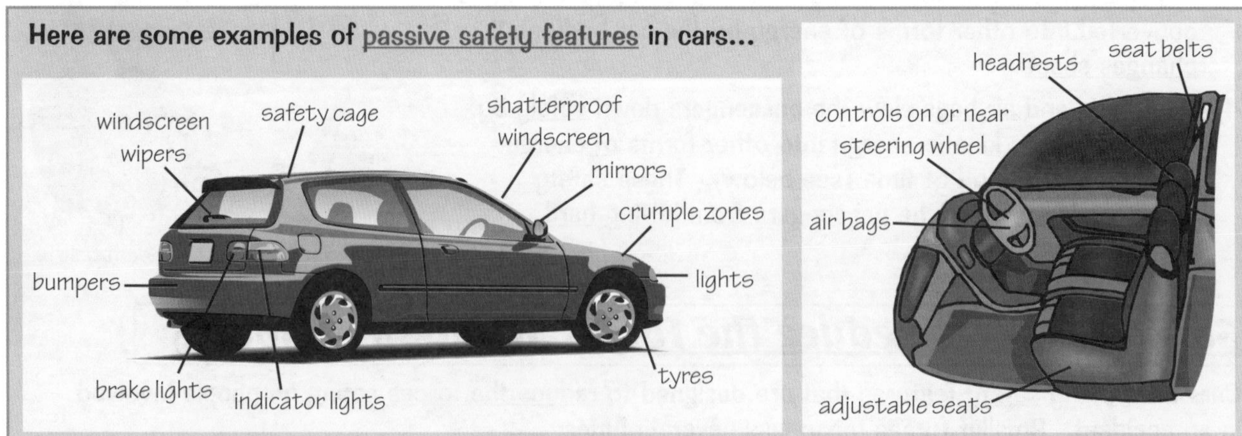

Safety Features Save Lives

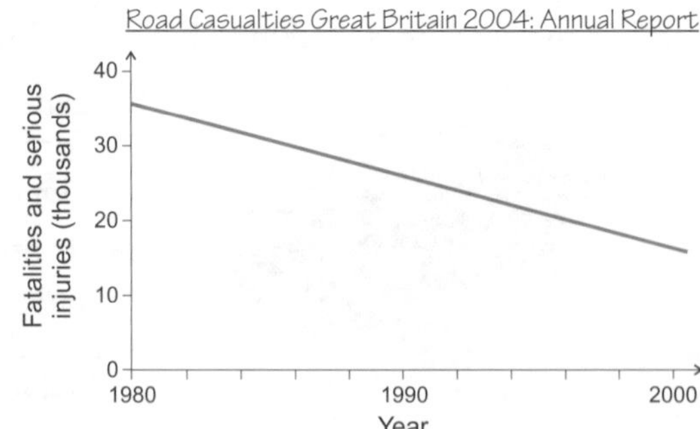

1) Safety features are rigorously tested by car manufacturers and government organisations to see how effectively they save lives or prevent injuries in an accident.
2) Crash tests have shown that wearing a seat belt reduces the number of fatalities (deaths) in car accidents by about 50% and that airbags reduce the number of fatalities by about 30% — so they're well worth using.
3) The graph (from the Department of Transport) shows the trend in the number of deaths and serious injuries from road traffic accidents in the UK since 1980. It shows that about half as many people are killed or seriously injured nowadays as in 1980 — this reduction is probably due to the wide range of safety features found in cars today.
4) But even though cars are loads safer than they used to be, lots of people still die on the roads every year — often because of bad driving (e.g. speeding, drink-driving etc.).

Belt up and start revising...

Passengers in the back of cars who don't wear a seat belt will hit the front seat with a force of between 30 to 60 times their body's weight in an accident at 30 mph — this is like the force you'd feel if you were sat on by an elephant (which I really wouldn't recommend).

Work and Potential Energy

When a force moves an object, ENERGY IS TRANSFERRED and WORK IS DONE.

That statement sounds far more complicated than it needs to. Try this:

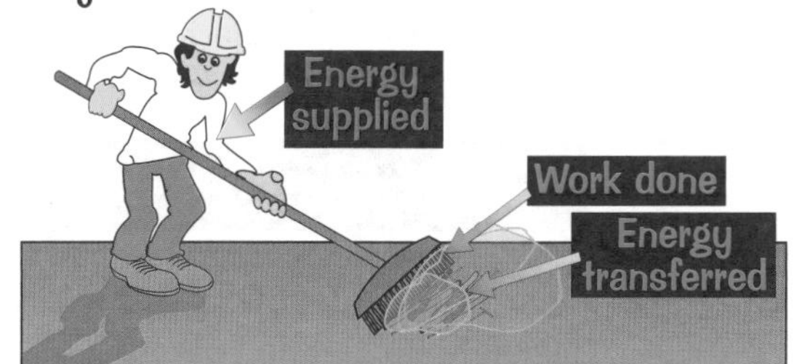

1) Whenever something moves, something else is providing some sort of 'effort' to move it.
2) The thing putting the effort in needs a supply of energy (like fuel or food or electricity etc.).
3) It then does 'work' by moving the object — and one way or another it transfers the energy it receives (as fuel) into other forms.
4) Whether this energy is transferred 'usefully' (e.g. by lifting a load) or is 'wasted' (e.g. lost as heat through friction), you can still say that 'work is done'. Just like Batman and Bruce Wayne, 'work done' and 'energy transferred' are indeed 'one and the same'. (And they're both given in joules.)

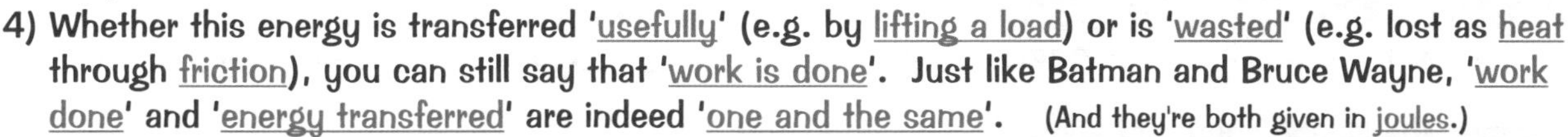

It's Just Another Trivial Formula:

Work Done = Force × Distance

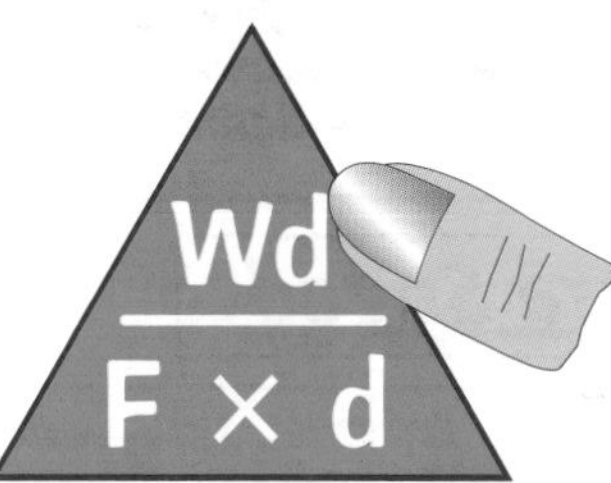

Whether the force is friction or weight or tension in a rope, it's always the same. To find how much energy has been transferred (in joules), you just multiply the force in N by the distance moved in m. Easy as that. I'll show you...

EXAMPLE: Some hooligan kids drag an old tractor tyre 5 m over rough ground. They pull with a total force of 340 N. Find the energy transferred.

ANSWER: Wd = F×d = 340 × 5 = 1700 J. Phew — easy peasy isn't it?

Potential Energy is Energy Due to Height

Potential Energy = mass × g × height

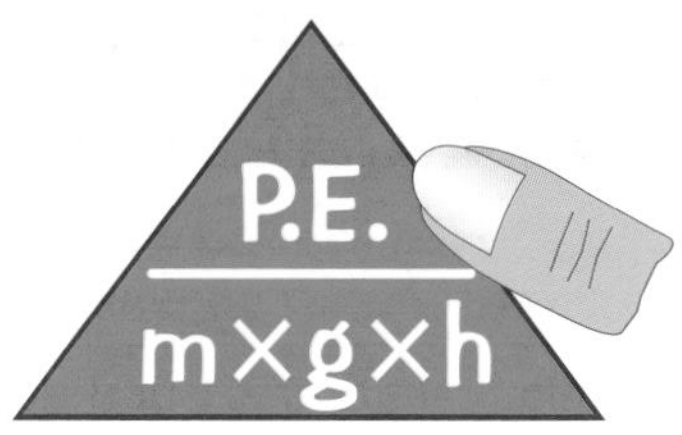

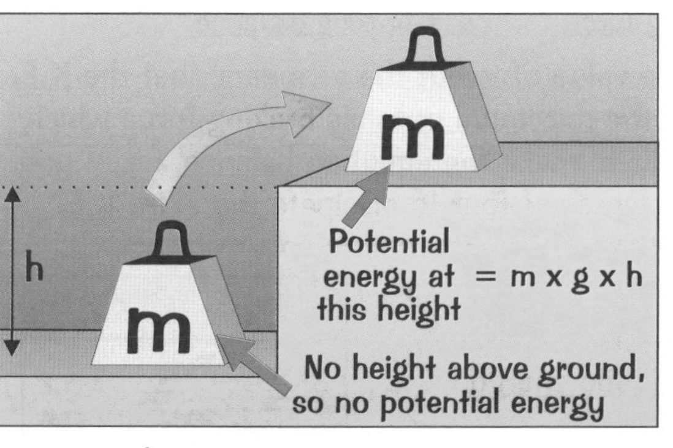

The proper name for this kind of 'potential energy' is gravitational potential energy, (as opposed to 'elastic potential energy' or 'chemical potential energy' etc.). The proper name for g is 'gravitational field strength'. On Earth, g is approximately 10 N/kg.

EXAMPLE: A sheep of mass 47 kg is slowly raised through 6.3 m. Find the gain in potential energy.

ANSWER: Just plug the numbers into the formula:
PE = mgh = 47 × 10 × 6.3 = 2961 J
(Joules because it's energy.)

!
What do you call a sheep with no eyes and no legs?
Dunno?
A Cloud!

Revise work done — what else...

Remember "energy transferred" and "work done" are the same thing. If you need a force to make something speed up (P.46), all that means is that you need to give it a bit of energy. Makes sense.

Kinetic Energy

Kinetic Energy is Energy of Movement

Anything that's moving has kinetic energy.
There's a slightly tricky formula for it, so you have to concentrate a little bit harder for this one.
But hey, that's life — it can be real tough sometimes:

Kinetic Energy = ½ × mass × speed²

K.E. / $\frac{1}{2}\times m\times v^2$

EXAMPLE: A car of mass 2450 kg is travelling at 38 m/s.
Calculate its kinetic energy.

ANSWER: It's pretty easy. You just plug the numbers into the formula — but watch the 'v²'!
K.E. = $\frac{1}{2}mv^2 = \frac{1}{2} \times 2450 \times 38^2$ = 1 768 900 J (Joules because it's energy.)

Remember, the kinetic energy of something depends both on mass and speed.
The more it weighs and the faster it's going, the bigger its kinetic energy will be.

Stopping Distances Increase Alarmingly with Extra Speed

— Mainly Because of the v^2 Bit in K.E.=½mv^2

To stop a car, the kinetic energy, $\frac{1}{2}mv^2$, has to be converted to heat energy at the brakes and tyres:

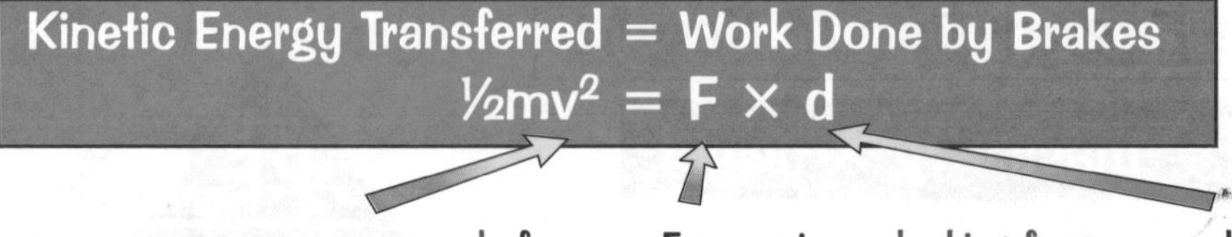

$$\frac{1}{2}mv^2 = F \times d$$

v = speed of car   F = maximum braking force   d = braking distance

Learn this real good: if you double the speed, you double the value of v, but the v^2 means that the K.E. is then increased by a factor of four. However, 'F' is always the maximum possible braking force which can't be increased, so d must also increase by a factor of four to make the equation balance, i.e. if you go twice as fast, the braking distance 'd' must increase by a factor of four to dissipate the extra K.E.

Falling Objects Convert P.E. into K.E.

When something falls, its potential energy is converted into kinetic energy.
So the further it falls, the faster it goes.
In practice, some of the P.E. will be dissipated as heat due to air resistance, but in exam questions they'll likely say you can ignore air resistance, in which case you'll just need to remember this simple and really quite obvious formula:

Kinetic energy gained = Potential Energy lost

Kinetic energy — just get a move on and learn it, OK...

So that's why braking distance goes up so much with speed. Bet you've been dying to find that out — and now you know. What you probably don't know yet, though, is that rather lovely formula at the top of the page. I mean, gosh, it's got more than three letters in it. Get learning.

Gravity and Roller Coasters

Gravity attracts all masses, but you only notice it when one of the masses is really, really big — like a planet. It makes everything accelerate towards the mass. On Earth, it gives things weight.

The Very Important Formula Relating Mass, Weight and Gravity

$$W = m \times g$$

(Weight = mass × g)

1) Mass is the amount of 'stuff' in an object. For any given object, this will have the same value anywhere in the Universe. Mass is measured in kg.
2) Weight and mass are NOT the same. Weight is caused by the pull of gravity. It's a force and it's measured in newtons (N).
3) The letter 'g' represents the strength of the gravity and its value is different for different planets. On Earth g is about 10 N/kg. On the Moon, where the gravity is weaker, g is just 1.6 N/kg.
4) This formula is hideously easy to use:

   EXAMPLE: What is the weight, in newtons, of a 5 kg mass, both on Earth and on the Moon?
   ANSWER: $W = m \times g$. On Earth: $W = 5 \times 10 = 50$ N (The weight of the 5 kg mass is 50 N)
   On the Moon: $W = 5 \times 1.6 = 8$ N (The weight of the 5 kg mass is 8 N)
   See what I mean. Hideously easy — as long as you've learnt what all the letters mean.

Roller Coasters Transfer Energy

1) At the top of a roller coaster (position A) the carriage has lots of gravitational potential energy (P.E.)
2) As the carriage descends to position B, P.E. is transferred to kinetic energy (K.E.) and the carriage speeds up.

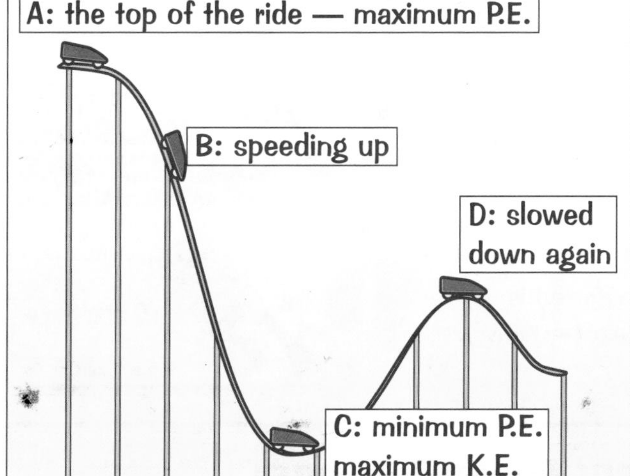

3) Between positions B and C the carriage keeps accelerating as its P.E. is converted into K.E.
4) If you ignore any air resistance or friction between the carriage and the track, then the carriage will have as much energy at C as it did at A. That energy must have been converted from P.E. to K.E. so at C the carriage has minimum P.E. and maximum K.E.
5) In a real roller coaster (that does have friction to deal with), the carriage has to have enough kinetic energy at point C to carry it up the hill again to D.

Learn about gravity NOW — no point in "weighting" around...

If the formula W = mg seems strangely familiar that's because it's just F = ma in disguise — where 'W' is just the force on an object due to gravity and 'g' is the acceleration of the object caused by gravity.

Power

Power is the 'Rate of Doing Work' — i.e. How Much per Second

POWER is not the same thing as force, nor energy. A powerful machine is not necessarily one which can exert a strong force (though it usually ends up that way).
A POWERFUL machine is one which transfers A LOT OF ENERGY IN A SHORT SPACE OF TIME.
This is the very easy formula for power:

$$\text{Power} = \frac{\text{Work done}}{\text{Time taken}}$$

EXAMPLE: A motor transfers 4.8 kJ of useful energy in 2 minutes. Find its power output.
ANSWER: P = Wd / t = 4800/120 = 40 W (or 40 J/s)
(Note that the kJ had to be turned into J, and the minutes into seconds.)

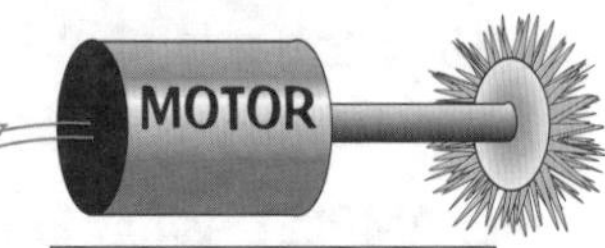

4.8 kJ of useful energy in 2 minutes

Power is Measured in Watts (or J/s)

The proper unit of power is the watt. One watt = 1 joule of energy transferred per second. Power means 'how much energy per second', so watts are the same as 'joules per second' (J/s). Don't ever say 'watts per second' — it's nonsense.

Calculating Your Power Output

Both cases use the same formula:

$$\text{POWER} = \frac{\text{ENERGY TRANSFERRED}}{\text{TIME TAKEN}} \quad \text{or} \quad P = \frac{E}{t}$$

a) The Timed Run Upstairs:

In this case the 'energy transferred' is simply the potential energy you gain (= mgh).
Hence, power = mgh/t

Power output
= En. transferred/time
= mgh/t
= (62×10×12)÷14
= 531 W

b) The Timed Acceleration:

This time the energy transferred is the kinetic energy you gain (= ½mv^2).
Hence, power = ½mv^2/t

Power output
= En. transferred/time
= ½mv^2/t
= (½×62×8^2)÷4
= 496 W

Cars Have Different Power Ratings

1) The size and design of car engines determine how powerful they are.
2) The more powerful an engine, the more energy it transfers from its fuel every second, so (usually) the higher the fuel consumption, see next page).
3) E.g. the power output of a typical small car will be around 50 kW and a sports car will be about 100 kW (some are much higher).

Sports car power = 100 kW

Small car power = 50 kW

Watt are you waiting for — revise this stuff now...

The power of a car isn't always measured in watts — sometimes you'll see it in a funny unit called brake horsepower. James Watt defined 1 horsepower as the work done when a horse raises a mass of 550 lb (250 kg) through a height of 1 ft (0.3 m) in 1 second... as you do. I'd stick to watts if I were you.

Fuels for Cars

A lot of us use cars to get us around and about, and lorries transport stuff around the country — but these forms of transport would be pretty useless if they didn't have any fuel to get them moving...

Most Cars Run on Fossil Fuels

1) All vehicles need a fuel to make them move — e.g. most cars and lorries use petrol or diesel.
2) Petrol and diesel are fuels that are made from oil, which is a fossil fuel. The pollution released when these fuels are burnt can cause environmental problems like acid rain and climate change.
3) Fossil fuels are non-renewable, so one day they'll run out — not good news if your car runs on petrol.
4) To get around some of the problems with petrol and diesel fuels, scientists are developing engines that run on alternative types of fuel, such as alcohol, liquid petroleum gas (LPG), hydrogen and 'bio-diesel'. They're not perfect, though. LPG still comes from fossil fuels — it just has lower emissions. Hydrogen can be produced by the electrolysis of a very dilute acid, but that takes energy that's likely to come from fossil fuels.

5) A few vehicles use large batteries to power electric motors. These vehicles don't release any pollution when they're driven, but their batteries need to be charged using electricity. This electricity is likely to come from power stations that do pollute.

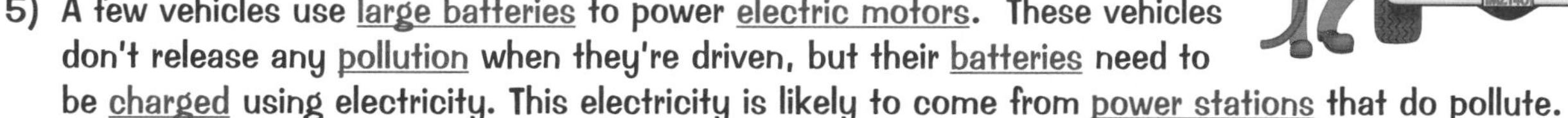

Fuel Consumption is All About the Amount of Fuel Used...

1) The fuel consumption of a car is usually stated as the distance travelled using a certain amount of fuel. Fuel consumption is often given in miles per gallon (mpg) or litres per 100 km (l/100 km) — e.g. a car with a fuel consumption of 5 l/100 km will travel 100 km on 5 litres of fuel.
2) A car's fuel consumption depends on many different things — e.g. the type and size of the engine, how the car is driven, the shape and weight of the car etc.
3) A car will have a high fuel consumption (i.e. use a lot of fuel) if a large force is needed to move it. Using $F = ma$, you can see that the force needed to move a car depends on the mass of the car and its acceleration.
4) A heavy car will need a greater force to accelerate it by a given amount than a lighter car, so the fuel consumption will be higher for the heavy car.
5) Driving style will also affect the fuel consumption — larger accelerations need a greater force and so use more fuel. Frequent braking and acceleration (e.g. when driving in a town) will increase the fuel consumption.
6) Opening the windows will increase a car's fuel consumption — this is because more energy will be needed to overcome the increase in air resistance.
7) The speed a car's travelling at affects fuel consumption as well. Cars work more efficiently at some speeds than others — the most efficient speed is usually between 40 and 55 mph.

Examples of how car design can improve fuel consumption:

The shape of modern cars reduces air resistance.
Cars are made from lightweight materials.
Engines with better fuel efficiency are constantly being designed.

I bet this page has fuelled your enthusiasm...

You might get asked how to reduce the fuel consumption of a car, so it's important that you remember the different ways that fuel consumption can be affected — e.g. friction, air resistance, weight etc.

Revision Summary for Module P3

Well done, you've made it to the end of another section. There are loads of bits and bobs about forces, motion and fast cars which you definitely have to learn — and the best way to find out what you know is to get stuck in to these lovely revision questions, which you're going to really enjoy (honest)...

1)* Write down the formula for working out speed. Find the speed of a partly chewed mouse which hobbles 3.2 metres in 35 seconds. Find how far he would go in 25 minutes.
2)* A speed camera is set up in a 30 mph (13.4 m/s) zone. It takes two photographs 0.5 s apart. A car travels 6.3 m between the two photographs. Was the car breaking the speed limit?
3) Sketch a typical distance-time graph and point out all the important parts of it.
4) Explain how to calculate speed from a distance-time graph.
5) What is acceleration? What are its units?
6)* Write down the formula for acceleration. What's the acceleration of a soggy pea flicked from rest to a speed of 14 m/s in 0.4 seconds?
7) Sketch a typical speed-time graph and point out all the important parts of it.
8) Explain how to find speed, distance and acceleration from a speed-time graph.
9) What could you do to reduce the friction between two surfaces?
10) Describe how air resistance is affected by speed.
11) Describe the effect on the top speed of a car of adding a roof box. Explain your answer.
12) What is "terminal speed"? What two main factors affect the terminal speed of a falling object?
13) If an object has zero resultant force on it, can it be moving? Can it be accelerating?
14)* Write down the formula relating resultant force and acceleration. A force of 30 N pushes a trolley of mass 4 kg. What will be its acceleration?
15) Explain what a reaction force is and where it pops up.
16) What are the two different parts of the overall stopping distance of a car?
17) List the three of four factors which affect each of the two parts of the stopping distance.
18) Explain how seat belts, crumple zones and air bags are useful in a crash.
19) List three active safety features and three passive safety features of cars. Describe how each one makes driving safer.
20) What's the connection between "work done" and "energy transferred"?
21)* Write down the formula for work done. A crazy dog drags a big branch 12 m over the next-door neighbour's front lawn, pulling with a force of 535 N. How much work was done?
22)* Write down the formula for potential energy. Calculate the increase in potential energy when a box of mass 12 kg is raised through 4.5 m.
23)* What's the formula for kinetic energy? Find the kinetic energy of a 78 kg sheep moving at 23 m/s.
24) How does the kinetic energy formula explain the effect of speed on the stopping distance of a car?
25)* Calculate the kinetic energy of a 78 kg sheep just as it hits the floor after falling through 20 m.
26) Explain the difference between mass and weight. What's the formula for weight?
27)* At the top of a roller coaster ride a carriage has 150 kJ of gravitational P.E. Ignoring friction, how much K.E. will the carriage have at the bottom (where P.E. = 0)?
28) What's the formula for power? What are the units of power?
29)* An electric motor uses 540 kJ of electrical energy in 4.5 minutes. What is its power consumption?
30)* Calculate the power output of a 78 kg sheep which runs 20 m up a staircase in 16.5 seconds.
31) Describe the relationship between the power rating of a car and its fuel consumption.
32) What are the two main fuels used in cars?
33) Electric vehicles don't give out polluting gases directly, but they still cause pollution. Explain why.
34) Give three factors that affect the fuel consumption of a car.

* Answers on page 108

Leaf Structure

Carbon dioxide + water → glucose + oxygen. Remember that? Well, here's some more...

Leaves are Designed for Making Food by Photosynthesis

The whole structure of leaves is geared towards that. You need to know all the different parts of a typical leaf shown on the diagram:

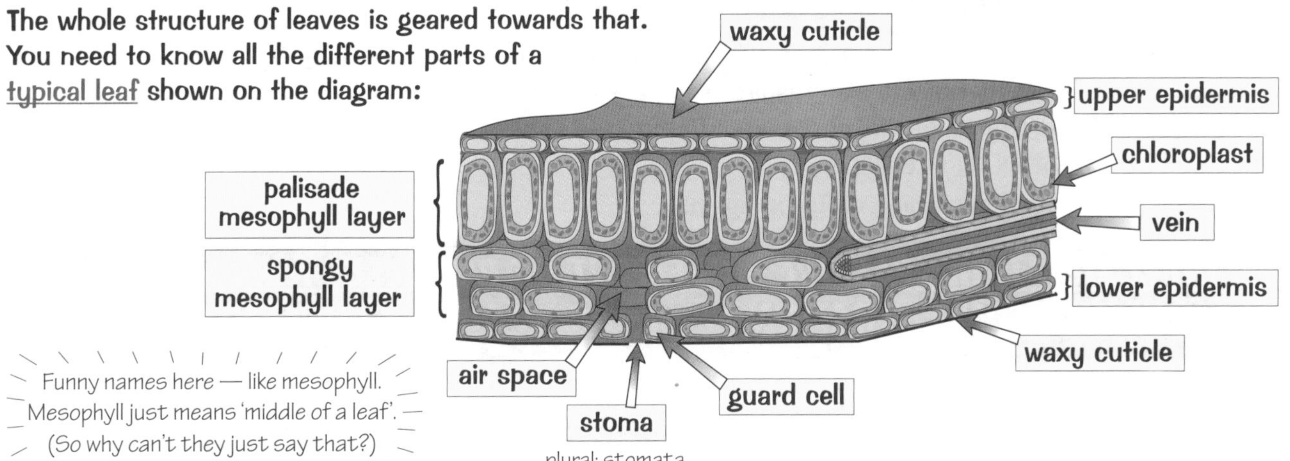

Learn These Important Features of Leaves

Leaves are adapted for efficient photosynthesis:

1) Leaves are broad, so there's a large surface area exposed to light.
2) They're also thin, which means carbon dioxide and water vapour only have to travel a short distance to reach the photosynthesising cells where it's needed.
3) There are air spaces in the spongy mesophyll layer. This allows gases like carbon dioxide (CO_2) and oxygen (O_2) to move easily between cells. This also means there's a large surface area for gas exchange — the technical phrase for this is "they have a very big internal surface area to volume ratio".
4) Leaves contain lots of chlorophyll, which is the pigment that absorbs light energy for photosynthesis. Chlorophyll is found in chloroplasts, and most of the chloroplasts are found in the palisade layer. This is so that they're near the top of the leaf where they can get the most light.
5) The upper epidermis is transparent so that light can pass through it to the palisade layer.
6) The lower surface is full of little holes called stomata. They're there to let gases like CO_2 and O_2 in and out. They also allow water to escape — which is known as transpiration (see page 60).
7) Leaves have a network of veins. These deliver water and other nutrients to every part of the leaf and take away the food produced by the leaf. They also help to support the leaf structure.

Leaf Palisade Cells are Designed for Photosynthesis

1) They're packed with chloroplasts for photosynthesis.
2) Their tall shape means a lot of surface area is exposed down the side for absorbing CO_2 from the air in the leaf.
3) Their tall shape also means there's a good chance of light hitting a chloroplast before it reaches the bottom of the cell.

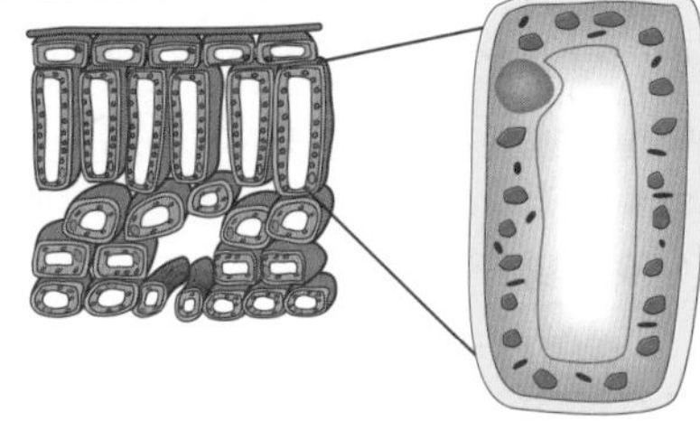

If you don't do much revision, it's time to turn over a new leaf...

So how the heck do they know all this stuff? Well, scientists know how leaves are adapted for photosynthesis because they've looked and seen the structure of leaves and the cells inside them. Not with the naked eye, of course — they used microscopes. So they're not just making it up, after all.

Diffusion in Leaves

You should remember diffusion from module B3 (page 5) — there was loads of it in there. Don't forget that diffusion is totally random and happens all by itself, so it doesn't use up any energy.

Plants Exchange Gases by Diffusion

When plants photosynthesise they use up CO_2 from the atmosphere and produce O_2 as a product. Don't forget that plants also respire (see page 1). During respiration they use up O_2 and produce CO_2 as a product. So there are lots of gases moving to and fro in plants, and this movement happens by diffusion.

Here's the posh way of explaining diffusion again:

DIFFUSION is the PASSIVE MOVEMENT OF PARTICLES from an area of HIGHER CONCENTRATION to an area of LOWER CONCENTRATION

Diffusion of Gases in Leaves is Vital for Photosynthesis

This is how diffusion of gases happens in leaves during photosynthesis:

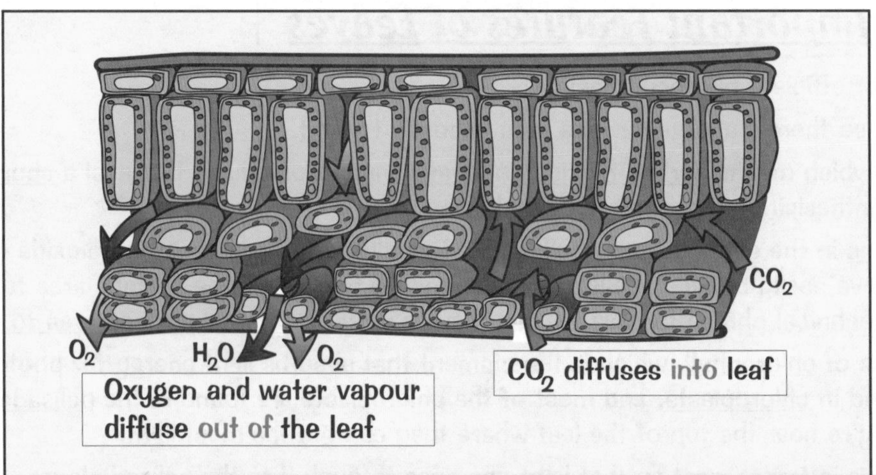

When the plant is photosynthesising it uses up lots of CO_2, so there's hardly any inside the leaf. Luckily this makes more CO_2 move into the leaf by diffusion (from an area of higher concentration to an area of lower concentration). At the same time lots of O_2 is being made as a waste product of photosynthesis. Some is used in respiration, and the rest diffuses out through the stomata (moving from an area of higher concentration to an area of lower concentration).

At night it's a different story — there's no photosynthesis going on because there's no light. Lots of carbon dioxide is made in respiration and lots of oxygen is used up. There's a lot of CO_2 in the leaf and not a lot of O_2, so now it's mainly carbon dioxide diffusing out and oxygen diffusing in.

Water vapour also escapes from the leaf by diffusion, because there's a lot of it inside the leaf and less of it in the air outside. This diffusion of water vapour out of leaves is known as transpiration (see page 60).

Diffusion — silent but deadly...

Particles whizz about so fast that they quickly spread out to cover as much space as possible — that's why they diffuse. An Austrian scientist called Ludwig Boltzmann developed the theory that gas particles do this in the 1860s. It's quite a tragic story actually — Ludwig was so upset when other scientists opposed his theory, he killed himself (he was suffering from depression). And he was right all along...

Osmosis

Osmosis is a Special Case of Diffusion, That's All

Osmosis is the movement of water molecules across a partially permeable membrane from a region of higher water concentration to a region of lower water concentration.

1) A partially permeable membrane is just one with very small holes in it. So small, in fact, that only tiny molecules (like water) can pass through them, and bigger molecules (e.g. sucrose) can't.
2) The water molecules actually pass both ways through the membrane during osmosis. This happens because water molecules move about randomly all the time.
3) But because there are more water molecules on one side than on the other, there's a steady net flow of water into the region with fewer water molecules, i.e. into the stronger sucrose solution.
4) This means the concentrated sucrose solution gets more dilute. The water acts like it's trying to 'even up' the concentration either side of the membrane.
5) Osmosis is a type of diffusion — passive movement of particles from an area of higher concentration to an area of lower concentration.

Water

Sucrose Solution

Net movement of water molecules

Turgor Pressure Supports Plant Tissues

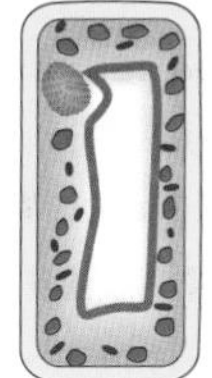
Normal Cell

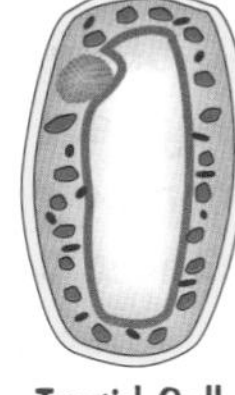
Turgid Cell

1) When a plant is well watered, all its cells will draw water in by osmosis and become plump and swollen. When the cells are like this, they're said to be turgid.
2) The contents of the cell push against the cell wall — this is called turgor pressure. Turgor pressure helps support the plant tissues.
3) If there's no water in the soil, a plant starts to wilt (droop). This is because the cells start to lose water and so lose their turgor pressure. The cells are then said to be flaccid.
4) If the plant's really short of water, the cytoplasm inside its cells starts to shrink and the membrane pulls away from the cell wall. The cell is now said to be plasmolysed. The plant doesn't totally lose its shape though, because the inelastic cell wall keeps things in position. It just droops a bit.

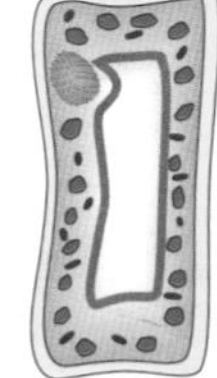
Flaccid Cell

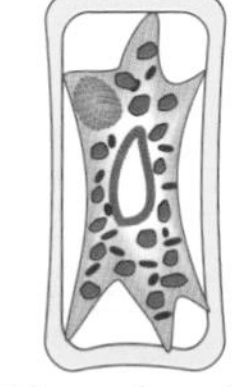
Plasmolysed Cell

Animal Cells Don't Have an Inelastic Cell Wall

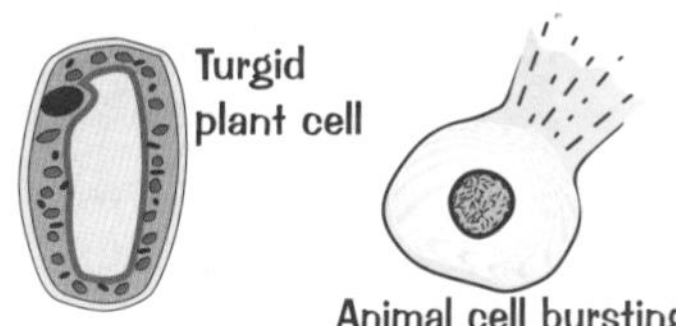

Plant cells aren't too bothered by changes in the amount of water because the inelastic cell wall keeps everything in place.

It's different in animal cells because they don't have a cell wall. If an animal cell takes in too much water, it bursts — this is known as lysis. If it loses too much water it gets all shrivelled up — this is known as crenation.

What all this means is that animals have to keep the amount of water in their cells pretty constant or they're in trouble, while plants are a bit more tolerant of periods of drought.

Revision by osmosis — you wish...

Wouldn't that be great — if all the ideas in this book would just gradually drift across into your mind, from an area of higher concentration (in the book) to an area of lower concentration (in your mind — no offence). Actually, that probably will happen if you read it again. Why don't you give it a go...

Water Flow Through Plants

If you don't water a house plant for a few days it starts to go all droopy. Then it dies, and the people from the Society for the Protection of Plants come round and have you arrested. Plants need water.

Root Hairs Take in Water by Osmosis

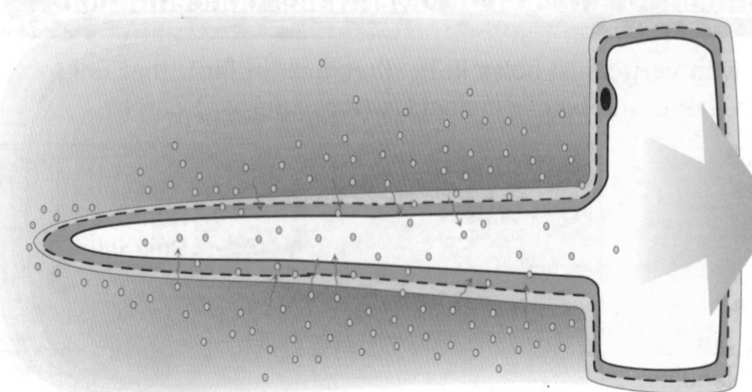

1) The cells on plant roots grow into long 'hairs' which stick out into the soil.
2) Each branch of a root will be covered in millions of these microscopic hairs.
3) This gives the plant a big surface area for absorbing water from the soil.
4) There's usually a higher concentration of water in the soil than there is inside the plant, so the water is drawn into the root hair cell by osmosis.

Transpiration is the Loss of Water from the Plant

1) Transpiration is caused by the evaporation and diffusion (see page 5) of water from inside the leaves.
2) This creates a slight shortage of water in the leaf, and so more water is drawn up from the rest of the plant through the xylem vessels (see page 62) to replace it.
3) This in turn means more water is drawn up from the roots, and so there's a constant transpiration stream of water through the plant.

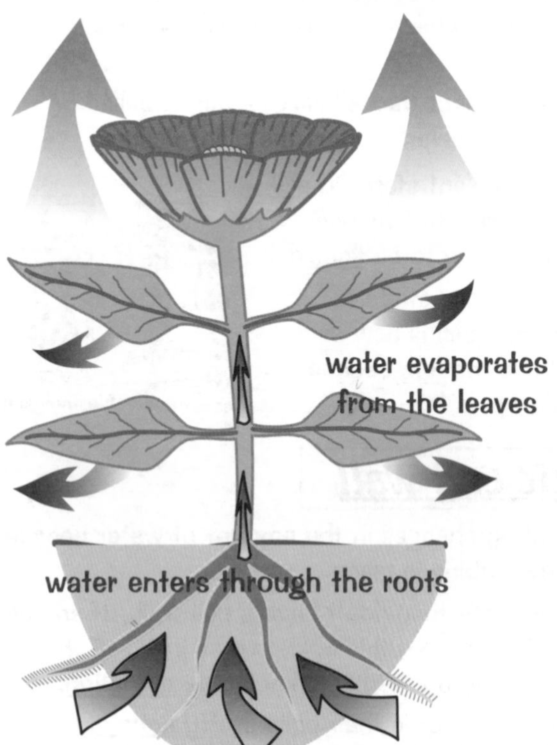
water evaporates from the leaves
water enters through the roots

Transpiration is just a side-effect of the way leaves are adapted for photosynthesis. They have to have stomata in them so that gases can be exchanged easily (see page 61). Because there's more water inside the plant than in the air outside, the water escapes from the leaves through the stomata.

The transpiration stream does have some benefits for the plants, however:

1) The constant stream of water from the ground helps to keep the plant cool.
2) It provides the plant with a constant supply of water for photosynthesis.
3) The water creates turgor pressure in the plant cells, which helps support the plant and stops it wilting (see page 59).
4) Minerals needed by the plant (see page 63) can be brought in from the soil along with the water.

Transpiration — the plant version of perspiration...

Here's an interesting fact — a biggish tree loses about a thousand litres of water from its leaves every single day. That's as much water as the average person drinks in a whole year, so the roots have to be very effective at drawing in water from the soil. Which is why they have all those root hairs, you see.

Water Flow Through Plants

Transpiration Rate is Affected by Four Main Things

1) LIGHT INTENSITY — the brighter the light, the greater the transpiration rate.
   Stomata begin to close as it gets darker. Photosynthesis can't happen in the dark, so they don't need to be open to let CO_2 in. When the stomata are closed, water can't escape.
2) TEMPERATURE — the warmer it is, the faster transpiration happens.
   When it's warm the water particles have more energy to evaporate and diffuse out of the stomata.
3) AIR MOVEMENT — if there's lots of air movement (wind) around a leaf, transpiration happens faster.
   If the air around a leaf is very still, the water vapour just surrounds the leaf and doesn't move away. This means there's a high concentration of water particles outside the leaf as well as inside it, so diffusion doesn't happen as quickly. If it's windy, the water vapour is swept away, maintaining a low concentration of water in the air outside the leaf. Diffusion then happens quickly, from an area of high concentration to an area of low concentration.
4) AIR HUMIDITY — if the air around the leaf is very dry, transpiration happens more quickly.
   This is like what happens with air movement. If the air is humid there's a lot of water in it already, so there's not much of a difference between the inside and the outside of the leaf. Diffusion happens fastest if there's a really high concentration in one place, and a really low concentration in the other.

Plants Need to Balance Water Loss with Water Uptake

Transpiration can help plants in some ways (see last page), but if it hasn't rained for a while and you're short of water it's not a good idea to have it rushing out of your leaves. So plants have adaptations to help reduce water loss from their leaves.

1) Leaves usually have a waxy cuticle covering the upper epidermis. This helps make the upper surface of the leaf waterproof.
2) Most stomata are found on the lower surface of a leaf where it's darker and cooler. This helps slow down diffusion of water out of the leaf (see above).
3) The bigger the stomata and the more stomata a leaf has, the more water the plant will lose. Plants in hot climates really need to conserve water, so they have fewer and smaller stomata on the underside of the leaf and no stomata on the upper epidermis.

Stomata Open and Close Automatically

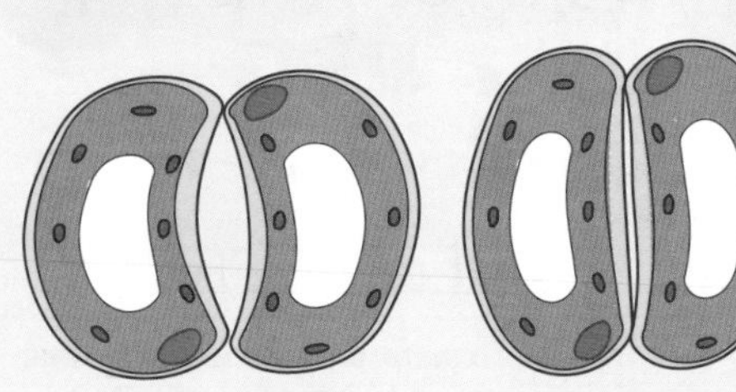
Cells turgid, stoma opens

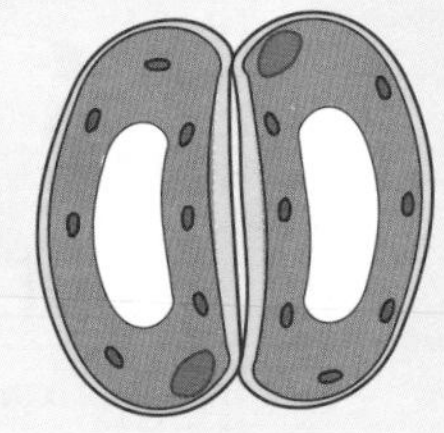
Cells flaccid, stoma closes

1) Stomata close automatically when supplies of water from the roots start to dry up.
2) The guard cells have a special kidney shape which opens and closes the stomata as the guard cells go turgid or flaccid.
3) Thin outer walls and thickened inner walls make this opening and closing function work properly.
4) Open stomata allow gases in and out for photosynthesis.
5) They're sensitive to light and close at night to conserve water without losing out on photosynthesis.

It always helps if you're quick on the uptake...

One good way to remember those four factors that affect the rate of transpiration is to think about drying washing. Then you'll realise there are far more boring things you could be doing than revision, and you'll try harder. No, only joking — it's the same stuff: sunny, warm, windy and dry.

Transport Systems in Plants

Where humans only have one circulatory system, plants have two.
They have two separate types of vessel — xylem and phloem — for transporting stuff around.
Both types of vessel go to every part of the plant, but they are totally separate.

Phloem Tubes Transport Food:

1) Made of columns of living cells with perforated end-plates to allow stuff to flow through.
2) They transport food substances (mainly sugars) made in the leaves to growing and storage tissues, in both directions.
3) This movement of food substances around the plant is known as translocation.

Xylem Tubes Take Water UP:

1) Made of dead cells joined end to end with no end walls between them and a hole (lumen) down the middle.
2) The thick side walls are strong and stiff, which gives the plant support.
3) They carry water and minerals from the roots up the shoot to the leaves in the transpiration stream.

You can Recognise Xylem and Phloem by Where They Are

1) They usually run alongside each other in vascular bundles (like veins).
2) Where they're found in each type of plant structure is related to xylem's other function — support.

You need to learn these three examples:

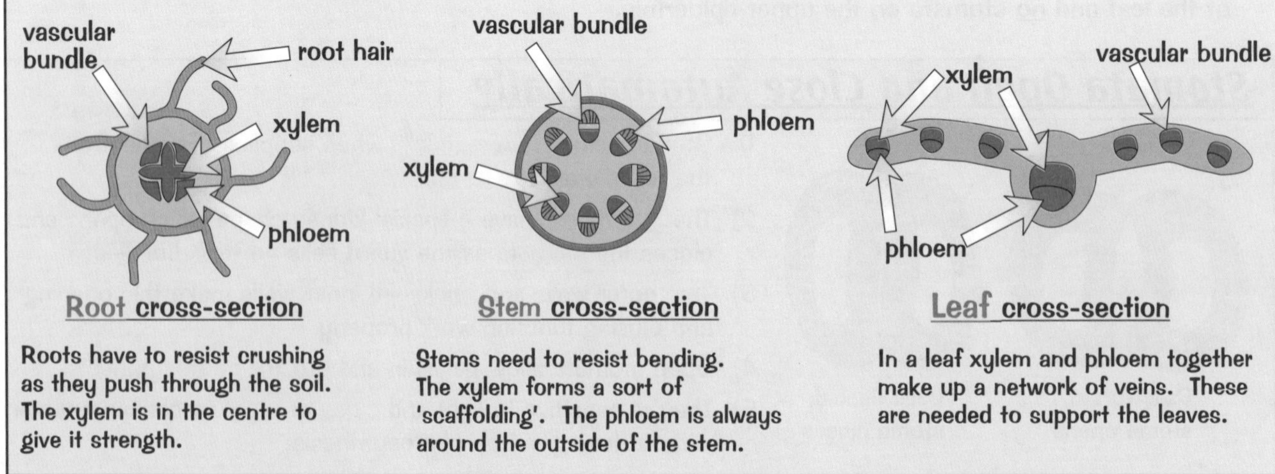

Root cross-section

Roots have to resist crushing as they push through the soil. The xylem is in the centre to give it strength.

Stem cross-section

Stems need to resist bending. The xylem forms a sort of 'scaffolding'. The phloem is always around the outside of the stem.

Leaf cross-section

In a leaf xylem and phloem together make up a network of veins. These are needed to support the leaves.

Don't let revision stress you out — just go with the phloem...

You probably did that really dull experiment at school where you stick a piece of celery in a beaker of water with red food colouring in it. Then you stare at it for half an hour, and once the time is up, hey presto, the red has reached the top of the celery. That's because it travelled there in the xylem.

Minerals Needed for Healthy Growth

Plants are important in food chains and nutrient cycles because they can take minerals from the soil and energy from the Sun and turn it into food. And then, after all that hard work, we eat them.

Plants Need Three Main Minerals

Plants need certain elements so they can produce important compounds. They get these elements from minerals in the soil. If there aren't enough of these minerals in the soil, plants suffer deficiency symptoms.

1) Nitrates

Contain nitrogen for making amino acids and proteins. These are needed for cell growth. If a plant can't get enough nitrates it will be stunted and will have yellow older leaves.

2) Phosphates

Contain phosphorus for making DNA and cell membranes and they're needed for respiration and growth. Plants without enough phosphate have poor root growth and purple older leaves.

3) Potassium

To help the enzymes needed for photosynthesis and respiration. If there's not enough potassium in the soil, plants have poor flower and fruit growth and discoloured leaves.

Magnesium is Also Needed in Small Amounts

The three main minerals are needed in fairly large amounts, but there are other elements which are needed in much smaller amounts. Magnesium is one of the most significant as it's required for making chlorophyll (needed for photosynthesis). Plants without enough magnesium have yellow leaves.

Root Hairs Take In Minerals Using Active Transport

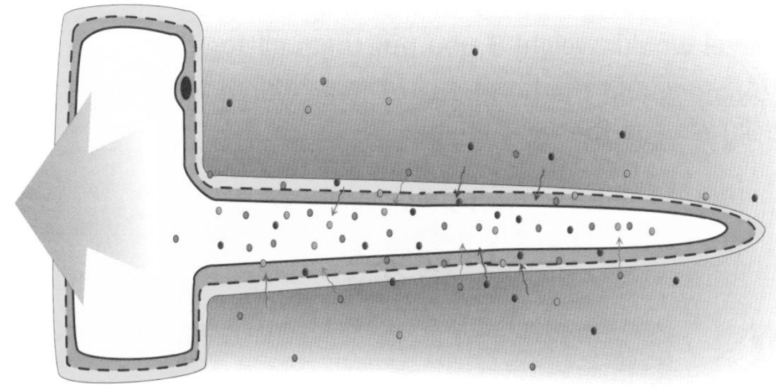

1) Root hairs (see page 60) give the plant a big surface area for absorbing minerals from the soil.
2) But the concentration of minerals in the soil is usually pretty low. It's normally higher in the root hair cell than in the soil around it.
3) So normal diffusion doesn't explain how minerals are taken up into the root hair cell.
4) They should go the other way if they followed the rules of diffusion.
5) The answer is that a different process called 'active transport' is responsible.
6) Active transport uses energy from respiration to help the plant pull minerals into the root hair against the concentration gradient. This is essential for its growth.

Nitrogen and phosphorus and potassium — oh my...

When a farmer or a gardener buys fertiliser, that's pretty much what he or she is buying — nitrates, phosphates and potassium. A fertiliser's NPK label tells you the relative proportions of nitrogen (N), phosphorus (P) and potassium (K) it contains, so you can choose the right one for your plants and soil.

Pyramids of Number and Biomass

A trophic level is a feeding level. It comes from the Greek word trophe meaning 'nourishment'. The amount of energy, biomass and usually the number of organisms all decrease as you move up a trophic level.

You Need to be Able to Construct Pyramids of Number

Luckily it's pretty easy — they'll give you all the information you need to do it in the exam. Here's an example:

5000 dandelions... feed... 100 rabbits... which feed... 1 fox.

1) Each bar on a pyramid of numbers shows the number of organisms at that stage of the food chain.
2) So the 'dandelions' bar on this pyramid would need to be longer than the 'rabbits' bar, which in turn should be longer than the 'fox' bar.
3) Dandelions go at the bottom because they're at the bottom of the food chain.

This gives a typical pyramid of numbers, where every time you go up a trophic (feeding) level, the number of organisms goes down. This is because it takes a lot of food from the level below to keep one animal alive.

But there are cases where a number pyramid is not a pyramid at all, like these ones:

500 Fleas
1 Fox
100 Rabbits
5000 Dandelions

1 Partridge
500 Ladybirds
3000 Aphids
1 Pear tree

You'll Have to Construct Pyramids of Biomass Too

1) Each bar on a pyramid of biomass shows the mass of living material at that stage of the food chain — basically how much all the organisms at each level would 'weigh' if you put them all together.
2) So the one pear tree above would have a big biomass and the hundreds of fleas would have a very small biomass. Biomass pyramids are practically always the right shape:

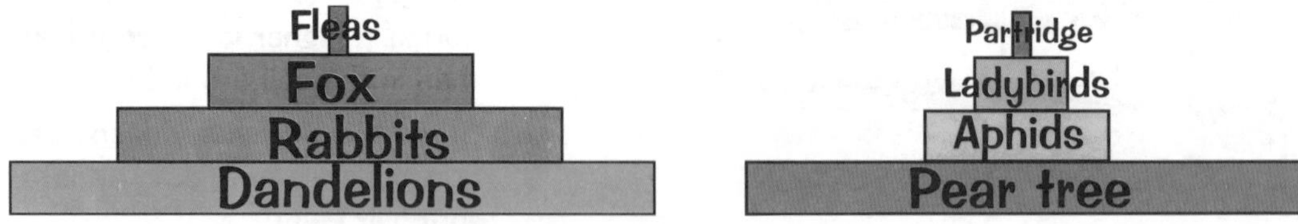

Even if you know nothing about the natural world, you're probably aware that a tree is quite a bit bigger than an aphid. So what's going on here is that lots (probably thousands) of aphids are feeding on a few great big trees. Quite a lot of ladybirds are then eating the aphids, and a few partridges are eating the ladybirds. Biomass and energy are still decreasing as you go up the levels — it's just that one tree can have a very big biomass, and can fix a lot of the Sun's energy using all those leaves.

Constructing pyramids is a breeze — just ask the Egyptians...

There are actually a couple of exceptions where pyramids of biomass aren't quite pyramid-shaped. It happens when the producer has a very short life but reproduces loads, like with plankton at certain times of year. But it's rare, and you don't need to know about it. Forget I ever mentioned it. Sorry.

Energy Transfer and Energy Flow

All That Energy Just Disappears Somehow...

1) Energy from the Sun is the source of energy for nearly all life on Earth.

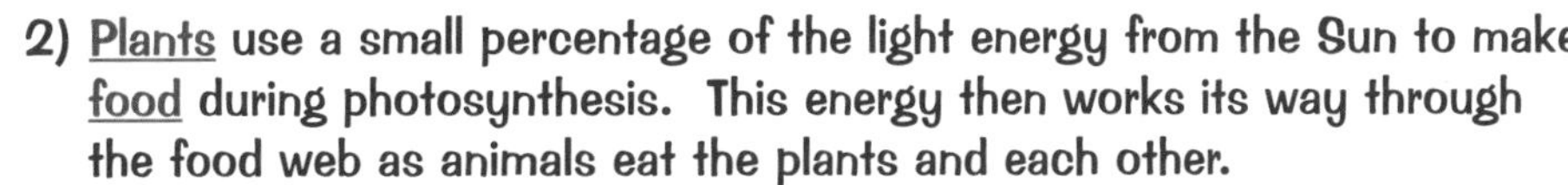

2) Plants use a small percentage of the light energy from the Sun to make food during photosynthesis. This energy then works its way through the food web as animals eat the plants and each other.

3) The energy lost at each stage is used for staying alive, i.e. in respiration (see page 1), which powers all life processes.

4) Most of this energy is eventually lost to the surroundings as heat. This is especially true for mammals and birds, whose bodies must be kept at a constant temperature which is normally higher than their surroundings.

HEAT LOSS

5) Material and energy are also lost from the food chain in the droppings — you'll need to remember the posh word for producing droppings, which is egestion.

MATERIALS LOST IN ANIMAL'S WASTE

Material and energy are both lost at each stage of the food chain.

This explains why you get biomass pyramids. Most of the biomass is lost and so does not become biomass in the next level up.

(There's more about the energy stored in biomass on page 64.)

It also explains why you hardly ever get food chains with more than about five trophic levels. So much energy is lost at each stage that there's not enough left to support more organisms after four or five stages.

You Need to be Able to Interpret Data on Energy Flow

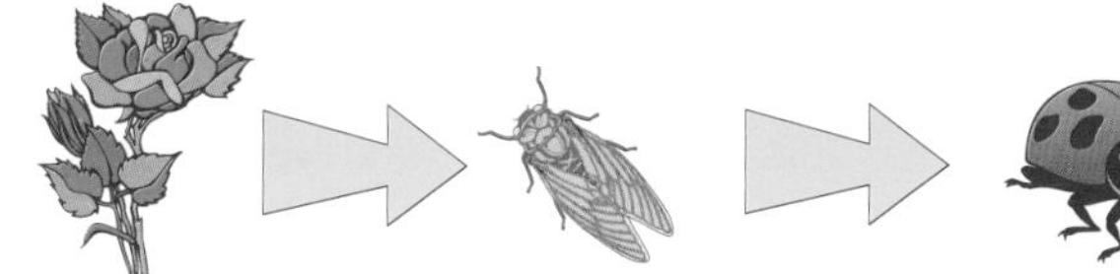

rosebush: 80 000 kJ — greenfly: 10 000 kJ — ladybird: 900 kJ — bird: 40 kJ

1) The numbers show the amount of energy available to the next level. So 80 000 kJ is the amount of energy available to the greenfly, and 10 000 kJ is the amount available to the ladybird.
2) You can work out how much energy has been lost at each level by taking away the energy that is available to the next level from the energy that was available from the previous level. Like this:
   Energy lost at 1st trophic level as heat and in egestion = 80 000 kJ – 10 000 kJ = 70 000 kJ lost.
3) You can also calculate the efficiency of energy transfer — this just means how good it is at passing on energy from one level to the next.

$$\text{efficiency} = \frac{\text{energy available to the next level}}{\text{energy that was available to the previous level}} \times 100$$

So at the 1st trophic level, efficiency of energy transfer = 10 000 kJ ÷ 80 000 kJ × 100
= 12.5% efficient.

So when revising, put the fire on and don't take toilet breaks...

No, I'm being silly — go if you have to. We're talking in general terms about whole food chains here — you won't lose your concentration as a direct result of, erm, egestion.

Biomass and Intensive Farming

Energy Stored in Biomass Can be Used for Other Things

There are many different ways to release the energy stored in biomass — including eating it, feeding it to livestock, growing the seeds of plants and using it as a fuel.

For a given area of land, you can produce a lot more food for humans by growing crops than by grazing animals — only about 10% of the biomass eaten by beef cattle becomes useful meat for people to eat. It's important to get a balanced diet, though, which is difficult from crops only. It's also worth remembering that some land, like moorland or fellsides, isn't suitable for growing crops. In these places, animals like sheep and deer can be the best way to get food from the land.

As well as using biomass as food, you can use it as fuel. Learn these two examples of biofuels:

1) Fast-growing trees — people tend to think burning trees is a bad thing, but it's not as long as they're fast-growing and planted especially for that purpose. Each time trees are cut down, more can be planted to replace them. There's no overall contribution to CO_2 emissions because the replacement trees are still removing carbon from the atmosphere.
2) Fermenting biomass using bacteria or yeast — fermenting means breaking down by anaerobic respiration. You can use micro-organisms to make biogas from plant and animal waste in a simple fermenter called a digester. The biogas can then be burned to release the energy for heating, powering a turbine, etc.

Developing biofuels is a great idea, for these three important reasons:

- Unlike coal, oil and the like, biofuels are renewable — they're not going to run out one day.
- Using biofuels reduces air pollution — no acid rain gases are produced when wood and biogas burn.
- You can be energy self-reliant. Theoretically, you could supply all your energy from household waste.

Intensive Farming is Used to Produce More Food

Intensive farming means trying to produce as much food as possible from your land, animals and plants. Farmers can do this in different ways, but they all involve reducing the energy losses that happen at each stage in a food chain (see last page). Here are some examples of how they do it:

1) They use herbicides to kill weeds. This means that more of the energy from the Sun falling on their fields goes to the crops, and not to any other competing plants that they don't want.
2) They use pesticides to kill insects that eat the crops. This makes sure no energy is transferred into a different food chain — it's all saved for growing the crops.
3) Animals are battery farmed. They're kept close together indoors in small pens, so that they're warm and can't move about. This saves them wasting energy as they move around, and stops them using up so much energy keeping warm.

Intensive farming allows us to produce a lot of food from less and less land, which means a huge variety of top quality foods, all year round, at cheap prices.

Intensive Farming Can Destroy the Environment

Intensive farming methods are efficient, but they raise ethical dilemmas because they can damage the world we live in, making it polluted, unattractive and devoid of wildlife. The main effects are:

1) Removal of hedges to make huge great fields for maximum efficiency. This destroys the natural habitat of wild creatures and can lead to serious soil erosion.
2) Careless use of fertilisers pollutes rivers and lakes (known as eutrophication).
3) Pesticides disturb food chains — see next page.
4) Lots of people think that intensive farming of animals such as battery-hens is cruel.

Be energy self-reliant — burn poo...

One of the saddest things about intensive farming methods is that it reduces the wildlife in the countryside. If there are no plants (except crops) and few insects, there's not much around to eat...

Pesticides and Biological Control

Biological control is growing more popular, as people get fed up with all the problems caused by pesticides.

Pesticides Disturb Food Chains

1) Pesticides are sprayed onto crops to kill the creatures that damage them, but unfortunately they also kill lots of harmless animals such as bees and beetles.
2) This can cause a shortage of food for animals further up the food chain.
3) Pesticides also tend to be toxic to creatures that aren't pests and there's a danger of the poison passing on through the food chain to other animals. There's even a risk that they could harm humans.

This is well illustrated by the case of otters which were almost wiped out over much of crop-dominated southern England by a pesticide called DDT in the early 1960s. The diagram shows the food chain which ends with the otter. DDT can't be excreted, so it accumulates along the food chain and the otter ends up with most of the DDT collected by all the other animals.

③ Each little tiny animal eats lots of small plants
⑤ Each eel eats lots of small fish
① Insecticide seeps into the river
② Small water plants take up a little insecticide
④ Each small fish eats lots of tiny animals
⑥ Each otter eats lots of eels

You Can Use Biological Control Instead of Pesticides

Biological control means using living things instead of chemicals to control a pest.
You could use a predator, a parasite or a disease to kill the pest. For example:

1) Aphids are a pest because they eat roses and vegetables. Ladybirds are aphid predators, so people release them into their fields and gardens to keep aphid numbers down.
2) Certain types of wasps and flies produce larvae which develop on (or in, yuck) a host insect. This eventually kills the insect host. Lots of insect pests have parasites like this.
3) Myxomatosis is a disease which kills rabbits. The myxoma virus was released in Australia as a biological control when the rabbit population there grew out of control and ruined crops.

You need to be able to explain the advantages and disadvantages of biological control:

ADVANTAGES:

- The predator, parasite or disease usually only affects the pest animal. You don't kill all the harmless and helpful creatures as well like you often do with a pesticide.
- No chemicals are used, so there's less pollution, disruption of food chains and risk to people eating the food that's been sprayed.

DISADVANTAGES:

- It's slower than pesticides — you have to wait for your control organism to build up its numbers.
- Biological control won't kill all the pests, and it usually only kills one type of pest.
- It takes more management and planning, and workers might need training or educating.
- Control organisms can drive out native species, or become pests in their own right.

Remember that removing an organism from a food web, whether you use biological control or pesticides, can affect all the other organisms too. For example, if you remove a pest insect, you're removing a source of food from all the organisms that normally eat it. These might die out, and another insect that they normally feed on could breed out of control and become a pest instead. You have to be very careful.

Don't get bugged by biological pest control...

In the exam you might be asked to interpret data related to biological control, e.g. tables showing the population sizes of pest species when using biological control and when using pesticides. Or they might give you a food web and ask you to predict the effect of removing different organisms.

Alternatives to Intensive Farming

Intensive farming methods are still used, a lot. But people are also using other methods more and more.

Hydroponics is Where Plants are Grown Without Soil

Most commercially grown tomatoes and cucumbers are grown in nutrient solutions (water and fertilisers) instead of in soil — this is called hydroponics.

There are advantages and disadvantages of using hydroponics instead of growing crops in soil:

ADVANTAGES	DISADVANTAGES
Takes up less space so less land required	It can be expensive to set up and run
No soil preparation or weeding needed	Need to use specially formulated soluble nutrients
Can still grow plants even in areas with poor soil	Growers need to be skilled and properly trained
Many pest species live in soil, so it avoids these	There's no soil to anchor the roots so plants need support
Mineral levels can be controlled more accurately	

Organic Farming is Still Perfectly Viable

Modern intensive farming produces lots of food and we all appreciate it on the supermarket shelves. But traditional organic farming methods do still work (amazingly!), and they have their benefits too. You need to know about these organic farming techniques:

1) Use of organic fertilisers (i.e. animal manure and compost). This recycles the nutrients left in plant and animal waste. It doesn't work as well as artificial fertilisers, but it is better for the environment.
2) Crop rotation — growing a cycle of different crops in a field each year. This stops the pests and diseases of one crop building up, and stops nutrients running out (as each crop has slightly different needs). Most crop rotations include a legume plant like peas or beans, as they help put nitrates back in the soil (see page 63).
3) Weeding — this means physically removing the weeds, rather than just spraying them with a herbicide. Obviously it's a lot more labour intensive, but there are no nasty chemicals involved.
4) Varying seed planting times — sowing seeds later or earlier in the season will avoid the major pests for that crop. This means the farmer won't need to use pesticides.
5) Biological control — this is covered on the previous page.

You also need to be able to discuss the advantages and disadvantages of organic farming. Always try to give a balanced point of view, unless you're specifically asked to argue one way or another. You can include your own opinion in a conclusion at the end. Here are a few points you could mention:

1) Organic farming takes up more space than intensive farming — so more land has to be farmland, rather than being set aside for wildlife or for other uses.
2) It's more labour-intensive. This provides more jobs, but it also makes the food more expensive.
3) You can't grow as much food. But on the other hand, Europe over-produces food these days anyway.
4) Organic farming uses fewer chemicals, so there's less risk of toxic chemicals remaining on food.
5) It's better for the environment. There's less chance of polluting rivers with fertiliser. Organic farmers also avoid using pesticides, so don't disrupt food chains and harm wildlife.
6) For a farm to be classed as organic, it will usually have to follow guidelines on the ethical treatment of animals. This means no battery farming.

Plants without soil? It's not like when I was a lad...

You can't just learn about the methods used in different types of farming — you have to think about their impact too. That means weighing up the advantages and disadvantages and being able to discuss them.

Decay

Micro-organisms are great because they break down plant and animal remains which are lying around and looking unsightly. But they also break down plant and animal remains that we just bought at the shops.

Things Decay Because of Micro-organisms

1) Living things are made of materials they take from the world around them.
2) When they die and decompose, or release material as waste, the elements they contain are returned to the soil or air where they originally came from.
3) These elements are then used by plants to grow and the whole cycle repeats over and over again.
4) Nearly all the decomposition is done by soil bacteria and fungi (see next page).
5) This happens everywhere in nature, and also in compost heaps and sewage works.
6) All the important elements are thus recycled, including carbon, hydrogen, oxygen and nitrogen.
7) The rate of decay depends on three main things:
    a) Temperature — a warm temperature makes things decay faster because it speeds up respiration in decomposers.
    b) Moisture — things decay faster when they're moist because decomposers need water.
    c) Oxygen (air) — decay is faster when there's oxygen available. The decomposers can respire aerobically, providing more energy.
8) These factors cause decomposers (bacteria and fungi) to grow and reproduce more quickly, so there'll be more of them to decay other living things.

An energetic decomposer

Food Preservation Methods Reduce the Rate of Decay

Decomposers are good for returning nutrients to the soil, but they're not so good when they start decomposing your lunch. So people have come up with ways to stop them:

1) Canning — basically, this involves putting food in an airtight can. This keeps the decomposers out. After canning, the tin and its contents are heated to a high temperature to kill any micro-organisms that might have been lurking in there already.
2) Cooling — the easiest way to keep food cool is put it in a fridge. Cooling slows down decay because it slows down respiration in the micro-organisms. They can't reproduce as fast either.
3) Freezing — food lasts longer in the freezer than in the fridge because the micro-organisms can't respire or reproduce at all at such low temperatures. Some (but not all) are killed when the water inside them expands as it freezes.
4) Drying — dried food lasts longer because micro-organisms need water. Lots of fruits are preserved by drying them out, and sometimes meat is too.
5) Adding salt — if there's a high concentration of salt around decomposers, they'll lose water by osmosis. This damages them and means they can't work properly. Things like tuna and olives are often stored in brine (salt water).
6) Adding vinegar — mmm, pickled onions. Vinegar is acidic, and the low pH inhibits the enzymes inside the micro-organisms. This stops them decomposing the delicious onions.

Decomposers — they're just misunderstood...

OK, so it's annoying when you go to the cupboard and find that everything has turned a funny green colour. But imagine the alternative — when a plant or animal died, it would just stay there, hanging around. Soon we'd be up to our eyes in dead things, and there'd be no nutrients in the soil. Not good.

The Carbon Cycle

Carbon is constantly moving between the atmosphere, the soil and living things in the carbon cycle.

Detritivores and Saprophytes Feed on Decaying Material

Detritivores and saprophytes are both types of organism that are important in decay. They're grouped into those two types depending on how they feed.

1) Detritivores feed on dead and decaying material (detritus). Examples of detritivores include earthworms, maggots and woodlice. As these detritivores feed on the decaying material, they break it up into smaller bits. This gives a bigger surface area for smaller decomposers to work on and so speeds up decay.
2) Saprophytes feed on decaying material by extracellular digestion, i.e. they feed by secreting digestive enzymes on to the material outside of their cells. The enzymes break down the material into smaller bits which can then be absorbed by the saprophyte. Most saprophytes are bacteria and fungi.

The Carbon Cycle Shows How Carbon is Recycled

Carbon is an important element in the materials that living things are made from. It's constantly recycled:

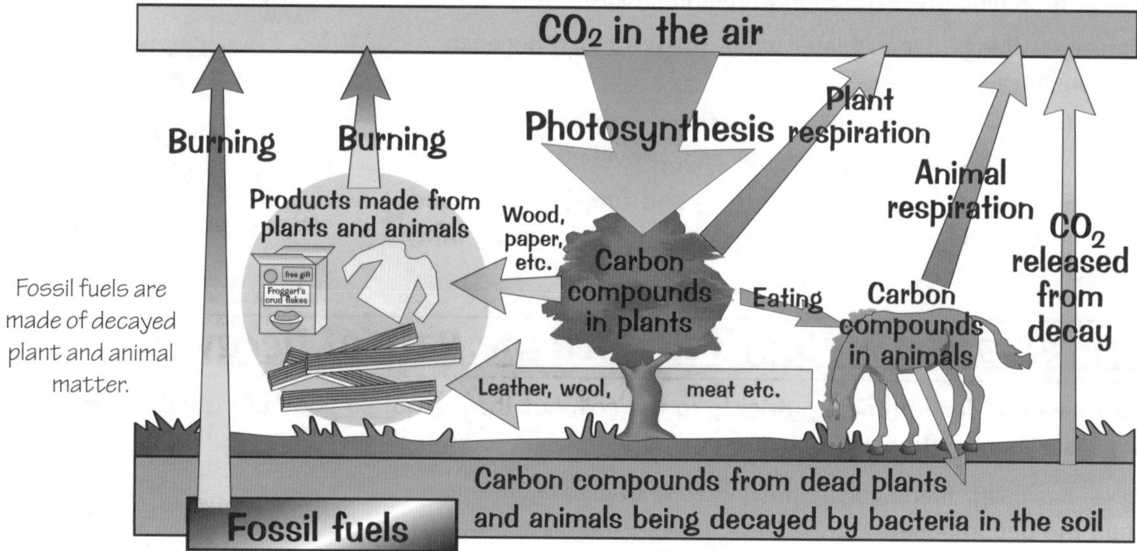

This diagram isn't half as bad as it looks. Learn these important points:

1) There's only one arrow going down. The whole thing is 'powered' by photosynthesis.
2) In photosynthesis plants convert the carbon from CO_2 in the air into sugars. Plants can now incorporate this carbon into carbohydrates, fats and proteins as well.
3) Eating passes the carbon compounds in the plant along to animals in a food chain or web.
4) Both plant and animal respiration while the organisms are alive releases CO_2 back into the air.
5) Plants and animals eventually die and decay, or are killed and turned into useful products.
6) When plants and animals decay they're broken down by bacteria and fungi. These decomposers release CO_2 back into the air by respiration as they break down the material.
7) Some useful plant and animal products, e.g. wood and fossil fuels, are burned (combustion). This also releases CO_2 back into the air.

There's another major recycling pathway for carbon in the sea. Marine organisms make shells made of carbonates. When they die the shells fall to the ocean floor and eventually form limestone rocks. The carbon in these rocks may return to the atmosphere as CO_2 during volcanic eruptions or weathering.

Come on out, it's only a little carbon cycle, it can't hurt you...

Carbon is a very important element for living things — it's the basis for all the organic molecules (fats, proteins, carbohydrates etc.) in our bodies. In sci-fi programmes the aliens are sometimes silicon-based instead, but then they're usually defeated in the end by some Bruce Willis type anyway.

The Nitrogen Cycle

Nitrogen, just like carbon, is constantly being recycled. So the nitrogen in your proteins might once have been in the air. And before that it might have been in a plant. Or even in some horse wee. Nice.

Nitrogen is Also Recycled in the Nitrogen Cycle

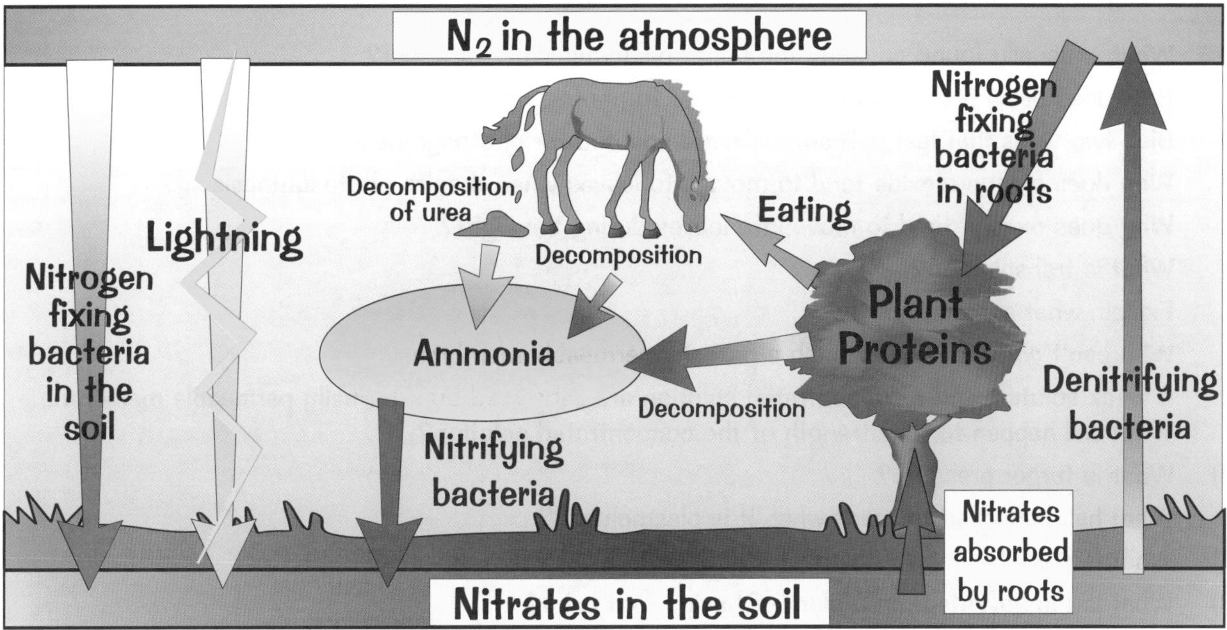

1) The atmosphere contains 78% nitrogen gas, N_2. This is very unreactive and so it can't be used directly by plants or animals.
2) Nitrogen is needed for making proteins for growth, so living organisms have to get it somehow.
3) Plants get their nitrogen from the soil, so nitrogen in the air has to be turned into nitrates before plants can use it. Animals can only get proteins by eating plants (or each other).
4) Decomposers break down proteins in rotting plants and animals, and urea in animal waste, into ammonia. So the nitrogen in these organisms is recycled.
5) Nitrogen fixation isn't an obsession with nitrogen — it's the process of turning N_2 from the air into nitrogen compounds in the soil which plants can use. There are two main ways that this happens:
   a) Lightning — there's so much energy in a bolt of lightning that it's enough to make nitrogen react with oxygen in the air to give nitrates.
   b) Nitrogen-fixing bacteria in roots and soil (see below).
6) There are four different types of bacteria involved in the nitrogen cycle:
   a) DECOMPOSERS — decompose proteins and urea and turn them into ammonia.
   b) NITRIFYING BACTERIA — turn ammonia in decaying matter into nitrates.
   c) NITROGEN-FIXING BACTERIA — turn atmospheric N_2 into nitrogen compounds that plants can use.
   d) DENITRIFYING BACTERIA — turn nitrates back into N_2 gas. This is of no benefit to living organisms.
7) Some nitrogen-fixing bacteria live in the soil. Others live in nodules on the roots of legume plants. This is why legume plants are so good at putting nitrogen back into the soil (see page 68). The plants have a mutualistic relationship with the bacteria — the bacteria get food (sugars) from the plant, and the plant gets nitrogen compounds from the bacteria to make into proteins. So the relationship benefits both of them.

It's the cyyyycle of liiiiife...

People sometimes forget that when we breathe in, we're breathing in mainly nitrogen. It's a pretty boring gas, colourless and with no taste or smell. But nitrogen is vital to living things, because the amino acids that join together to make proteins (like enzymes) all contain nitrogen.

Revision Summary for Module B4

What a nice leafy section that was. Things started to get a bit mouldy towards the end, but that's life I suppose. Now, just to make sure you've taken in all the leafiness and mouldiness, here's a little revision summary so you can check what you've learned. You know the routine by now — whizz through the questions and make a note of any you can't answer. Then go back and find the answer in the section. It's actually kind of fun, like a treasure hunt... well, okay, it's not — but it works.

1) What is usually found covering the upper epidermis layer of a leaf?
2) How does being broad and thin help a leaf to photosynthesise?
3) Give two ways that leaf palisade cells are adapted for photosynthesis.
4) Why does carbon dioxide tend to move into leaves when they're photosynthesising?
5) Why does oxygen tend to move into leaves during the night?
6) What is transpiration?
7) Explain what osmosis is.
8) Why can't glucose pass through a partially permeable membrane?
9) A weak solution and a concentrated solution are separated by a partially permeable membrane. What will happen to the strength of the concentrated solution?
10) What is turgor pressure?
11) What has happened to a cell when it is plasmolysed?
12) What is crenation? Why doesn't it happen to plant cells?
13) What is the advantage to a plant of having root hairs?
14) Give three ways that the transpiration stream benefits a plant.
15) How is the transpiration rate affected by: a) increased temperature, b) increased air humidity?
16) What causes stomata to close when a plant is short of water? How does this benefit the plant?
17) Give the term for the transport of sugars around a plant.
18) How are xylem vessels adapted to their function?
19) What is a vascular bundle?
20) Where are the xylem and phloem found in a root?
21) Name the three main minerals plants need for healthy growth.
22) How can you tell by looking at a plant that it isn't getting enough phosphates?
23) What is magnesium needed for in a plant?
24) What is active transport? Why is it used in the roots of a plant?
25) Explain why number pyramids are not always pyramid-shaped.
26) What does each bar on a pyramid of biomass represent?
27) What is the source of all the energy in a typical food chain?
28) Why is it unusual to find a food chain with more than five trophic levels?
29) Give three ways that intensive farming methods reduce the energy lost at each stage in a food chain.
30) Give three problems associated with intensive farming.
31) What is meant by the term hydroponics?
32) What is crop rotation?
33) Give two advantages and two disadvantages of organic farming methods.
34) Why do dead organisms decay faster when it is warm?
35) Why does pickling food in vinegar help it to last for longer without decaying?
36) Give an example of a detritivore.
37) How does carbon enter the carbon cycle from the air?
38) What important role do nitrogen-fixing bacteria play in the nitrogen cycle?

Acids and Bases

You'll find acids and bases at home, in industry and in the lab — they're an important set of chemicals.

The pH Scale and Universal Indicator

An Indicator is Just a Dye That Changes Colour

The dye in the indicator changes colour depending on whether it's above or below a certain pH. Universal indicator is a very useful combination of dyes which gives the colours shown above.

It's very useful for estimating the pH of a solution.

The pH Scale Goes from 0 to 14

1) A very strong acid has pH 0. A very strong alkali has pH 14.
2) A neutral substance has pH 7 (e.g. pure water).

Acids and Bases Neutralise Each Other

An ACID is a substance with a pH of less than 7. Acids form H^+ ions in water.
A BASE is a substance with a pH of greater than 7.
An ALKALI is a base that DISSOLVES IN WATER. Alkalis form OH^- ions in water.

The reaction between acids and bases is called neutralisation. Make sure you learn it:

$$\text{acid} + \text{base} \rightarrow \text{salt} + \text{water}$$

Neutralisation can also be seen in terms of H^+ and OH^- ions like this, so learn it too:

$$H^+ + OH^- \rightarrow H_2O$$

When an acid neutralises a base (or vice versa), the products are neutral, i.e. they have a pH of 7.

Modern Industry Uses Tonnes of Sulfuric Acid

1) Sulfuric acid is used in car batteries, where it's concentrated enough to cause severe burns.
2) It's also used in many manufacturing processes, such as making fertilisers and detergents.
3) You can also use it to clean and prepare metal surfaces, e.g. before painting or welding. A metal surface is usually covered with a layer of insoluble metal oxide. Sulfuric acid reacts with these, forming soluble metal salts which wash away, nice and easily.

This'll give you a firm base for Chemistry...

There's no getting away from acids and bases in Chemistry, or even in real life. They are everywhere — acids are found in loads of foods, like vinegar and fruit, and as food flavourings and preservatives, whilst alkalis (particularly sodium hydroxide) are used to help make all sorts of things from soaps to ceramics.

Reactions of Acids

Metal Oxides and Metal Hydroxides are Bases

1) Some metal oxides and metal hydroxides dissolve in water. These soluble compounds are alkalis.
2) Even bases that won't dissolve in water will still react with acids.
3) So, all metal oxides and metal hydroxides react with acids to form a salt and water.

Acid + Metal Oxide → Salt + Water

Acid + Metal Hydroxide → Salt + Water

(These are neutralisation reactions, of course.)

Hydrochloric acid	+	Copper oxide	→	Copper chloride	+	water
2HCl	+	CuO	→	$CuCl_2$	+	H_2O
Sulfuric acid	+	Potassium hydroxide	→	Potassium sulfate	+	water
H_2SO_4	+	2KOH	→	K_2SO_4	+	$2H_2O$
Nitric acid	+	Sodium hydroxide	→	Sodium nitrate	+	water
HNO_3	+	NaOH	→	$NaNO_3$	+	H_2O

Acids and Carbonates Produce Carbon Dioxide

These are very like the ones above — they just produce carbon dioxide as well.

Acid + Carbonate → Salt + Water + Carbon dioxide

Hydrochloric acid	+	Sodium carbonate	→	Sodium chloride	+	water	+	carbon dioxide
2HCl	+	Na_2CO_3	→	2NaCl	+	H_2O	+	CO_2
Hydrochloric acid	+	Calcium carbonate	→	Calcium chloride	+	water	+	carbon dioxide
2HCl	+	$CaCO_3$	→	$CaCl_2$	+	H_2O	+	CO_2

Acids and Ammonia Produce Ammonium Salts

And lastly...

Acid + Ammonia → Ammonium salt

Hydrochloric acid	+	Ammonia	→	Ammonium chloride
HCl	+	NH_3	→	NH_4Cl
Sulfuric acid	+	Ammonia	→	Ammonium sulfate
H_2SO_4	+	$2NH_3$	→	$(NH_4)_2SO_4$
Nitric acid	+	Ammonia	→	Ammonium nitrate
HNO_3	+	NH_3	→	NH_4NO_3

This last reaction with nitric acid produces the famous ammonium nitrate fertiliser, much appreciated for its double dose of essential nitrogen. (See P. 63.)

Acid + Revision → Insomnia Cure...

Some of these reactions are really useful, and some are just for fun (who said chemistry was dull). Try doing different combinations of acids and alkalis, acids and carbonates, acids and ammonia. Balance them. Cover the page and scribble all the equations down. If you make any mistakes, try again...

Relative Formula Mass

The biggest trouble with relative atomic mass and relative formula mass is that they sound so blood-curdling. You need them for the calculations on the next page though, so take a few deep breaths, and just enjoy, as the mists slowly clear...

Relative Atomic Mass, A_r — Easy Peasy

1) This is just a way of saying how heavy different atoms are compared with the mass of an atom of carbon-12. So carbon-12 has A_r of exactly 12.
2) It turns out that the relative atomic mass A_r is usually just the same as the mass number of the element.
3) In the periodic table, the elements all have two numbers. The smaller one is the atomic number (how many protons it has). The bigger one is the relative atomic mass. Easy peasy, I'd say.

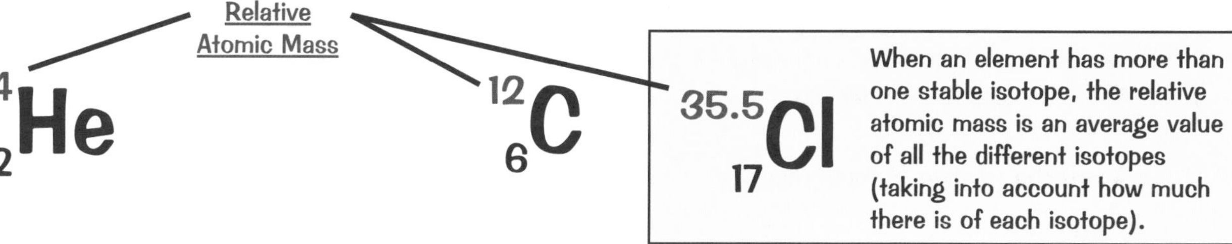

When an element has more than one stable isotope, the relative atomic mass is an average value of all the different isotopes (taking into account how much there is of each isotope).

Helium has A_r = 4. Carbon has A_r = 12. Chlorine has A_r = 35.5.

Relative Formula Mass, M_r — Also Easy Peasy

If you have a compound like $MgCl_2$ then it has a relative formula mass, M_r, which is just all the relative atomic masses added together.

For $MgCl_2$ it would be:

$$MgCl_2$$
$$24 + (35.5 \times 2) = 95$$

So M_r for $MgCl_2$ is simply 95.

You can easily get A_r for any element from the periodic table (see inside front cover), but in a lot of questions they give you them anyway. I tell you what, since it's nearly Christmas I'll run through another example for you:

Compounds with Brackets in...

Find the relative formula mass for calcium hydroxide, $Ca(OH)_2$

ANSWER: The small number 2 after the bracket in the formula $Ca(OH)_2$ means that there's two of everything inside the brackets. But that doesn't make the question any harder really.

The brackets in the sum are in the same place as the brackets in the chemical formula.

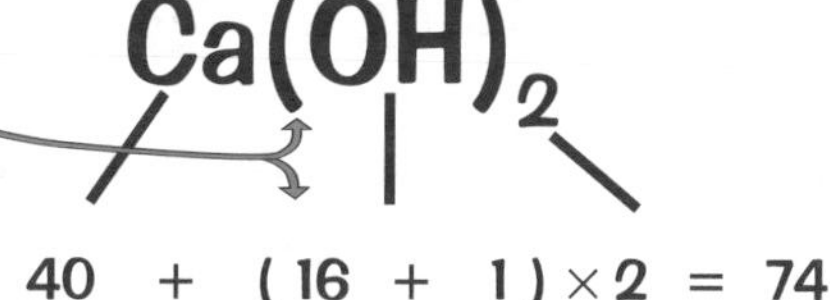

$$40 + (16 + 1) \times 2 = 74$$

So the Relative Formula Mass for $Ca(OH)_2$ is 74.

Phew, Chemistry — scary stuff sometimes, innit...

Learn the definitions of relative atomic mass and relative formula mass, then have a go at these:

1) Use the periodic table to find the relative atomic mass of these elements: Cu, K, Kr, Cl
2) Find the relative formula mass of: NaOH, Fe_2O_3, C_6H_{14}, $Mg(NO_3)_2$

Answers on page 108

Calculating Masses in Reactions

These can be kinda scary too, but chill out, little trembling one — just relax and enjoy.

The Three Important Steps — Not to Be Missed...

(Miss one out and it'll all go horribly wrong, believe me.)

1) Write out the balanced equation
2) Work out M_r — just for the two bits you want
3) Apply the rule: Divide to get one, then multiply to get all
   (But you have to apply this first to the substance they give information about, and then the other one!)

Don't worry — these steps should all make sense when you look at the example below.

Example: What mass of magnesium oxide is produced when 60 g of magnesium is burned in air?

Answer:

1) Write out the balanced equation:

$$2Mg + O_2 \rightarrow 2MgO$$

2) Work out the relative formula masses:

(don't do the oxygen — we don't need it)

$$2 \times 24 \rightarrow 2 \times (24 + 16)$$
$$48 \rightarrow 80$$

3) Apply the rule: Divide to get one, then multiply to get all

The two numbers, 48 and 80, tell us that 48 g of Mg react to give 80 g of MgO.
Here's the tricky bit. You've now got to be able to write this down:

48 g of Mg ......reacts to give.....80 g of MgO
1 g of Mg ......reacts to give.....
60 g of Mg .....reacts to give......

The big clue is that in the question they've said we want to burn '60 g of magnesium', i.e. they've told us how much magnesium to have, and that's how you know to write down the left-hand side of it first, because:

We'll first need to divide by 48 to get 1 g of Mg
and then need to multiply by 60 to get 60 g of Mg.

Then you can work out the numbers on the other side (shown in orange below) by realising that you must divide both sides by 48 and then multiply both sides by 60. It's tricky.

÷48	48 g of Mg .... 80 g of MgO	÷48	
	1 g of Mg .... 1.67 g of MgO		
×60	60 g of Mg .... 100 g of MgO	×60	

The mass of product is called the yield of a reaction. You should realise that in practice you never get 100% of the yield, so the amount of product will be slightly less than calculated (see p.77).

This finally tells us that 60 g of magnesium will produce 100 g of magnesium oxide.
If the question had said 'Find how much magnesium gives 500 g of magnesium oxide', you'd fill in the MgO side first, because that's the one you'd have the information about. Got it? Good-O!

Reaction mass calculations? — no worries, matey...

Calculating masses is a very useful skill to have. If you're trying to get 10 g of magnesium oxide, say, for use in a medicine or fertiliser, you're going to need to be able to work out how much magnesium to use, or you could get too much or too little. A wrong calculation could be an expensive mistake...

Percentage Yield

Of course, things are never simple. Not even the most efficient reaction will have a 100% yield.

Percentage Yield Compares Actual and Predicted Yield

The more reactants you start with, the higher the actual yield will be — that's pretty obvious. But the percentage yield doesn't depend on the amount of reactants you started with — it's a percentage.

1) The predicted yield of a reaction can be calculated from the balanced reaction equation (see page 76).
2) Percentage yield is given by the formula:

$$\text{percentage yield} = \frac{\text{actual yield (grams)}}{\text{predicted yield (grams)}} \times 100$$

3) Percentage yield is always somewhere between 0 and 100%.
4) 100% yield means that you got all the product you expected to get.
5) 0% yield means that no reactants were converted into product, i.e. no product at all was made.

Yields are Always Less Than 100%

In real life, you never get a 100% yield. Some product or reactant always gets lost along the way — and that goes for big industrial processes as well as school lab experiments.
How this happens depends on what sort of reaction it is and what apparatus is being used.
Lots of things can go wrong, but the four you need to know about are:

1) Evaporation

Liquids evaporate all the time — not just while they're being heated.

2) Heating

Losses while heating can be due to evaporation, or for more complicated reasons.

In reversible reactions, increasing the temperature moves the equilibrium position.

So heating the reaction to speed it up might mean a lower yield.

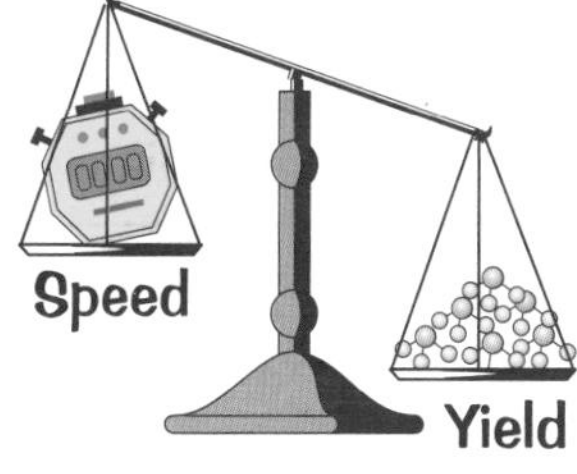

3) Filtration

When you filter a liquid to remove solid particles, you nearly always lose a bit of liquid or a bit of solid.

1) If you want to keep the liquid, you lose the bit that remains with the solid and filter paper (as they always stay a bit wet).
2) If you want to keep the solid, some of it usually gets left behind when you scrape it off the filter paper — even if you're really careful.

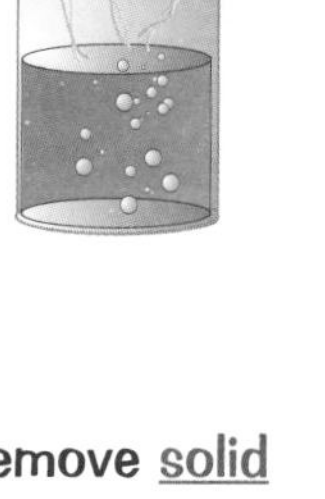

4) Transferring Liquids

You always lose a bit of liquid when you transfer it from one container to another — even if you manage not to spill it.

Some of it always gets left behind on the inside surface of the old container. Think about it — it's always wet when you finish.

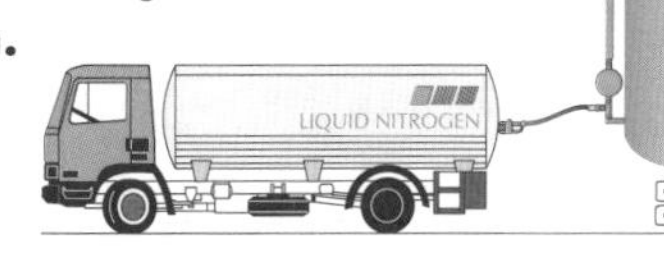

You can't always get what you want...

Unfortunately, no matter how careful you are, you're not going to get a 100% yield in any reaction. So you'll always get a little loss of product. In industry, people work very hard to keep wastage as low as possible — so reactants that don't react first time are collected and recycled whenever possible.

Fertilisers

There's a lot more to using fertilisers than making your garden look nice and pretty...

Fertilisers Provide Plants with the Essential Elements for Growth

1) The three main essential elements in fertilisers are nitrogen, phosphorus and potassium. If plants don't get enough of these elements, their growth and life processes are affected. For example, nitrogen is used to make plant proteins, which are essential for growth.
2) Sometimes these elements are missing from the soil because they've been used up by a previous crop.
3) Fertilisers replace these missing elements or provide more of them. This helps to increase the crop yield.
4) The fertiliser must first dissolve in water before it can be taken in by the crop roots.

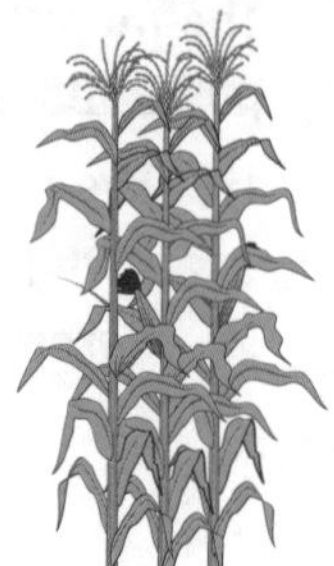

Ammonia Can be Neutralised with Acids to Produce Fertilisers

1) Ammonia is a base, and can be neutralised by acids to make ammonium salts.
2) Ammonium nitrate is an especially good fertiliser because it has nitrogen from two sources, the ammonia and the nitric acid. Kind of a double dose.

Ammonia + Nitric acid → Ammonium nitrate

3) Ammonium sulfate can also be used as a fertiliser, and is made by neutralising sulfuric acid with ammonia:

Ammonia + Sulfuric acid → Ammonium sulfate

These are neutralisation reactions, but using ammonia as the base you only get an ammonium salt — not salt + water.

4) Two other fertilisers manufactured using ammonia are ammonium phosphate and urea.
5) Potassium nitrate is also a fertiliser.

Preparing Ammonium Nitrate in the Lab

You can make most fertilisers using this titration method — just choose the right acid (nitric, sulfuric or phosphoric) and alkali (ammonia or potassium hydroxide) to get the salt you want. You'll need ammonia and nitric acid to make ammonium nitrate.

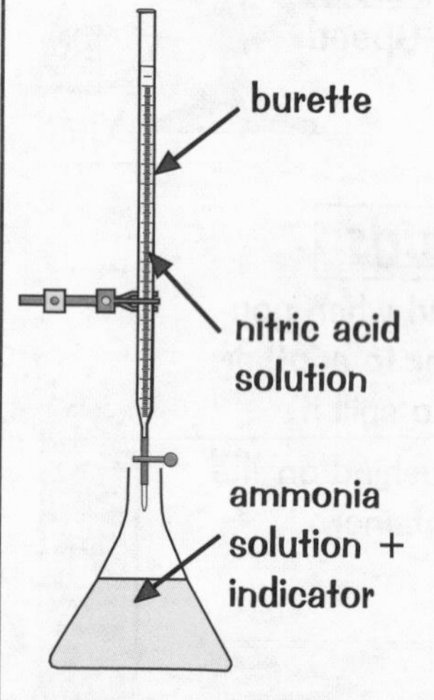

1) Set up your apparatus as in the diagram. Add a few drops of methyl orange indicator to the ammonia — it'll turn yellow.
2) Slowly add the nitric acid from the burette into the ammonia, until the yellow colour just changes to red. Gently swirl the flask as you add the acid. Go especially slowly when you think the alkali's almost neutralised. Methyl orange is yellow in alkalis, but red in acids, so this colour change means all the ammonia has been neutralised and you've got ammonium nitrate solution.
3) To get solid ammonium nitrate crystals, gently evaporate the solution until only a little bit is left. Leave it to crystallise.
4) The ammonium nitrate crystals aren't pure — they've got methyl orange in them. To get pure ammonium nitrate crystals, you need to note exactly how much nitric acid it took to neutralise the ammonia, and then repeat the titration using that volume of acid, but no indicator.

Using urea as a fertiliser — you must be taking the...

Fertilisers are really useful. With increasing population sizes we need to be able to produce bigger, better crops to feed everyone. Famine is a major problem in some places, like parts of Africa. The high temperatures and droughts decrease their crop yield, and they just can't make enough to go around.

Fertilisers

Calculating Relative Formula Mass of a Fertiliser

This is exactly the same as calculating any other relative formula mass — see page 75.
It's all the relative atomic masses added together.

Find the relative formula mass for ammonium nitrate, NH_4NO_3, using the following data:
A_r for H = 1 A_r for N = 14 A_r for O = 16

ANSWER:

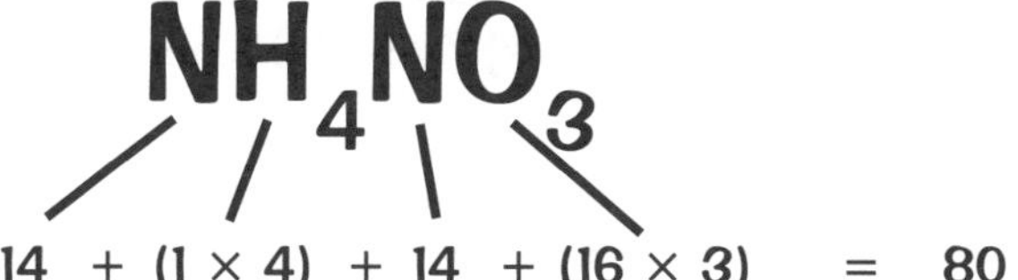

So the M_r for NH_4NO_3 is 80.

Calculating the % Mass of an Essential Element in a Fertiliser

This is actually dead easy — so long as you've learnt this formula:

$$\text{PERCENTAGE MASS OF AN ELEMENT IN A COMPOUND} = \frac{A_r \times \text{No. of atoms (of that element)}}{M_r \text{ (of whole compound)}} \times 100$$

Find the percentage mass of nitrogen in ammonium sulfate, $(NH_4)_2SO_4$, using the following data:
A_r for H = 1 A_r for N = 14 A_r for O = 16 A_r for S = 32

ANSWER: M_r of $(NH_4)_2SO_4 = 2 \times [14 + (1 \times 4)] + 32 + (16 \times 4) = 132$

Now use the formula:

$$\text{Percentage mass} = \frac{A_r \times n}{M_r} \times 100 = \frac{14 \times 2}{132} \times 100 = 21.2\%$$

So there you have it. Nitrogen represents 21.2% of the mass of ammonium sulfate.

Fertilisers Damage Lakes and Rivers — Eutrophication

1) Fertilisers which contain nitrates are essential to modern farming.
2) But you get problems if some of the rich fertiliser finds its way into rivers and streams.
3) This happens quite easily if too much fertiliser is applied, especially if it rains soon afterwards.
4) The result is EUTROPHICATION, which basically means 'too much of a good thing'.

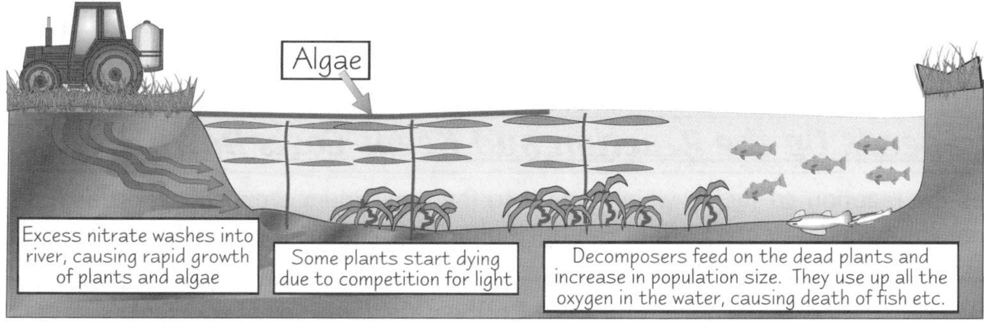

As the picture shows, too many nitrates in the water cause a sequence of 'mega-growth', 'mega-death' and 'mega-decay' involving most of the plant and animal life in the water.

5) Farmers need to take a lot more care when spreading artificial fertilisers.

There's nowt wrong wi' just spreadin' muck on it...

Unfortunately, no matter how good something is, there's always a downside. It's a good idea to learn the diagram really, really well, and make sure you understand it. Learn it mini-essay style.

The Haber Process

This is an important industrial process. It produces ammonia (NH_3), which is needed for making fertilisers.

The Haber Process is a Reversible Reaction:

$$N_2 + 3H_2 \rightleftharpoons 2NH_3 \quad (+\text{ heat})$$

1) The nitrogen is obtained easily from the air, which is 78% nitrogen (and 21% oxygen).
2) The hydrogen comes from the cracking of oil fractions or natural gas.
3) Because the reaction is reversible (it goes in both directions), not all the nitrogen and hydrogen will convert to ammonia.
4) The N_2 and H_2 which don't react are recycled and passed through again so none is wasted.

Industrial conditions:

PRESSURE: 200 atmospheres; TEMPERATURE: 450 °C; CATALYST: Iron

Because the Reaction is Reversible, There's a Compromise to be Made:

1) Higher pressures favour the forward reaction (since there are four molecules of gas on the left-hand side, but only two molecules on the right).
2) So the pressure is set as high as possible to give the best % yield, without making the plant too expensive to build (it'd be too expensive to build a plant that'd stand pressures of over 1000 atmospheres, for example). Hence the 200 atmospheres operating pressure.
3) The forward reaction is exothermic, which means that increasing the temperature will actually move the equilibrium the wrong way — away from ammonia and towards N_2 and H_2.
   So the yield of ammonia would be greater at lower temperatures.
4) The trouble is, lower temperatures mean a slower rate of reaction. So what they do is increase the temperature anyway, to get a much faster rate of reaction.

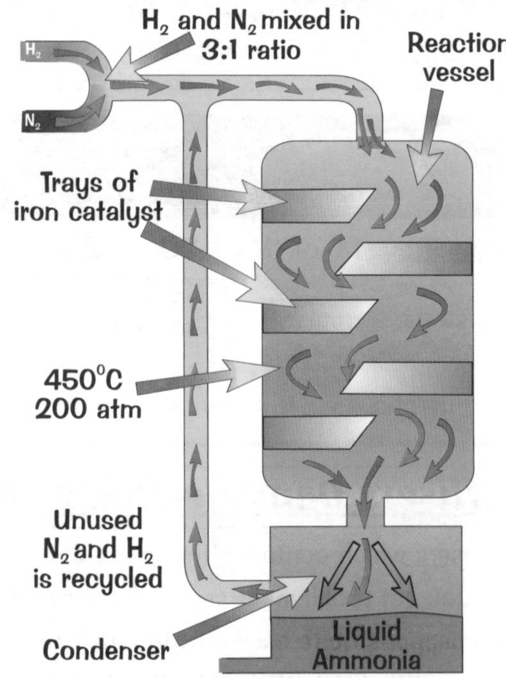

5) The 450 °C is a compromise between maximum yield and speed of reaction.
   It's better to wait just 20 seconds for a 10% yield than to have to wait 60 seconds for a 20% yield.
6) Remember, the unused hydrogen and nitrogen are recycled, so nothing is wasted.

The Iron Catalyst Speeds Up the Reaction and Keeps Costs Down

1) The iron catalyst makes the reaction go faster, which gets it to the equilibrium proportions more quickly. But remember, the catalyst doesn't affect the position of equilibrium (i.e. the % yield).
2) Without the catalyst the temperature would have to be raised even further to get a quick enough reaction, and that would reduce the % yield even further. So the catalyst is very important.

200 atmospheres? — that could give you a headache...

The Haber process makes ammonia, which is used to make fertilisers, which are great. Because it's a reversible reaction, certain factors need to be controlled to increase the percentage yield. Remember — the temperature is increased to improve speed, not the equilibrium position. Learn it mini-essay style.

Minimising the Cost of Production

Things like fast reaction rates and high % yields are nice in industry — but in the end, the important thing is keeping costs down. It all comes down to maximum efficiency...

Production Cost Depends on Several Different Factors

There are five main things that affect the cost of making a new substance. It's these five factors that companies have to consider when deciding if, and then how, to produce a chemical.

1) Price of Energy

a) Industry needs to keep its energy bills as low as possible.

b) If a reaction needs a high temperature, the running costs will be higher.

2) Cost of Raw Materials

a) This is kept to a minimum by recycling any materials that haven't reacted.

b) A good example of this is the Haber process. The % yield of the reaction is quite low (about 10%), but the unreacted N_2 and H_2 can be recycled to keep waste to a minimum.

3) Labour Costs (Wages)

a) Everyone who works for a company has got to be paid.

b) Labour-intensive processes (i.e. those that involve many people), can be very expensive.

c) Automation cuts running costs by reducing the number of people involved.

d) But companies have always got to weigh any savings they make on their wage bill against the initial cost and running costs of the machinery.

4) Plant Costs (Equipment)

a) The cost of equipment depends on the conditions it has to cope with.

b) For example, it costs far more to make something to withstand very high pressures than something which only needs to work at atmospheric pressure.

5) Rate of Production

a) Generally speaking, the faster the reaction goes, the better it is in terms of reducing the time and costs of production.

b) So rates of reaction are often increased by using catalysts.

c) But the increase in production rate has to balance the cost of buying the catalyst in the first place and replacing any that gets lost.

Optimum Conditions are Chosen to Give the Lowest Cost

1) Optimum conditions are those that give the lowest production cost per kg of product — even if this means compromising on the speed of reaction or % yield. Learn the definition:

OPTIMUM CONDITIONS are those that give the LOWEST PRODUCTION COST.

2) However, the rate of reaction and percentage yield must both be high enough to make a sufficient amount of product each day.

3) Don't forget, a low percentage yield is okay, as long as the starting materials can be recycled.

This will make it as cheap as chips...

In industry, compromises must be made, just like in life, and the Haber process is a prime example of this. You need to learn those five different factors affecting cost, and the definition of 'optimum conditions'. Cover the page and scribble it all down — keep doing it until you get it all right.

Detergents and Dry-Cleaning

Cleanliness is next to godliness... or so they say.

Washing at Low Temperatures Saves Energy (and Your Clothes)

1) When you're washing clothes, high temperatures usually work best for getting things clean. They melt greasy dirt deposits, so your detergent can break up and remove the stain more easily.
2) But some natural fabrics (e.g. wool) shrink, and some artificial fabrics (e.g. nylon) quickly lose their shape, if they're washed at too high a temperature.
3) Also, some dyes will run in high-temperature washes. Brightly coloured clothes can quickly fade and stop looking new.
4) Nowadays you can get biological detergents, with enzymes in them. The enzymes digest protein-based and fat-based stains without the need for high temperatures, which protects your clothes. If you heat biological detergents above 40 °C, the enzymes denature (see p.4) and stop working.
5) Low-temperature washes also save energy, which is great for the environment and your energy bill. Less energy used means less carbon dioxide emissions, reducing the greenhouse effect and climate change.

Detergents Work by Sticking to Both Water and Grease

1) Some dirt will dissolve in water without the help of a detergent, but most won't. Anything that's oil-based won't dissolve in water at all (see next page).
2) Detergents help water and oil to mix.
3) Detergents contain molecules that have a hydrophilic (water-loving) head, and a hydrophobic (water-hating) tail.
4) The hydrophilic heads form intermolecular bonds with water.
5) And the hydrophobic tails bond to the fat molecules in greasy dirt.

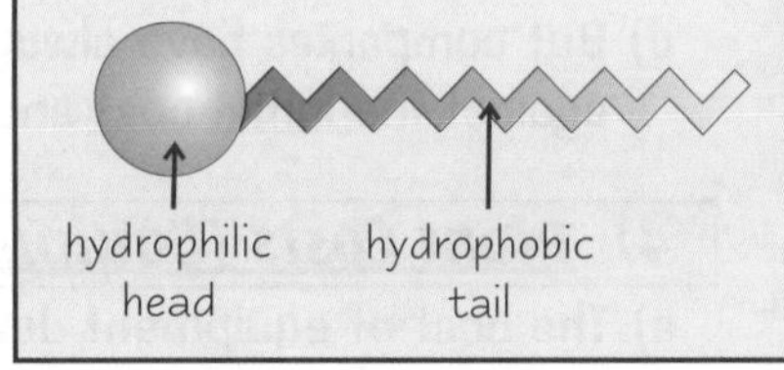

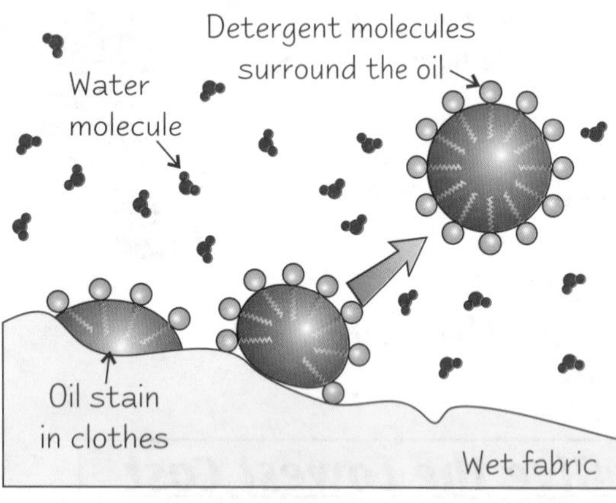

6) When you (or a washing machine) swish the fabric around, the detergent molecules find their way in between the grease and the wet fabric.
7) The detergent molecules eventually surround the grease completely, and bond to it, with their hydrophilic heads around the outside like a coat.
8) This hydrophilic coat stops the grease droplets reattaching themselves to the fabric, and they're pulled away into the wash water.
9) Then, when you rinse the fabric, the grease and dirt are rinsed away along with the water.

Most Detergents are Salts

1) The original detergents were soaps, which are made from fats. Soaps form a scum with hard water which can build up on your clothes — so they're not used so much nowadays.
2) Modern synthetic (soapless) detergents are mostly made using big organic molecules from crude oil. An acid group is added to one end of the molecule to make an organic acid. This is then neutralised with a strong alkali, usually sodium or potassium hydroxide, to form a salt:

   organic acid + strong alkali → salt (detergent) + water

   Soapless detergents don't form a scum with hard water, which is handy.
3) Both kinds of detergent work in the same way. The covalent hydrocarbon chain is the hydrophobic tail. The ionic bit on the end is the hydrophilic head.

Detergents and Dry-Cleaning

Different Solvents Dissolve Different Stains

1) When a solid dissolves in a liquid, a clear solution is formed. The liquid is called the solvent, and the solid is called the solute.
2) Here's how it works. If the solvent is water and the solute is a sugar lump:
   - the water molecules form strong intermolecular bonds with the sugar molecules,
   - as water-sugar bonds form, they pull apart the sugar-sugar bonds and the sugar lump breaks up,
   - the water molecules completely surround the sugar molecules, and you have a solution.
3) You can't dissolve every solid in every liquid — they have to be able to form the right sort of intermolecular bond. So different solids need different solvents.
4) To successfully remove a stain, you have to use the right solvent to dissolve it off the fabric.
5) A lot of stains aren't soluble in water — especially greasy stains, paints and varnishes. Sometimes using a detergent can remove the stain (see previous page), but sometimes you need to use a different, dry-cleaning solvent.

Dry-Cleaning Uses a Solvent That isn't Water

1) There are quite a few dry-cleaning solvents around, but the most common one is tetrachloroethene.
2) Dry-cleaning is usually used for clothes that would get damaged if you washed them in water — e.g. clothes with fibres that swell up and change shape when they get wet.
3) But it's also handy if you have a stain that won't dissolve in water or detergent — dry-cleaning might work. Paints, varnishes and other organic chemicals often dissolve in an organic dry-cleaning solvent.
4) It works because the solvent is strongly attracted to the oily molecules in the stain. The intermolecular bonds between the 'stain' molecules break and are replaced by bonds with the solvent. The stain dissolves.

Some Cleaners are Better than Others

All washing powders claim to clean better than their rivals. You've got to be able to compare the results of lab tests to work out which one really cleans better. You can do a test something like this:

1) Take some white cotton cloth and cut it into pieces.
2) Measure out equal amounts of some substances to test your washing powder with, e.g. egg yolk, engine oil, blackcurrant, chocolate. Stain each bit of cloth with a different substance and leave to dry.
3) Set up a 'washing machine' — a beaker of water over a Bunsen burner. Heat the water to 40 °C and dissolve some washing powder in it.
4) Add a piece of stained cloth and 'wash' (stir) for 5 minutes.
5) Remove the cloth with tongs (enzymes are irritants), rinse under a running tap, and let it dry.
6) Repeat for each washing powder, keeping the volume of water, the amount of powder, the temperature and the wash time the same.

Compare the washed cloth pieces:

Which cloth is whitest? Which detergent lived up to its claims the best? Which was best for protein stains (e.g. egg, milk, blood)? Which was best on fats (e.g. butter, engine oil, suntan lotion)?

Would your whites pass the OCR exam challenge...

Yes, I'm afraid you are going to have to do some washing at some point — you will run out of clothes eventually. And when you do, you'll have the pleasure of knowing how it all works. Isn't that nice. ☺

Chemical Production

The Type of Manufacturing Process Depends on the Product

Continuous production: large-scale industrial manufacture of popular chemicals, e.g. the Haber process for making ammonia (see p.80).

1) Production never stops, so you don't waste time emptying the reactor and setting it up again.
2) It runs automatically — you only need to interfere if something goes wrong.
3) The quality of the product is very consistent.
4) Usually the manufacturing plant only makes one product, so there's little risk of contamination.
5) Start-up costs to build the plant are huge, and it isn't cost-effective to run at less than full capacity.

Batch production: small quantities of specialist chemicals, e.g. pharmaceutical drugs, often on demand.

1) It's flexible — several different products can be made using the same equipment.
2) Start-up costs are relatively low — small-scale, multi-purpose equipment can be bought off the shelf.
3) It's labour-intensive — the equipment needs to be set up and manually controlled for each batch and then cleaned out at the end.
4) 'Downtime' between batches means there are times when you're not producing anything.
5) It's trickier to keep the same quality from batch to batch. Also, there's more chance of contamination because the same equipment is used to make more than one thing. On the other hand, any problems can be traced to a specific batch, which can be recalled.

Pharmaceutical drugs are complicated to make and there's relatively low demand for them. So, batch production is often the most cost-effective way for a company to produce small quantities of different drugs to order.

Several Factors Affect the Cost of Pharmaceutical Drugs

1) Market Research — identifying a possible new drug. Is there any competition already out there? Is there enough demand for it to make it worthwhile developing?
2) Research and Development — finding a suitable compound, testing it, modifying it, testing again, until it's ready. This involves the work of lots of highly paid scientists.
3) Trialling — no drug can be sold until it's gone through loads of time-consuming tests including animal trials and human trials to prove that it works and it's safe.
4) Marketing — advertising in medical magazines and buttering up doctors.
5) Manufacture — multi-step batch production is labour-intensive and can't be automated. Other costs include energy and raw materials. The raw materials for pharmaceuticals are often rare and sometimes need to be extracted from plants (an expensive process).

It takes about 12 years and £900 million to develop a new drug and get it onto the market. Ouch.

To extract a substance from a plant, it has to be crushed and dissolved in a suitable solvent. Then, you can extract the substance you want by chromatography.

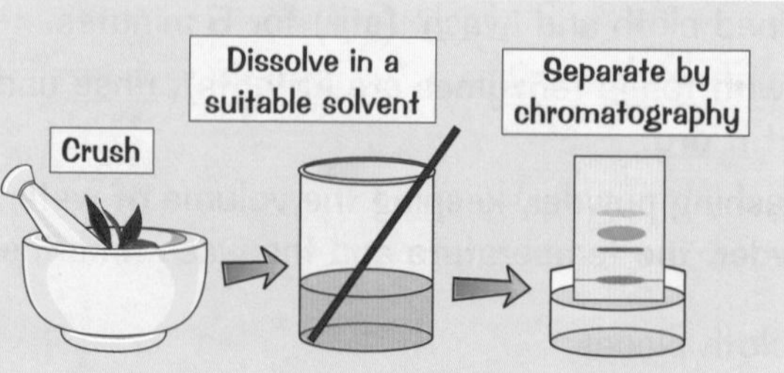
Crush
Dissolve in a suitable solvent
Separate by chromatography

Once the active ingredient has been isolated, it can be analysed, and its chemical structure worked out.

It's often possible to make a synthetic version of the chemical.

6) The actual price per dose depends on the demand and how long the company is willing to wait to get back its initial investment. A company only holds a drug patent for 20 years — after that anyone can make it. Some drugs can cost thousands of pounds for just one dose.

I wish they'd find a drug to cure exams...

£900 million. You could buy yourself an island. And one for your mum. And a couple for your mates...

Allotropes of Carbon

Allotropes are just different structural forms of the same element — carbon has quite a few:

Diamond is Used in Jewellery and Cutting Tools

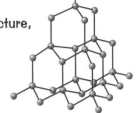

1) Diamonds are sparkly, colourless and clear. Ideal for jewellery.
2) Each carbon atom forms four covalent bonds in a very rigid giant covalent structure, which makes diamond really hard. This makes diamonds ideal as cutting tools.
3) All those strong covalent bonds give diamond a very high melting point.
4) It doesn't conduct electricity because it has no free electrons.

Graphite Makes the Lead of Your Pencil

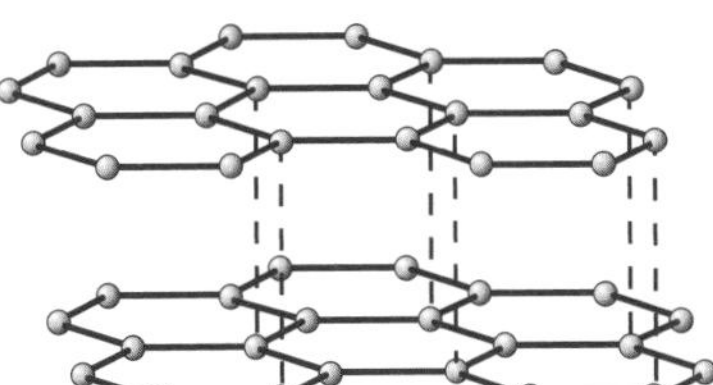

1) Graphite is black and opaque, but still kind of shiny.
2) Each carbon atom only forms three covalent bonds, creating sheets of carbon atoms which are free to slide over each other.
3) The layers are held together so loosely that they can be rubbed off onto paper to leave a black mark — that's how a pencil works. This also makes graphite slippery, so it's ideal as a lubricating material.
4) Graphite's got a high melting point — the covalent bonds need loads of energy to break.
5) Since only three out of each carbon's four outer electrons are used in bonds, there are lots of spare electrons. This means graphite conducts electricity — it's used for electrodes. See page 34.

Fullerenes are Nanoparticles

Nanoparticles are only a few nanometres (nm) across (1 nm = 0.000 000 001 m).

1) Fullerenes are molecules of carbon, shaped like hollow balls or closed tubes. Each carbon atom forms three covalent bonds with its neighbours, leaving free electrons that can conduct electricity.
2) The smallest fullerene is buckminsterfullerene, which has 60 carbon atoms joined in a ball — its molecular formula is C_{60}.
3) Fullerenes can be used to 'cage' other molecules. The fullerene structure forms around another atom or molecule, which is then trapped inside. This could be a new way of delivering a drug into the body, e.g. for slow release.

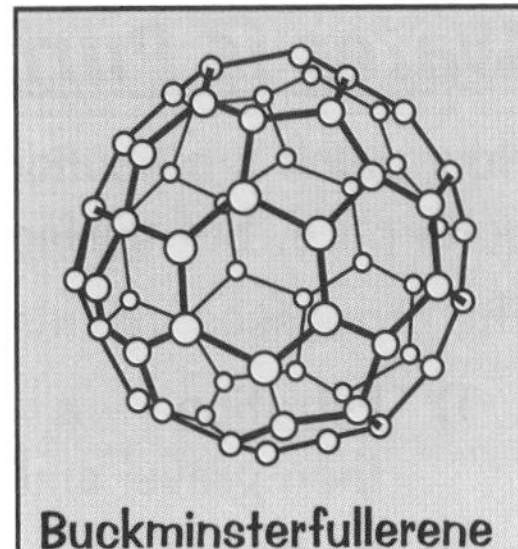
Buckminsterfullerene

Fullerenes can be joined together to form nanotubes — teeny tiny hollow carbon tubes:

a) All those covalent bonds make carbon nanotubes very strong. They can be used to reinforce graphite in tennis rackets and to make stronger, lighter building materials.

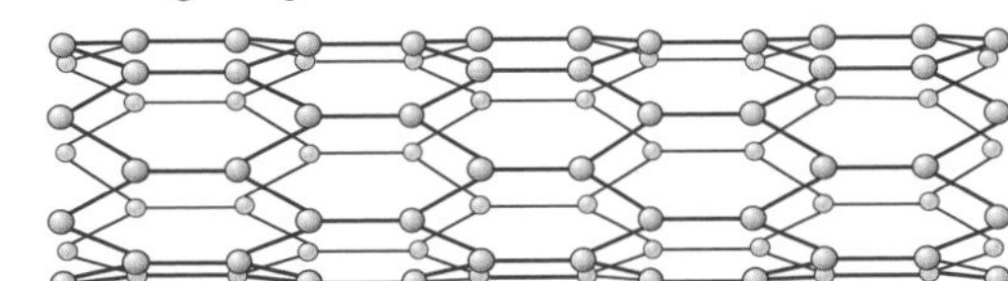

b) Nanotubes conduct electricity, so they can be used in tiny electric circuits for computer chips.
c) They have a huge surface area, so they could help make great industrial catalysts — individual catalyst molecules could be attached to the nanotubes (the bigger the surface area the better).

Nanoparticles have very different properties from the 'bulk' chemical. Nanoparticles of normally unreactive silver can kill bacteria. The colour of gold nanoparticles actually varies from red to purple.

Nanoparticles can be made by molecular engineering, but this is really hard. Molecular engineering is building a product molecule-by-molecule to a specific design — either by positioning each molecule exactly where you want it or by starting with a bigger structure and taking bits off it.

Carbon is a girl's best friend...

Nanoparticles. Confused? Just think of it as knitting teeny weeny atomic footballs, and you'll be fine...

Water Purity

Water, water, everywhere... well, there is if you live in Cumbria.

There are a Variety of Limited Water Resources in the UK

1) As well as for drinking, we need water for loads of domestic uses (mainly washing things).
2) Industrially, water is important as a cheap raw material, a coolant (especially in power stations) and a solvent. Between half and two thirds of all the fresh water used in the UK goes into industry.

In the UK, we get our water from:
1) SURFACE WATER: lakes, rivers and reservoirs (artificial lakes). In much of England and Wales, these sources start to run dry during the summer months.
2) GROUNDWATER: aquifers (rocks that trap water underground). In parts of the south-east where surface water is very limited, as much as 70% of the domestic water supply comes from groundwater.

All these resources are limited, depending on annual rainfall, and demand for water increases every year. Experts worry that, unless we limit our water use, by 2025 we might not have enough water to supply everybody's needs. Ways to conserve water include:

1) Stopping leaks in pipes. About 20% of all the water that enters the mains is lost through leaks.
2) Not wasting water at home, e.g. not leaving taps running, using a bucket instead of a hose to wash the car, avoiding sprinklers in the garden (they use up to 1000 litres per hour), washing up by hand rather than using a dishwasher, using a water-efficient washing machine (fully loaded each time).
3) Recycling water, e.g. collecting rainwater to use in the garden.
4) Installing a water meter — you tend to waste less water if you're paying for it by the bath-full.

Water is Purified in Water Treatment Plants

How much purification the water needs depends on the source. Groundwater from aquifers is usually quite pure, but surface water needs a lot of treatment.

The processes include:

1) Filtration — a wire mesh screens out large twigs etc., and then gravel and sand beds filter out any other solid bits.
2) Sedimentation — iron sulfate or aluminium sulfate is added to the water, which makes fine particles clump together and settle at the bottom.
3) Chlorination — chlorine gas is bubbled through to kill harmful bacteria and other microbes.

Other processes can be used to break down and remove some chemical pollutants, but it's too difficult to get rid of all the dissolved impurities, including minerals which cause water hardness and some harmful or toxic chemicals such as pesticides and fertilisers (see below).

Tap Water Can Still Contain Impurities

The water that comes out of our taps has to meet strict safety standards, but low levels of pollutants are still found. These pollutants come from various sources:

1) Nitrate residues from excess fertiliser 'run-off' into rivers and lakes. If too many nitrates get into drinking water it can cause serious health problems, especially for young babies. Nitrates prevent the blood from carrying oxygen properly.
2) Lead compounds from old lead pipes. Lead is very poisonous, particularly in children.
3) Pesticide residues from spraying too near to rivers and lakes.

Water Purity

You Can Test Water for Various Dissolved Ions

Water companies have to test their water regularly to make sure that pollutant levels don't exceed strict limits. You can test for some dissolved ions very easily using precipitation reactions (where two dissolved compounds react to form an insoluble solid — the precipitate).

1) TEST FOR SULFATE IONS: add some dilute hydrochloric acid, then 10 drops of barium chloride solution to the test sample. If you see a white precipitate, there are sulfate ions in the sample.

add $BaCl_2$ solution

white precipitate of $BaSO_4$

barium chloride + sulfate ions → barium sulfate + chloride ions

$$BaCl_2 + SO_4^{2-} \rightarrow BaSO_4 + 2Cl^-$$

e.g. if potassium sulfate (K_2SO_4) was present, you'd get $BaSO_4$ and KCl produced.

2) TEST FOR HALIDE IONS: add some dilute nitric acid, then 10 drops of silver nitrate solution to the test sample.
Chloride ions will produce a white precipitate.
Bromide ions will produce a cream precipitate.
Iodide ions will produce a pale yellow precipitate.

e.g. if sodium iodide (NaI) is present in the water, you'll get the following reaction:

$$AgNO_3 + NaI \rightarrow AgI + NaNO_3$$

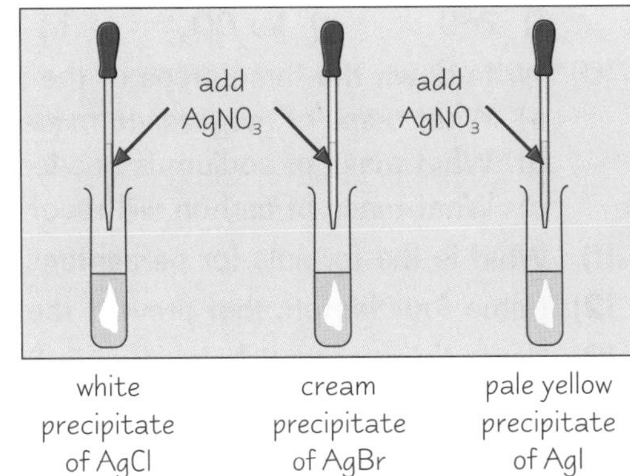

white precipitate of AgCl — cream precipitate of AgBr — pale yellow precipitate of AgI

1.4 Billion People Worldwide Can't Get Clean Water to Drink

1) Communities in some developing countries often don't have access to sources of clean water, such as local wells or distribution networks.
2) People from these communities often have to walk for miles every day to fetch water from sources which may be contaminated.
3) Dirty water can carry dangerous microbes which cause outbreaks of serious diseases such as cholera and dysentery. About 3.4 million people (mainly children) die from water-borne diseases each year.
4) Giving a community a clean water source and teaching them the skills to maintain it can save many lives. It doesn't have to be complicated — sinking a well and adding a pump is often all that's needed.

You Can Get Fresh Water by Distilling Sea Water

1) In some very dry countries, e.g. Kuwait, sea water is distilled to produce drinking water.
2) Distillation needs loads of energy, so it's really expensive and not practical for producing large quantities of fresh water.
3) Kuwait has so much oil (in other words, cheap energy) that it's the only country in the world which uses distilled water for agriculture.

Who'd have thought there'd be so much to learn about water...

In the UK we're very lucky to have clean water available at the turn of a tap — but it's not a never-ending supply. Fresh water is quite hard to come by at the end of a dry summer. Learn how water is purified and tested in the UK, and what pollutants get through the cleaning process. Cover. Scribble.

Revision Summary for Module C4

Some more tricky questions to stress you out. The thing is though, why bother doing easy questions? These meaty monsters find out what you really know, and worse, what you really don't. Yeah, I know, it's kinda scary, but if you want to get anywhere in life you've got to face up to a bit of hardship. That's just the way it is. Take a few deep breaths and then try these.

1) Describe fully the colour of universal indicator for every pH from 0 to 14.
2) Is the pH of nitric acid less than or greater than 7? What about the pH of ammonia?
3) What are acids and bases? What is an alkali?
4) What type of ions are always present when: a) acids, and b) alkalis dissolve in water?
5) Write the equation of a neutralisation reaction in terms of these ions.
6) Describe three uses of sulfuric acid in industry.
7) What type of salts do: a) hydrochloric, and b) sulfuric acid produce?
8)* Write a balanced symbol equation for the reaction between dilute nitric acid and ammonia.
9)* Find A_r or M_r for each of these (use the periodic table inside the front cover):
    a) Ca b) Ag c) CO_2 d) $MgCO_3$ e) $Al(OH)_3$
    f) ZnO g) Na_2CO_3 h) sodium chloride
10)* Write down the three steps of the method for calculating reacting masses.
    a) What mass of magnesium oxide is produced when 112.1 g of magnesium burns in air?
    b) What mass of sodium is needed to produce 108.2 g of sodium oxide?
    c) What mass of carbon will react with hydrogen to produce 24.6 g of propane (C_3H_8)?
11) What is the formula for percentage yield? How does percentage yield differ from actual yield?
12) Name four factors that prevent the percentage yield being 100%
13) Name three essential elements in fertilisers.
14) How does nitrogen increase the growth of plants?
15) Name two fertilisers which are manufactured from ammonia.
16) Describe how you could produce one of these fertilisers in the lab.
17) Describe what can happen if too much fertiliser is put onto fields. How can it be avoided?
18) What determines the choice of operating temperature for the Haber process?
19) What effect does the catalyst have on the Haber process reaction?
20) In general, how can the cost of raw materials be kept as low as possible?
21) In industry, how are the 'optimum conditions' for a process decided?
22) Explain the advantages of washing clothes at low temperatures.
23) Describe how a detergent helps remove greasy dirt from clothes.
24) Explain, in terms of intermolecular forces, how dry-cleaning works.
25) What are 'batch production' and 'continuous production'.
26) Explain the advantages of using batch production to make pharmaceutical drugs.
    What are the disadvantages?
27) It can take 12 years and about £900 million to bring a new drug to market. Explain why.
28) In terms of intermolecular bonds, explain why diamond makes a good cutting tool.
29) Why does graphite conduct electricity?
30) What properties of carbon nanotubes make them suitable for the following applications:
    a) reinforcing tennis rackets, b) computer chips, c) catalysts?
31) How might fullerenes be used to deliver drugs to the body?
32) Why is it important to preserve water. List four ways to preserve water in the home.
33) A student adds dilute hydrochloric acid and barium chloride to a water sample and a white precipitate is produced. What ions were present in the water?

* Answers on page 108

Static Electricity

Static electricity is all about charges which are NOT free to move. This causes them to build up in one place, and it often ends with a spark or a shock when they do finally move.

1) Build-up of Static is Caused by Friction

1) When two insulating materials are rubbed together, electrons will be scraped off one and dumped on the other.
2) This'll leave a positive static charge on one and a negative static charge on the other.
3) Which way the electrons are transferred depends on the two materials involved.
4) Electrically charged objects attract small neutral objects placed near them. (Try this: rub a balloon on a woolly pully – then put it near tiddly bits of paper and watch them jump.)
5) The classic examples are polythene and acetate rods being rubbed with a cloth duster, as shown in the diagrams.

With the polythene rod, electrons move from the duster to the rod.

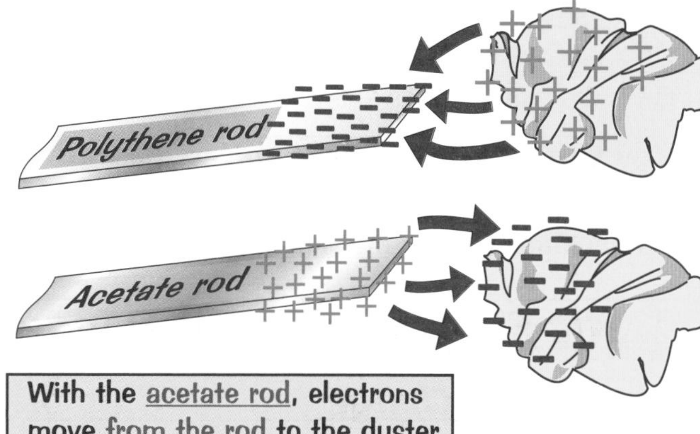

With the acetate rod, electrons move from the rod to the duster.

2) Only Electrons Move — Never the Positive Charges

Watch out for this in exams. Both +ve and –ve electrostatic charges are only ever produced by the movement of electrons. The positive charges definitely do not move. A positive static charge is always caused by electrons moving away elsewhere, as shown above. Don't forget!

A charged conductor can be discharged safely by connecting it to earth with a metal strap. The electrons flow down the strap to the ground if the charge is negative and flow up the strap from the ground if the charge is positive.

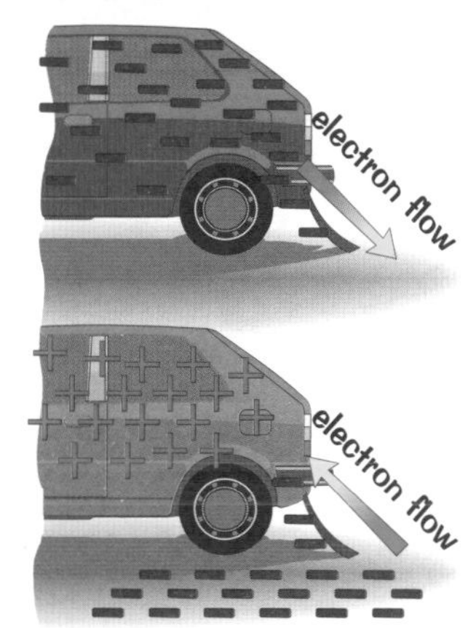

3) Like Charges Repel, Opposite Charges Attract

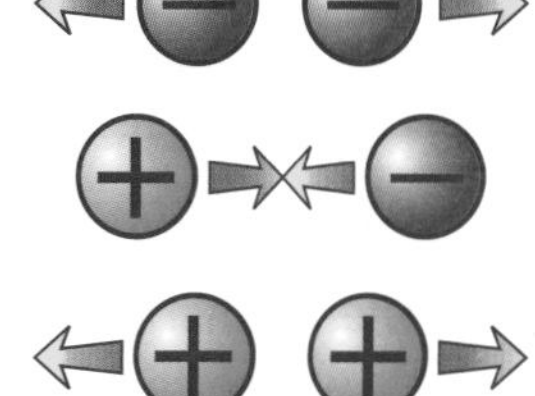

Hopefully this is kind of obvious.
Two things with opposite electric charges are attracted to each other.
Two things with the same electric charge will repel each other.
These forces get weaker the further apart the two things are.

Come on, be +ve — this is the last section in the book...

Static electricity's great fun. You must have tried it — rubbing a balloon against your clothes and trying to get it to stick to the ceiling. It really works... well, sometimes. And it's all due to the build-up of static. Bad hair days are also caused by static — it builds up on your hair, so your strands of hair repel each other. Conditioners try to decrease this, but they don't always work...

Static Electricity

They like asking you to give quite detailed examples in exams. Make sure you learn all these details.

Static Electricity Being a Little Joker:

1) Attracting Dust

Dust particles are charged and will be attracted to anything with the opposite charge. Unfortunately, many objects around the house are made out of insulators (e.g. TV screen, wood, plastic containers etc.) that get easily charged and attract the dust particles — this makes cleaning a nightmare.

2) Clothing Cling and Crackles

When synthetic clothes are dragged over each other (like in a tumble drier) or over your head, electrons get scraped off, leaving static charges on both parts, and that leads to the inevitable — attraction (they stick together and cling to you) and little sparks / shocks as the charges rearrange themselves.

3) Shocks From Door Handles

If you walk on a nylon carpet wearing shoes with insulating soles, charge builds up on your body. Then if you touch a metal door handle, the charge flows to the conductor and you get a little shock.

Static Electricity Can be Dangerous:

1) A Lot of Charge Can Build Up on Clothes

1) A large amount of static charge can build up on clothes made out of synthetic materials if they rub against other synthetic fabrics — like wriggling about on a car seat.
2) Eventually, this charge can become large enough to make a spark — which is really bad news if it happens near any inflammable gases or fuel fumes... KABOOM!

2) Grain Chutes, Paper Rollers and the Fuel Filling Nightmare:

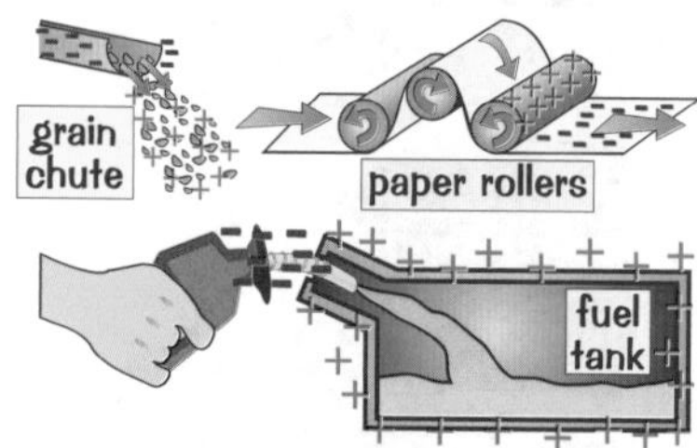

1) As fuel flows out of a filler pipe, or paper drags over rollers, or grain shoots out of pipes, then static can build up.
2) This can easily lead to a spark and might cause an explosion in dusty or fumey places — like when filling up a car with fuel at a petrol station.
3) All these problems with sparks can be solved by earthing charged objects...

Objects Can be Earthed or Insulated to Prevent Sparks

1) Dangerous sparks can be prevented by connecting a charged object to the ground using a conductor (e.g. a copper wire) — this is called earthing and it provides an easy route for the static charges to travel into the ground. This means no charge can build up to give you a shock or make a spark.
2) Fuel tankers must be earthed to prevent any sparks that might cause the fuel to explode.
3) Static charges are also a big problem in places where sparks could ignite inflammable gases, or where there are high concentrations of oxygen (e.g. in a hospital operating theatre).
4) Anti-static sprays and liquids work by making the surface of a charged object conductive — this provides an easy path for the charges to move away and not cause a problem.

Static electricity — it's really shocking stuff...

Lightning always chooses the easiest path between the sky and the ground — even if that means going through tall buildings, trees or you. That's why it's never a good idea to fly a kite in a thunderstorm...

Uses of Static Electricity

Static electricity isn't always a nuisance. It's got loads of applications in medicine and industry, and now's your chance to learn all about them, you lucky thing...

1) Paint Sprayers — Getting an Even Coat

1) Bikes and cars are painted using electrostatic paint sprayers.
2) The spray gun is charged, which charges up the small drops of paint. Each paint drop repels all the others, since they've all got the same charge, so you get a very fine spray.

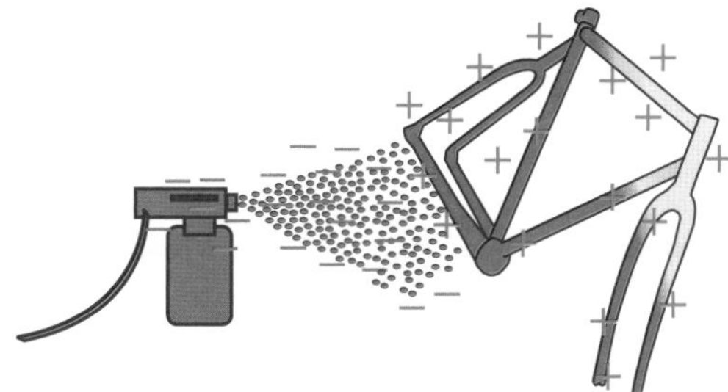

3) The object to be painted is given an opposite charge to the gun. This attracts the fine spray of paint.
4) This method gives an even coat and hardly any paint is wasted. In addition parts of the bicycle or car pointing away from the spray gun still receive paint, i.e. there are no paint shadows.

2) Dust Precipitators — Cleaning Up Emissions

Smoke is made up of tiny particles which can be removed with a precipitator. There are several different designs of precipitator — here's a very simple one:

1) As smoke particles reach the bottom of the chimney, they meet a wire grid with a high negative charge, which charges the particles negatively.
2) The charged smoke particles are attracted to positively charged metal plates. The smoke particles stick together to form larger particles.
3) When heavy enough, the particles fall off the plates or are knocked off by a hammer. The dust falls to the bottom of the chimney and can be removed.
4) The gases coming out of the chimney have very few smoke particles in them.

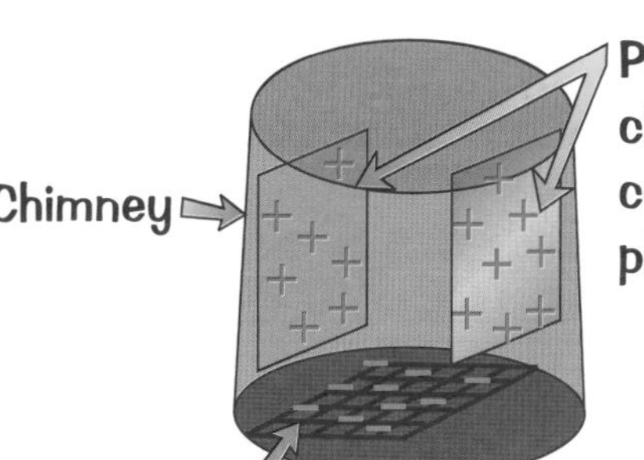

3) Defibrillators — Restarting a Heart

1) The beating of your heart is controlled by tiny little electrical pulses inside your body. So an electric shock to a stopped heart can make it start beating again.
2) Hospitals and ambulances have machines called defibrillators which can be used to shock a stopped heart back into operation.
3) The defibrillator consists of two paddles connected to a power supply.
4) The paddles of the defibrillator are placed firmly on the patient's chest to get a good electrical contact and then the defibrillator is charged up.
5) Everyone moves away from the patient except for the defibrillator operator who holds insulated handles. This means only the patient gets a shock.

If this doesn't get your heart going — nothing will...

You can get your very own special defibrillator now. One to carry around in your handbag, just in case. No, really, you can (okay, maybe it wouldn't fit in your handbag unless you're Mary Poppins, but still...). And the really clever thing is that they don't work unless they're needed. Amazing eh...

Charge in Circuits

If you've got a complete loop (a circuit) of conducting stuff (e.g. metal) connected to an electric power source (like a battery), electricity flows round it. Isn't electricity great.

Mind you it's pretty bad news if the words don't mean anything to you... Hey, I know — learn them now!

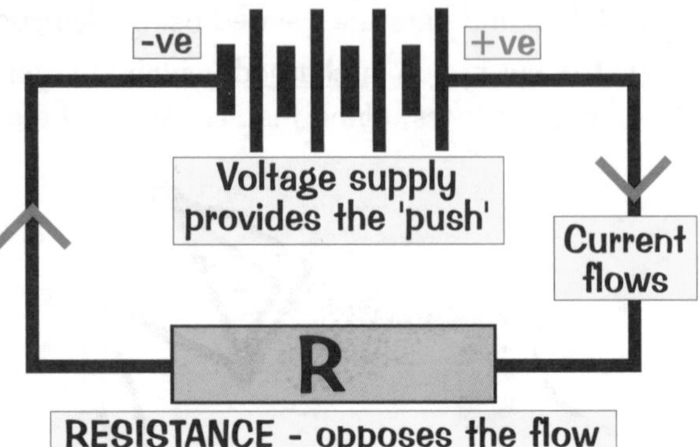

1) **CURRENT** is the flow of electrons around the circuit and it's measured in amps, A. Current will only flow through a component if there is a voltage across that component [unless the component is a superconductor (see p.39)].

2) **VOLTAGE** is the driving force that pushes the current round — kind of like "electrical pressure". Voltage is measured in volts, V.

3) **RESISTANCE** is anything in the circuit which slows the flow down. Resistance is measured in ohms, Ω.

4) **THERE'S A BALANCE:** the voltage is trying to push the current round the circuit, and the resistance is opposing it — the relative sizes of the voltage and resistance decide how big the current will be:

> If you increase the VOLTAGE — then MORE CURRENT will flow.
> If you increase the RESISTANCE — then LESS CURRENT will flow (or MORE VOLTAGE will be needed to keep the SAME CURRENT flowing).

It's Just Like the Flow of Water Around a Set of Pipes

1) The current is simply like the flow of water.
2) The voltage is like the force provided by a pump which pushes the stuff round.
3) Resistance is any sort of constriction in the flow, which is what the pressure has to work against.
4) If you turn up the pump and provide more force (or "voltage"), the flow will increase.
5) If you put in more constrictions ("resistance"), the flow (current) will decrease.

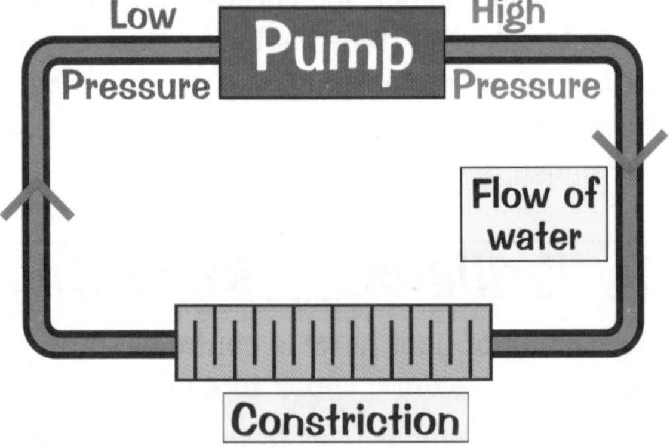

If You Break the Circuit, the Current Stops Flowing

1) Current only flows in a circuit as long as there's a complete loop for it to flow around. Break the circuit and the current stops.
2) Wire fuses and circuit breakers (resettable fuses) are safety features that break a circuit if there's a fault (see p.93).

Teachers — the driving force of revision...

The funny thing is — the electrons in circuits actually move from –ve to +ve... but scientists always think of current as flowing from +ve to –ve. Basically it's just because that's how the early physicists thought of it (before they found out about the electrons), and now it's become convention.

Fuses and Safe Plugs

Now then, did you know... electricity is dangerous. It can kill you. Well just watch out for it, that's all.

Plugs and Cables — Learn the Safety Features

Get the Wiring Right:

1) The right coloured wire is connected to each pin, and firmly screwed in.
2) No bare wires showing inside the plug.
3) Cable grip tightly fastened over the cable outer layer.

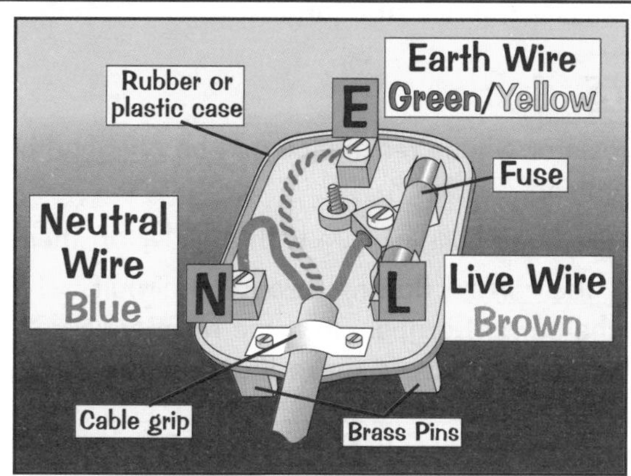

Plug Features:

1) The metal parts are made of copper or brass because these are very good conductors.
2) The case, cable grip and cable insulation are made of rubber or plastic because they're really good insulators, and flexible too.
3) This all keeps the electricity flowing where it should.

Earthing and Fuses Prevent Fires and Shocks

The LIVE WIRE alternates between a HIGH +VE AND –VE VOLTAGE of about 230 V.
The NEUTRAL WIRE is always at 0 V. Electricity normally flows in through the live wire and out through neutral wire.
The EARTH WIRE and fuse (or circuit breaker) are just for safety and work together like this:

1) If a fault develops in which the live somehow touches the metal case, then because the case is earthed, a big current flows in through the live, through the case and out down the earth wire.
2) This surge in current 'blows' the fuse (or trips the circuit breaker), which cuts off the live supply.
3) This isolates the whole appliance, making it impossible to get an electric shock from the case. It also prevents the risk of fire caused by the heating effect of a large current.
4) Fuses should be rated as near as possible but just higher than the normal operating current.

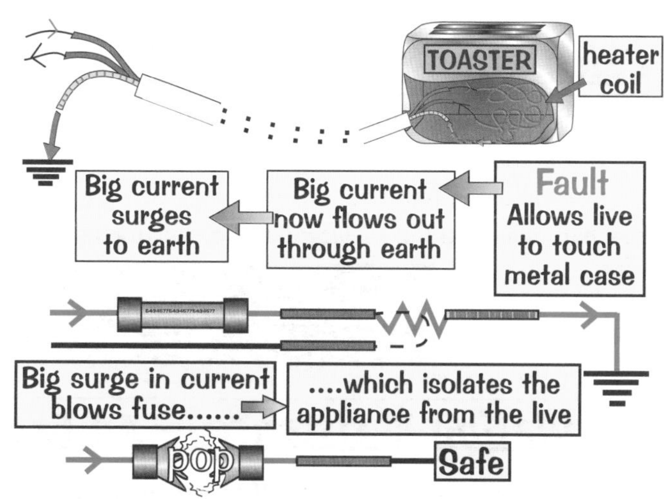

All appliances with metal cases must be "earthed" to reduce the danger of electric shock. "Earthing" just means the case must be attached to an earth wire. An earthed conductor can never become live. If the appliance has a plastic casing and no metal parts showing then it's said to be double insulated. Anything with double insulation like that doesn't need an earth wire — just a live and neutral.

CGP books are ACE — well, I had to get a plug in somewhere...

Have you ever noticed how if anything doesn't work in the house, it's always due to the fuse. The lights, the toaster, the car — always a little annoying, but it makes everything a whole load safer...

Resistance

A resistor is a component that reduces the current flowing in a circuit. The higher the resistance, the harder it is for the electricity to flow, and so the lower the current.
If you get an electric shock, it's the current that does the damage, not the voltage. So the higher the resistance in a circuit, the smaller the risk of injury.

Variable Resistors

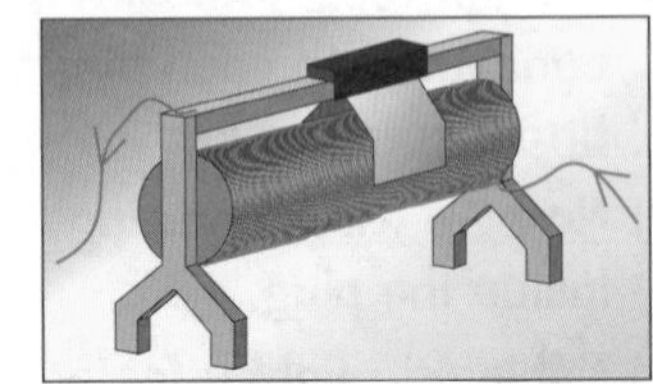

1) A variable resistor is a resistor whose resistance can be changed by twiddling a knob or something.
2) The old-fashioned ones are huge coils of wire with a slider on them.
3) They're great for altering the current flowing through a circuit. Turn the resistance up, the current drops. Turn the resistance down, the current goes up. You can use this to make the standard test circuit:

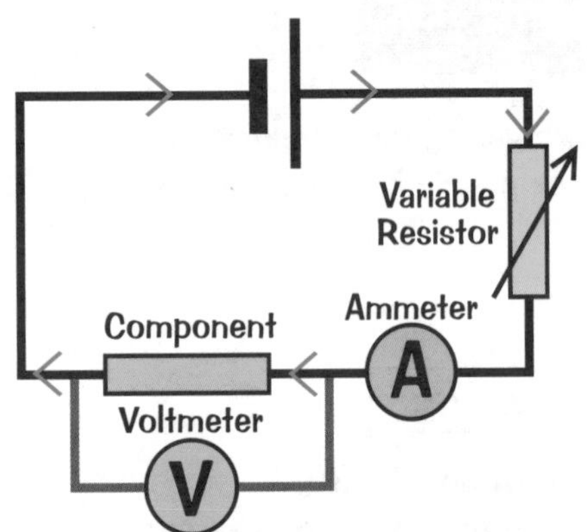

The Ammeter

1) Measures the current (in amps) through the component.
2) Can be put anywhere in series in the main circuit, but never in parallel like the voltmeter.

The Voltmeter

1) Measures the voltage (in volts) across the component.
2) Must be placed in parallel around the component under test — NOT around the variable resistor or the battery!
3) The proper name for voltage is "potential difference".

1) This very basic circuit is used for testing the resistance of components.
2) As you vary the variable resistor it alters the current flowing through the circuit.
3) This allows you to take several pairs of readings from the ammeter and voltmeter.

Calculating Resistance: R = V/I

The resistance of a (non-variable) resistor is steady (at constant temperature).
1) If you increase the voltage across a resistor, the current increases as well.
2) For the same potential difference (p.d.), current increases as resistance decreases.

You can calculate the resistance of a resistor using the formula:

$$\text{Resistance} = \frac{\text{Potential Difference}}{\text{Current}}$$

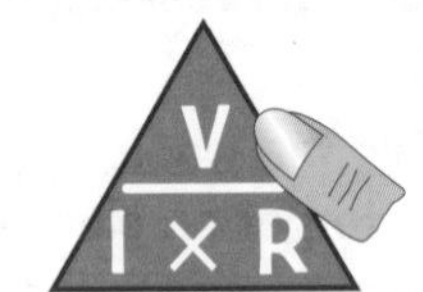

Calculating Resistance — An Example

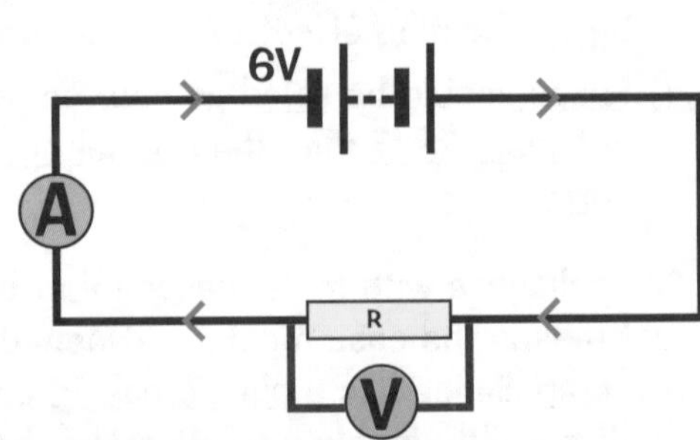

EXAMPLE. Voltmeter V reads 6 V and resistor R is 4 Ω. What is the current through ammeter A?

ANSWER. Rearrange the resistance formula to give:

I = V/R.

Then put in the values: I = 6/4 which is 1.5 A.

You have to learn this — resistance is futile...

Sometimes you can get funny light switches which fade the light in and out. Some of them work by resistance, and are perfect for getting that nice romantic atmosphere you want for your dinner for two. Learn the equation — you won't be given it in your exam, so you'll lose easy marks if you don't.

Ultrasound Scans and Treatment

Sound is a Longitudinal Wave

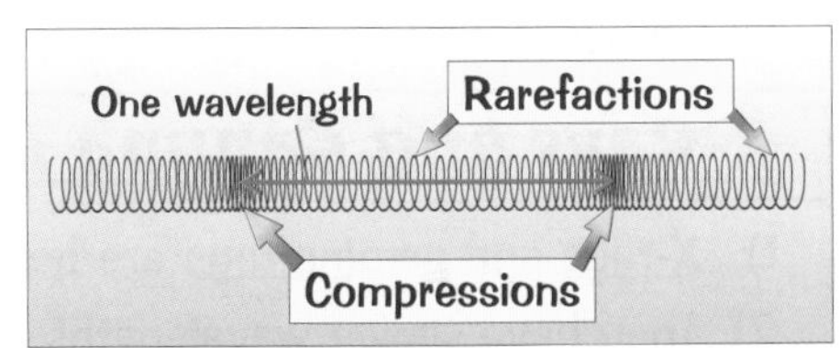

You need to know the features of longitudinal waves:

1) Sound waves squash up and stretch out the material they pass through, making compressions and rarefactions.
2) The WAVELENGTH is a full cycle of the wave, e.g. from crest to crest, not just from "two bits that are sort of separated a bit".
3) FREQUENCY is how many complete waves there are per second (passing a certain point). Frequency is measured in hertz. 1 Hz is 1 complete wave per second. For sound, high frequency = high pitch.
4) The AMPLITUDE tells you how much energy the wave is carrying, or how loud the sound is. You can see the amplitude of a sound on a CRO (oscilloscope). CRO displays show sounds as transverse waves so you can see what's going on. You measure the amplitude from the middle line to the crest, NOT from a trough to a crest.

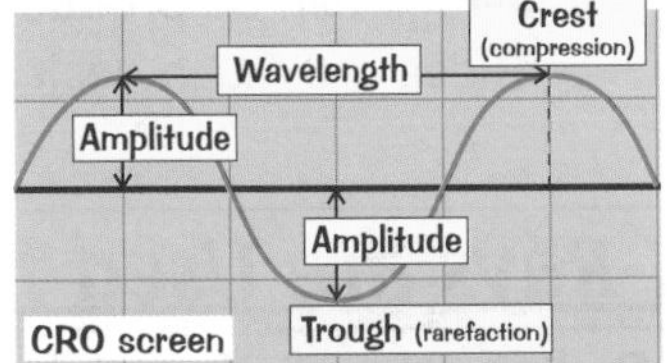

In LONGITUDINAL waves the vibrations are along the SAME DIRECTION as the wave is travelling.	In TRANSVERSE waves the vibrations are at 90° to the DIRECTION OF TRAVEL of the wave.

Ultrasound is Sound with a Higher Frequency Than We Can Hear

Electrical devices can be made which produce electrical oscillations of any frequency. These can easily be converted into mechanical vibrations to produce sound waves beyond the range of human hearing (i.e. frequencies above 20 kHz). This is called ultrasound and it has loads of uses in hospitals:

1) Breaking Down Kidney Stones

An ultrasound beam concentrates high energy waves at the kidney stone and turns it into sand-like particles. These particles then pass out of the body in urine. It's a good method because the patient doesn't need surgery and it's relatively painless.

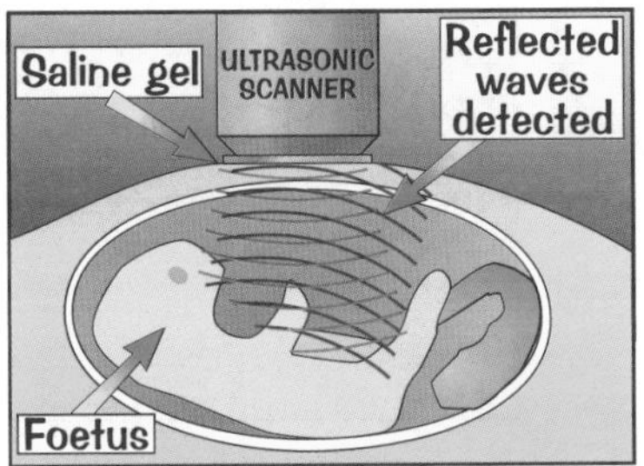

2) For Pre-Natal Scanning of a Foetus

Ultrasound waves can pass through the body, but whenever they reach a boundary between two different media (like fluid in the womb and the skin of the foetus) some of the wave is reflected back and detected. The exact timing and distribution of these echoes are processed by a computer to produce a video image of the foetus.
No one knows for sure whether ultrasound is safe in all cases but X-rays would definitely be dangerous to the foetus.

3) Measuring the Speed of Blood Flow

You don't need to know how they do that though.

Ultrasound Has Advantages over X-Rays

1) X-rays pass easily through soft tissues like muscle and skin, so you can usually only use them to make images of hard things like bone. Ultrasound is great for imaging soft tissue.
(It's no good for taking pictures of bones though — well, you win some, you lose some.)
2) The other advantage is that ultrasound is, as far as anyone can tell, safe.
X-rays are ionising radiation. They can cause cancer if you're exposed to too high a dose.

Looking at things with sound — weird if you ask me...

You can use ultrasound to get images of other things too — like shipwrecks. The time it takes for the wave to return also tells you the distance to the object. Dolphins use ultrasound as well (I always knew they were going to take over the world) to detect predators and food. Clever eh...

Ionising Radiation

Ionising radiation (e.g. alpha, beta, gamma and X-rays) damages living cells, but can be really useful if handled carefully...

X-Rays and Gamma Rays are Electromagnetic Waves

1) X-rays and gamma rays are both high frequency, short wavelength electromagnetic waves.
2) They have similar wavelengths, and so have similar properties, but are made in different ways:
   a) Gamma rays are released from some unstable atomic nuclei when they decay (see p.97). Nuclear decay is completely random, so there's no way to control when they're released.
   b) X-rays can be produced by firing high-speed electrons at a heavy metal like tungsten. These are much easier to control than gamma rays.

X-Rays are Used in Hospitals, but are Pretty Dangerous

1) Radiographers in hospitals take X-ray photographs of people to see whether they have any broken bones.
2) X-rays pass easily through flesh, but not so easily through denser material like bones or metal.
3) X-rays can cause cancer, so radiographers wear lead aprons and stand behind a lead screen, or leave the room, to keep their exposure to X-rays to a minimum.

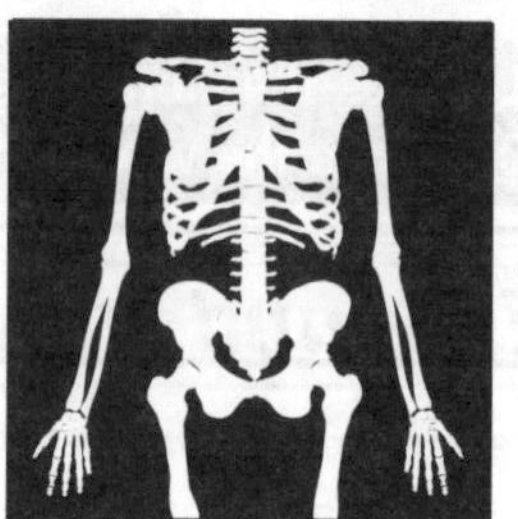

The brighter bits are where fewer X-rays get through. This is a negative image. The plate starts off all white.

Radiation Harms Living Cells

1) Nuclear radiation (alpha α, beta β, gamma γ) and X-rays will cheerfully enter living cells and collide with molecules.
2) These collisions cause ionisation, which damages or destroys the molecules.
3) Lower doses tend to cause minor damage without killing the cell. This can give rise to mutant cells which divide uncontrollably. This is cancer.
4) Higher doses tend to kill cells completely, which causes radiation sickness if a lot of body cells all get blatted at once.

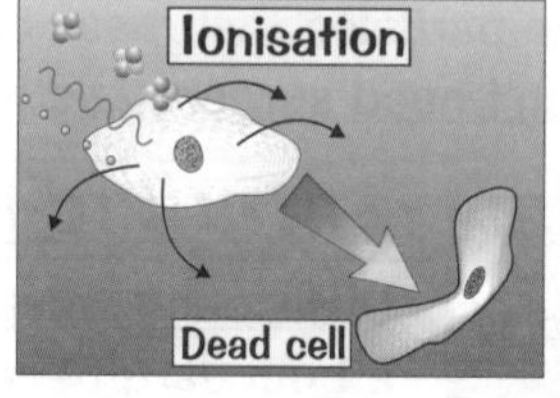

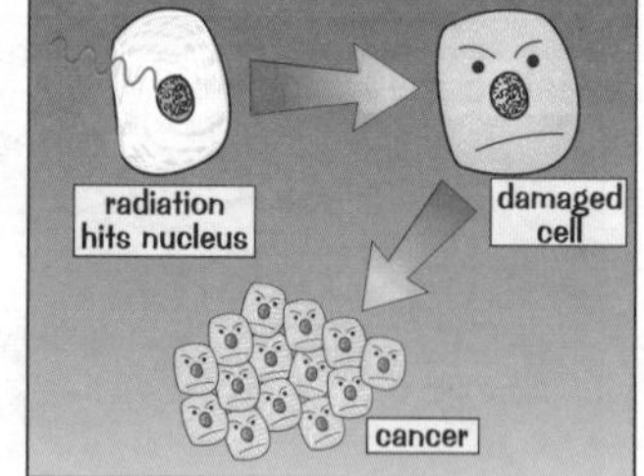

Outside the Body, β and γ Sources are the Most Dangerous

This is because beta and gamma can get inside to the delicate organs, whereas alpha is much less dangerous because it can't penetrate the skin.

Inside The Body, an α Source is the Most Dangerous

Inside the body alpha sources do all their damage in a very localised area. Beta and gamma sources on the other hand are less dangerous inside the body because they are less ionising, and mostly pass straight out without doing much damage.

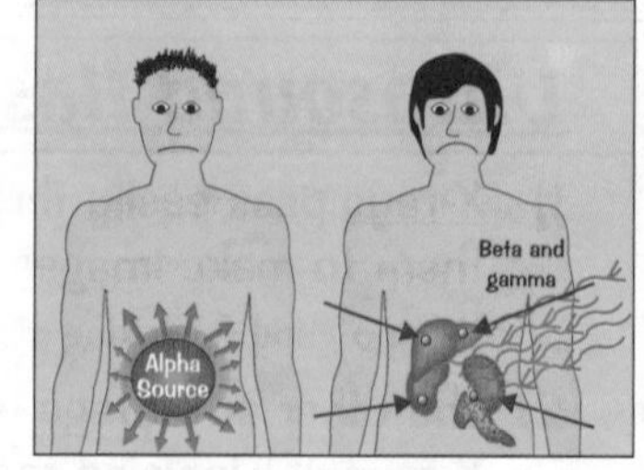

Radiation — easy as α, β, γ...

X-rays aren't just used for looking for broken bones — they have some other uses, such as working out the exact place, size and orientation of a cancer tumour. Several X-rays are needed though, so it's left to a last resort — you don't want to risk causing more damage to the person...

Radioactive Decay

Radioactive materials are made up of atoms that decay, giving out alpha, beta or gamma radiation.

You Need to Know What the Three Types of Radiation Are

ALPHA PARTICLES ARE HELIUM NUCLEI: $^{4}_{2}He$

They're relatively big, heavy and slow moving, so they don't penetrate very far into materials.

BETA PARTICLES ARE FAST-MOVING ELECTRONS: $^{0}_{-1}e$

They're quite fast and quite small.

GAMMA RAYS ARE ELECTROMAGNETIC RADIATION: $^{0}_{0}\gamma$

They don't have any mass or charge, so they penetrate a long way before they're stopped.

Radioactivity is a Totally Random Process

Unstable nuclei will decay, and in the process give out radiation. This happens entirely at random. This means that if you have 1000 unstable nuclei, you can't say when any one of them is going to decay, and neither can you do anything at all to make a decay happen.

Each nucleus will just decay quite spontaneously in its own good time. It's completely unaffected by physical conditions like temperature, or by any sort of chemical bonding etc.

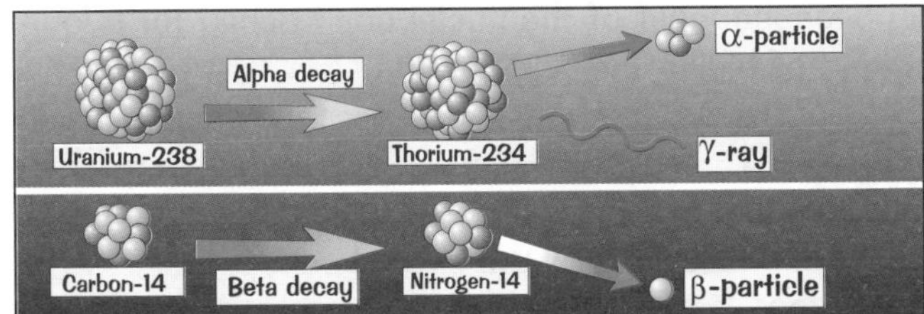

When the nucleus does decay it will spit out one or more of the three types of radiation, alpha, beta and gamma, and in the process the nucleus will often change into a new element.

Nuclear Equations — Not Half as Bad as They Sound

Nuclear equations are OK I think. In the end it's just a case of making sure the mass numbers and atomic numbers balance up on both sides, that's all. The trickiest bit is remembering the mass and atomic numbers for α, β and γ particles, and neutrons too. Make sure you can do all of these easily:

1) Alpha emission: An α-particle has a mass of 4 and charge of +2: $^{4}_{2}He$

A typical alpha emission: $^{226}_{88}Ra \rightarrow\, ^{222}_{86}Rn +\, ^{4}_{2}He$

2) Beta emission: A β-particle has (virtually) no mass and a charge of –1: $^{0}_{-1}e$

A typical beta emission: $^{14}_{6}C \rightarrow\, ^{14}_{7}N +\, ^{0}_{-1}e$

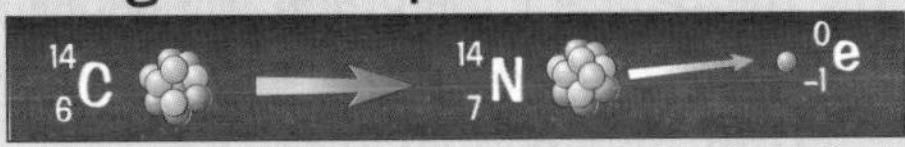

3) Gamma emission: A γ-ray is a photon with no mass and no charge: $^{0}_{0}\gamma$

After an alpha or beta emission the nucleus sometimes has extra energy to get rid of. It does this by emitting a gamma ray. Gamma emission never changes the atomic or mass numbers of the nucleus.

A typical combined α and γ emission: $^{238}_{92}U \rightarrow\, ^{234}_{90}Th +\, ^{4}_{2}He +\, ^{0}_{0}\gamma$

Sorry, no clear equations on this page...

The most important thing to remember is the symbol for each type of particle with its proton number and mass number. As long as you know those, you should be able to write down an equation for any type of radioactive decay they might throw at you in the exam — just keep everything balanced...

Radioactivity and Half-Life

The unit for measuring radioactivity is the becquerel (Bq). 1 Bq means one nucleus decaying per second.

The Radioactivity of a Sample Always Decreases Over Time

1) This is pretty obvious when you think about it. Each time a decay happens and an alpha, beta or gamma is given out, it means one more radioactive nucleus has disappeared.
2) Obviously, as the unstable nuclei all steadily disappear, the activity as a whole will decrease. So the older a sample becomes, the less radiation it will emit.

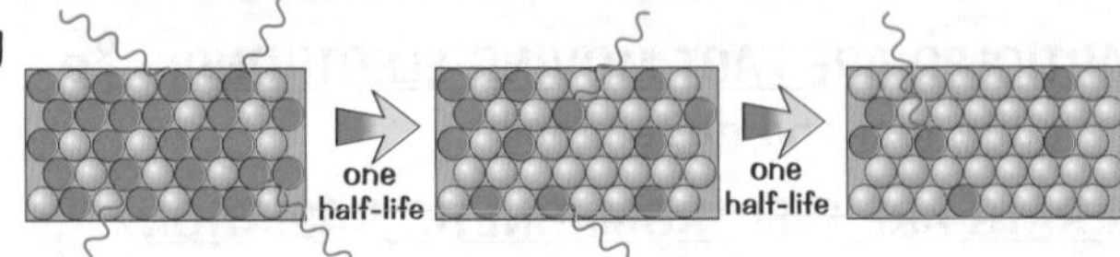

3) How quickly the activity drops off varies a lot. For some substances it takes just a few hours before nearly all the unstable nuclei have decayed, whilst for others it can take millions of years.
4) The problem with trying to measure this is that the activity never reaches zero, which is why we have to use the idea of half-life to measure how quickly the activity drops off.
5) Learn this definition of half-life:
6) A short half-life means the activity falls quickly, because lots of the nuclei decay quickly.

HALF-LIFE is the TIME TAKEN for HALF of the radioactive atoms now present to DECAY

7) A long half-life means the activity falls more slowly because most of the nuclei don't decay for a long time — they just sit there, basically unstable, but kind of biding their time.

Do Half-life Questions Step by Step

Half-life is maybe a little confusing, but exam calculations are straightforward so long as you do them slowly, STEP BY STEP. Like this one:

A VERY SIMPLE EXAMPLE: The activity of a radioisotope is 640 cpm (counts per minute). Two hours later it has fallen to 40 cpm. Find the half-life of the sample.

ANSWER: You must go through it in short simple steps like this:

INITIAL count:		after ONE half-life:		after TWO half-lives:		after THREE half-lives:		after FOUR half-lives:
640	$(\div 2)\rightarrow$	320	$(\div 2)\rightarrow$	160	$(\div 2)\rightarrow$	80	$(\div 2)\rightarrow$	40

Notice the careful step-by-step method, which tells us it takes four half-lives for the activity to fall from 640 to 40. Hence two hours represents four half-lives, so the half-life is 30 minutes.

Finding the Half-life of a Sample Using a Graph

1) The data for the graph will usually be several readings of count rate taken with a G-M tube and counter.
2) The graph will always be shaped like the one shown.
3) The half-life is found from the graph, by finding the time interval on the bottom axis corresponding to a halving of the activity on the vertical axis. Easy peasy really.

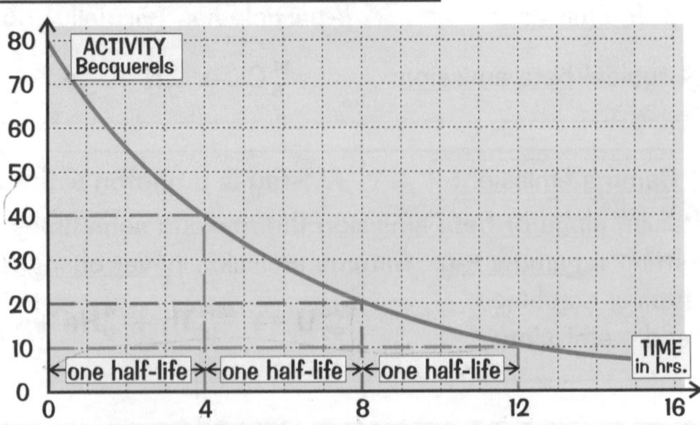

Half-life of a box of chocolates — about five minutes...

For medical applications, you need to use isotopes that have a suitable half-life. A radioactive tracer needs to have a short half-life to minimise the risk of damage to the patient. A source for sterilising equipment needs to have a long half-life, so you don't have to replace it too often (see p.100).

Background Radiation

Background Radiation Comes from Many Sources

The background radiation we receive comes from:

1) Radioactivity of naturally occurring unstable isotopes which are all around us — in the air, in food, in building materials and in the rocks under our feet.
2) Radiation from space, which is known as cosmic rays. These come mostly from the Sun.
3) Radiation due to human activity, e.g. fallout from nuclear explosions, or dumped nuclear waste. But this represents a tiny proportion of the total background radiation.

The RELATIVE PROPORTIONS of background radiation:

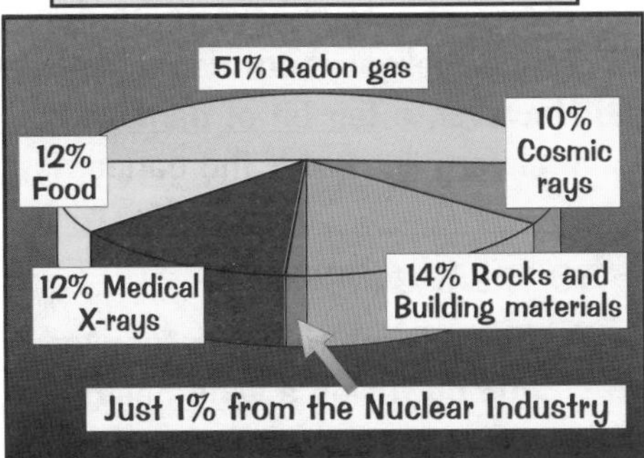

The Level of Background Radiation Changes Depending on Where You Are

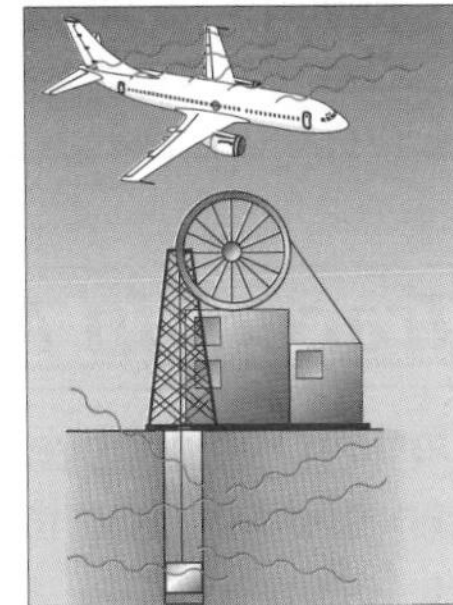

1) At high altitudes (e.g. in jet planes) the background radiation increases because of more exposure to cosmic rays. That means commercial pilots have an increased risk of getting some types of cancer.
2) Underground in mines, etc. it increases because of the rocks all around.
3) Certain underground rocks (e.g. granite) can cause higher levels at the surface, especially if they release radioactive radon gas, which tends to get trapped inside people's houses.

Radon Gas is the Subject of Scientific Debate

1) The radon concentration in people's houses varies widely across the UK, depending on what type of rock the house is built on.
2) Studies have shown that exposure to high doses of radon gas can cause lung cancer — and the greater the radon concentration, the higher the risk.
3) The scientific community is a bit divided on the effects of lower doses, and there's still a lot of debate over what the highest safe(ish) concentration is.
4) Evidence suggests that the risk of developing lung cancer from radon is much greater for smokers than non-smokers.
5) Some medical professionals reckon that about 1 in 20 deaths from lung cancer (about 2000 per year) are caused by radon exposure.
6) New houses in areas where high levels of radon gas might occur must be designed with good ventilation systems. These reduce the concentration of radon in the living space.
7) In existing houses, the Government recommends that ventilation systems are put in wherever the radiation due to radon is above a certain level.

Coloured bits indicate more radiation from rocks

Background radiation — it's like nasty wallpaper...

Did you know that background radiation was first discovered accidentally. Scientists were trying to work out which materials were radioactive, and couldn't understand why their reader still showed radioactivity when there was no material being tested. They realised it must be natural background radiation.

Medical Uses of Radiation

As well as X-ray scans, ionising radiation has loads of uses in hospitals, and you have to know about them.

1) Radiotherapy — the Treatment of Cancer Using Gamma Rays

1) Since high doses of gamma rays will kill all living cells, they can be used to treat cancers.
2) The gamma rays have to be directed carefully and at just the right dosage so as to kill the cancer cells without damaging too many normal cells.
3) However, a fair bit of damage is inevitably done to normal cells, which makes the patient feel very ill. But if the cancer is successfully killed off in the end, then it's worth it.

TO TREAT CANCER:

1) The gamma rays are focused on the tumour using a wide beam.
2) This beam is rotated round the patient with the tumour at the centre.
3) This minimises the exposure of normal cells to radiation, and so reduces the chances of damaging the rest of the body.

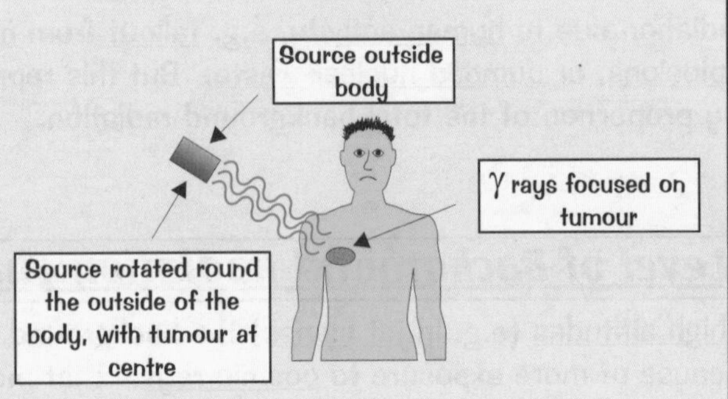

2) Tracers in Medicine — Always Short Half-life Gamma Emitters

1) Certain radioactive isotopes can be injected into people (or they can just swallow them) and their progress around the body can be followed using an external detector. A computer converts the reading to a display showing where the strongest reading is coming from.
2) A well-known example is the use of iodine-131, which is absorbed by the thyroid gland just like normal iodine-127, but it gives out radiation which can be detected to indicate whether or not the thyroid gland is taking in the iodine as it should.

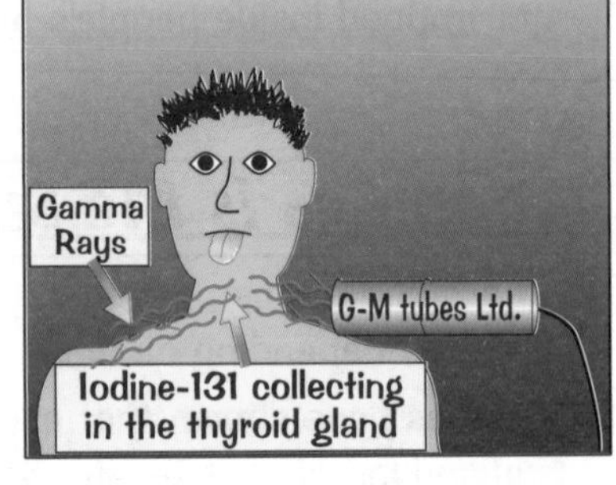

3) All isotopes which are taken into the body must be GAMMA or BETA (never alpha), so that the radiation passes out of the body — and they should only last a few hours, so that the radioactivity inside the patient quickly disappears (i.e. they should have a short half-life).

3) Sterilisation of Surgical Instruments Using Gamma Rays

1) Medical instruments can be sterilised by exposing them to a high dose of gamma rays, which will kill all microbes.
2) The great advantage of irradiation over boiling is that it doesn't involve high temperatures, so heat-sensitive things like thermometers and plastic instruments can be totally sterilised without damaging them.

Ionising radiation — just what the doctor ordered...

See — radiation isn't all bad. It also kills bad things, like disease-causing bacteria. Radiotherapy and chemotherapy (which uses chemicals instead of gamma rays) are commonly used to treat cancer. They both work in the same way — by killing lots and lots of cells, and trying to target the cancerous ones...

Non-Medical Uses of Radiation

Radioactive materials aren't just used in hospitals (p.100) — you've got to know these uses too.

1) Tracers in Industry — For Finding Leaks

G-M tubes Ltd.

This is much the same technique as the medical tracers.

1) Radioisotopes can be used to track the movement of waste materials, find the route of underground pipe systems or detect leaks or blockages in pipes.
2) To check a pipe, you just squirt it in, then go along the outside with a detector. If the radioactivity reduces or stops after a certain point, there must be a leak or blockage there. This is really useful for concealed or underground pipes, to save you digging up half the road trying to find the leak.
3) The isotope used must be a gamma emitter, so that the radiation can be detected even through metal or earth which may be surrounding the pipe. Alpha and beta radiation wouldn't be much use because they are easily blocked by any surrounding material.
4) It should also have a short half-life so as not to cause a hazard if it collects somewhere.

2) Smoke Detectors

1) A weak radioactive source is placed in the detector, close to two electrodes.
2) The source causes ionisation, and a current flows.
3) If there is a fire then smoke will absorb the radiation — the current falls and the alarm sounds.

3) Radioactive Dating of Rocks and Archaeological Specimens

The discovery of radioactivity and the idea of half-life gave scientists their first opportunity to accurately work out the age of some rocks and archaeological specimens. By measuring the amount of a radioactive isotope left in a sample, and knowing its half-life, you can work out how long the thing has been around.

Radiocarbon Dating — Carbon-14 Calculations

Carbon-14 makes up about 1/10 000 000 (one ten-millionth) of the carbon in the air. This level stays fairly constant in the atmosphere. The same proportion of C-14 is also found in living things. However, when they die, the C-14 is trapped inside the wood or wool or whatever, and it gradually decays with a half-life of 5730 years. By simply measuring the proportion of C-14 found in some old axe handle, burial shroud, etc. you can easily calculate how long ago the item was living material using the known half-life.

EXAMPLE: An axe handle was found to contain 1 part in 40 000 000 carbon-14. How old is the axe?

ANSWER: The C-14 was originally 1 part in 10 000 000. After one half-life it would be down to 1 part in 20 000 000. After two half-lives it would be down to 1 part in 40 000 000. Hence the axe handle is two C-14 half-lives old, i.e. $2 \times 5730 = 11\,460$ years old.
Note the same old stepwise method from page 98, going down one half-life at a time.

Dating Rocks — Relative Proportions Calculations

Uranium isotopes have very long half-lives and decay via a series of short-lived particles to produce stable isotopes of lead. The relative proportions of uranium and lead isotopes in a sample of igneous rock can therefore be used to date the rock, using the known half-life of the uranium. It's as simple as this:

Initially	After one half-life	After two half-lives
100% uranium	50% uranium	25% uranium
0% lead	50% lead	75% lead

Ratio of uranium to lead: (half-life of uranium-238 = 4.5 billion years)

Initially	After one half-life	After two half-lives
1:0	1:1	1:3

Will any of that be in your exam? — isotope so...

You wouldn't believe radioactive materials have so many uses. They're even used in genetics — remember radioactive markers for DNA fingerprinting on page 2. So radiation isn't all bad then...

Nuclear Power

Nuclear Fission — The Splitting Up of Uranium Atoms

Nuclear power stations are powered by nuclear reactors. In a nuclear reactor, a controlled chain reaction takes place in which uranium or plutonium atoms split up and release energy in the form of heat. This heat is then used to heat water to drive a steam turbine. So nuclear reactors are really just glorified steam engines!

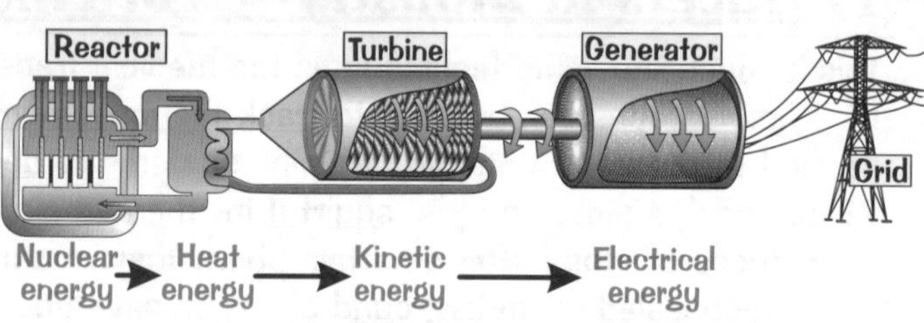

The Splitting of Uranium-235 Needs Neutrons

Uranium-235 (i.e. a uranium atom with a total of 235 protons and neutrons) is used in some nuclear reactors (and bombs — a nuclear bomb is an uncontrolled fission reaction).

1) Uranium-235 (U-235) is actually quite stable, so it needs to be made unstable before it'll split.
2) This is done by firing slow-moving neutrons at the U-235 atom.
3) The neutron joins the nucleus to create U-236, which is unstable.
4) The U-236 then splits into two smaller atoms, plus 2 or 3 fast-moving neutrons.
5) There are different pairs of atoms that U-236 can split into — e.g. krypton-90 and barium-144, which are radioactive.

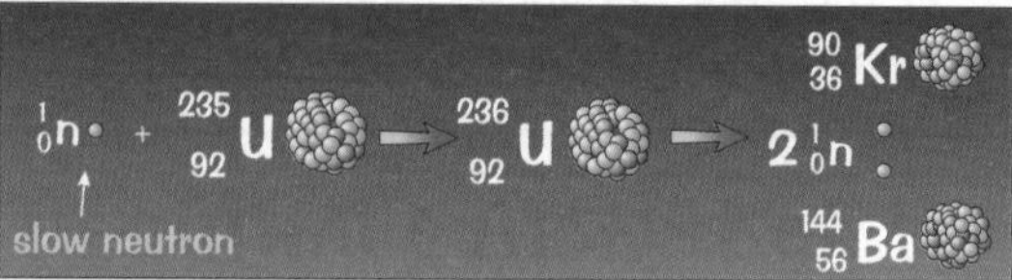

You Can Split More than One Atom — Chain Reactions

1) To get a useful amount of energy, loads of U-235 atoms have to be split. So neutrons released from previous fissions are used to hit other U-235 atoms.
2) These cause more atoms to split, releasing even more neutrons, which hit even more U-235 atoms... and so on and so on. This process is known as a chain reaction.
3) The fission of an atom of uranium releases loads of energy, in the form of the kinetic energy of the two new atoms (which is basically heat).

Inside a Gas-Cooled Nuclear Reactor

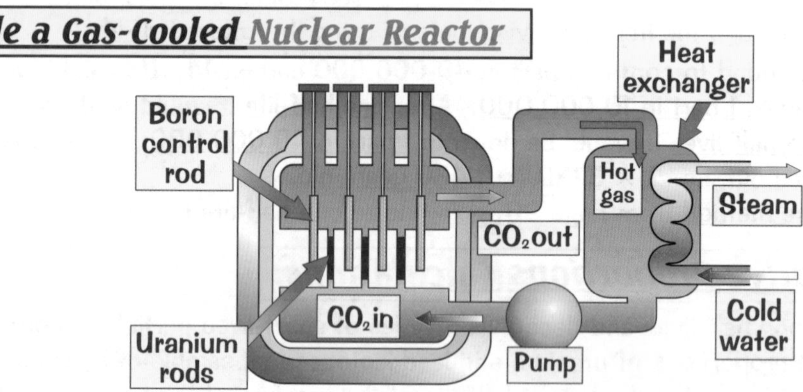

This is a gas-cooled nuclear reactor — but there are many other kinds.

1) Free neutrons in the reactor "kick-start" the fission process.
2) The two fission fragments then collide with surrounding atoms, causing the temperature in the reactor to rise.
3) Control rods, often made of boron, limit the rate of fission by absorbing excess neutrons.
4) A gas, typically carbon dioxide, is pumped through the reactor in order to carry away the heat generated.
5) The gas is then passed through the heat exchanger, where it gives its energy to water. This water is heated and turned into steam, which is then used to turn the turbines, generating electricity.

Uranium — gone fission, back after lunch...

The products left over after nuclear fission are generally radioactive, so they can't just be thrown away. Sometimes they're put in thick metal boxes, which are then placed in a deep hole, which is then filled with concrete. But some people worry that the materials could leak out after a number of years. Hmm.

Revision Summary for Module P4

Some of this stuff can be just learnt and regurgitated — other parts actually need thinking about.
It doesn't help that you can't see most of it happening — you'll just have to take my word for it.
If you can answer these questions, you should have no problem with anything the examiners throw at you.
But if any of these questions stump you, go back and learn the stuff, then give it another go.

1) What is static electricity? What causes it to build up?
2) Which particles move when static builds up? Which particles don't move?
3) Give two examples each of static electricity being: a) a nuisance, b) dangerous.
4) Explain how you can reduce the danger of getting a static electric shock.
5) Give three examples of how static electricity can be helpful. Write all the details.
6) Explain what current, voltage and resistance are in an electric circuit.
7) Sketch a properly wired three-pin plug.
8) Explain fully how fuses work.
9) Describe what earthing and double insulation are. Why are they useful?
10) A variable resistor is used to change the resistance in a circuit. What happens to the current flowing through a circuit if the resistance is increased?
11) Explain how you could work out the resistance of a resistor.
12) Define the frequency, wavelength and amplitude of a wave.
13) What's the relationship between frequency and pitch in a sound wave?
14) What is ultrasound? Give details of two medical applications of ultrasound.
15) Explain why ultrasound rather than X-rays are used to take images of a foetus.
16) What is the main difference between X-rays and gamma rays?
17) Explain what kind of damage radiation causes to body cells. What are the effects of high doses? What damage do lower doses do?
18) Which kinds of radioactive source are most dangerous: a) inside the body, b) outside the body?
19) Radioactivity is a totally random process. Explain what this means.
20)* Write down the nuclear equation for the alpha decay of: a) $^{234}_{92}U$, b) $^{230}_{90}Th$, and c) $^{226}_{88}Ra$.
21)* Write down the nuclear equation for the beta/gamma decay of: a) $^{234}_{90}Th$, b) $^{234}_{91}Pa$, and c) $^{14}_{6}C$.
22) Sketch a diagram to show how the activity of a radioactive sample decreases over time.
23) Give a proper definition of half-life.
24) Sketch a typical graph of activity against time. Show how you can find the half-life from your graph.
25) List three places where the level of background radiation is increased and explain why.
26) Describe in detail how radioactive sources are used in each of the following:
a) treating cancer, b) tracers in medicine, c) sterilisation.
27) Describe in detail how radioactive sources are used in each of the following:
a) tracers in industry, b) smoke alarms, c) dating archaeological samples, d) dating rocks.
28)* An old bit of cloth was found to have 1 atom of C-14 to 80 000 000 atoms of C-12.
If C-14 decays with a half-life of 5730 yrs, find the age of the cloth.
29) Describe in terms of energy transfers how electricity is produced from a nuclear power station.
30) What type of particle is U-235 bombarded with to make it split?
31) Explain how a chain reaction is created in a nuclear reactor.
32) What is used in a reactor to slow down neutrons which are moving too quickly?

* Answers on page 108

The Main Formulas for Each Topic

Whatever you might think about science being more understanding than rote learning... you've still got formulas to learn, and there's no getting away from it. Believe me, you don't want to be in the exam trying to answer Physics questions without knowing the formulas — it'll be a nightmare.

So I've rounded up all the formulas in the book and repeated them here — make sure you know EVERY LAST ONE before you go into the exam.

Additional Physics Has Ten Main Formulas...

Come on, surely you didn't expect Physics not to have the odd formula or two — that's what Physics IS...

	Quantity	Symbol	Standard Units	Formula	
1	Velocity or Speed	v or s	metres/sec, m/s	$s = d/t$	(see p42)
2	Acceleration	a	metres/sec^2, m/s^2	$A = \Delta v/t$ or $a = F/m$	(see p43)
3	Force	F	newtons, N	$F = m \times a$ or	(see p46)
4	Mass	m	kilograms, kg	$a = F/m$	
5	Weight (a force)	W	newtons, N	$W = m \times g$	(see p53)
6	Work done (energy)	Wd	joules, J	$Wd = F \times d$	(see p51)
7	Power	P	watts, W	$P = Wd/t$ or $P = E/t$	(see p54)
8	Potential Energy	PE	joules, J	$PE = m \times g \times h$	(see p51)
9	Kinetic Energy	KE	joules, J	$KE = ½ \times m \times v^2$	(see p52)
10	Resistance	R	ohms, Ω	$R = V/I$	(see p94)

Chemistry Has a Couple Too...

No units for these two — they're just percentages.

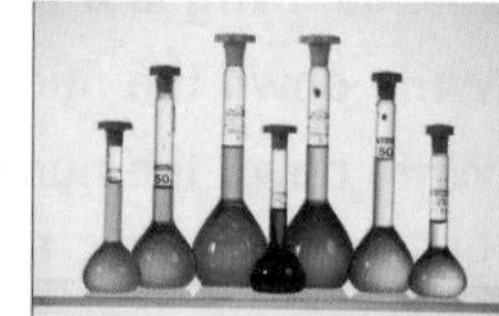

$$\text{PERCENTAGE YIELD} = \frac{\text{actual yield (grams)}}{\text{predicted yield (grams)}} \times 100$$

(see p77)

$$\text{PERCENTAGE MASS OF AN ELEMENT IN A COMPOUND} = \frac{A_r \times \text{No. of atoms (of that element)}}{M_r \text{ (of whole compound)}} \times 100$$

(see p79)

And Not Forgetting Biology...

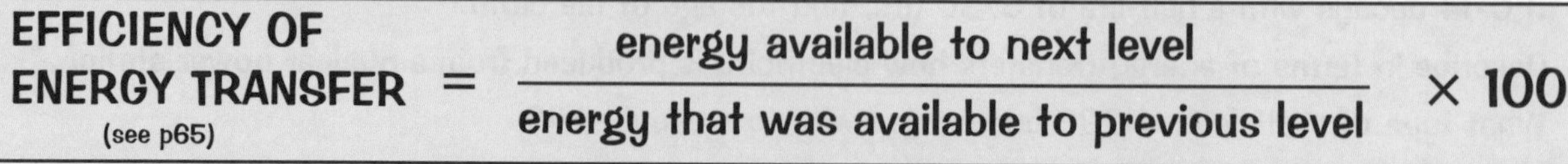

No units here either. In energy and ecosystems, you need to be able to calculate the percentage efficiency of energy transfer from one trophic level to the next:

$$\text{EFFICIENCY OF ENERGY TRANSFER} = \frac{\text{energy available to next level}}{\text{energy that was available to previous level}} \times 100$$

(see p65)

Formulas — all you've got to do is LEARN them...

Your task is simplicity itself. For the Physics list, leave the "Quantity" column exposed and cover up the other 3. Then simply fill in the 3 columns for each quantity. And just keep practising and practising till you can do it all. Then learn the Chemistry and Biology ones. This really is so important. So do it.

Index

Index

Index

Index and Answers

Answers

Revision Summary for Module C3 (page 41)

1) a) $CaCO_3 + 2HCl \rightarrow CaCl_2 + H_2O + CO_2$
   b) $Ca + 2H_2O \rightarrow Ca(OH)_2 + H_2$
   c) $H_2SO_4 + 2KOH \rightarrow K_2SO_4 + 2H_2O$
   d) $Fe_2O_3 + 3H_2 \rightarrow 2Fe + 3H_2O$

21) a) bromine + lithium → lithium bromide
   $Br_2 + 2Li \rightarrow 2LiBr$
   b) chlorine + potassium → potassium chloride
   $Cl_2 + 2K \rightarrow 2KCl$
   c) iodine + sodium → sodium iodide
   $I_2 + 2Na \rightarrow 2NaI$

Revision Summary for Module P3 (page 56)

1) 0.091 m/s; 137 m
2) The car was travelling at 12.6 m/s, so it wasn't breaking the speed limit.
6) 35 m/s^2
14) 17.5 m/s^2
21) 6420 J
22) 540 J
23) 20 631 J
25) 15 600 J
27) 150 kJ
29) 2000 W
30) 945 W

Bottom of page 75

1) Cu : 64, K : 39, Kr : 84, Cl : 35.5
2) NaOH : 40, Fe_2O_3 : 160, C_6H_{14} : 86, $Mg(NO_3)_2$: 148

Revision Summary for Module C4 (page 88)

8) $HNO_3 + NH_3 \rightarrow NH_4NO_3$
9) a) 40
   b) 108
   c) $12 + (16 \times 2) = 44$
   d) $24 + 12 + (16 \times 3) = 84$
   e) $27 + 3 \times (16 + 1) = 78$
   f) $65 + 16 = 81$
   g) $(23 \times 2) + 12 + (16 \times 3) = 106$
   h) $23 + 35.5 = 58.5$
10) a) 186.8 g
   b) 80.3 g
   c) 20.1 g

Revision Summary for Module P4 (page 103)

20) a) ${}^{234}_{92}U \rightarrow {}^{230}_{90}Th + {}^{4}_{2}He$
   b) ${}^{230}_{90}Th \rightarrow {}^{226}_{88}Ra + {}^{4}_{2}He$
   c) ${}^{226}_{88}Ra \rightarrow {}^{222}_{86}Rn + {}^{4}_{2}He$
21) a) ${}^{234}_{90}Th \rightarrow {}^{234}_{91}Pa + {}^{0}_{-1}e$
   b) ${}^{234}_{91}Pa \rightarrow {}^{234}_{92}U + {}^{0}_{-1}e$
   c) ${}^{14}_{6}C \rightarrow {}^{14}_{7}N + {}^{0}_{-1}e$
28) 17 190 years old (3 half-lives).